Clean Living under Difficult Circumstances

Clean Living under Difficult Circumstances

Finding a Home in the Ruins of Modernism

Owen Hatherley

VERSO
London • New York

First published by Verso 2021
© Owen Hatherley 2021

The publisher and author express their gratitude to the publications
in which some of the essays republished here first appeared. Complete
details of prior publication can be found in the acknowledgments.

1 3 5 7 9 10 8 6 4 2

Verso
UK: 6 Meard Street, London W1F 0EG
US: 20 Jay Street, Suite 1010, Brooklyn, NY 11201
versobooks.com

Verso is the imprint of New Left Books

ISBN-13: 978-1-83976-221-5
ISBN-13: 978-1-83976-224-6 (US EBK)
ISBN-13: 978-1-83976-223-9 (UK EBK)

British Library Cataloguing in Publication Data
A catalogue record for this book is available from the British Library

Library of Congress Cataloging-in-Publication Data

Names: Hatherley, Owen, author.
Title: Clean living under difficult circumstances : finding a home in the
    ruins of modernism / Owen Hatherley.
Description: Brooklyn, NY : Verso, 2021. | Summary: 'In this essay
    collection, essayist and author Owen Hatherley outlines a vision of the
    modern city as both a venue for political debate and a space for
    everyday experience – the city as a socialist project' – Provided by
    publisher.
Identifiers: LCCN 2021001634 (print) | LCCN 2021001635 (ebook) | ISBN
    9781839762215 (hardback) | ISBN 9781839762246 (US ebk) | ISBN
    9781839762239 (UK ebk)
Subjects: LCSH: City planning – Environmental aspects – Great Britain. |
    Housing – Great Britain. | Sound – Environmental aspects –Great Britain. |
    Socialism – Great Britain.
Classification: LCC HT169.G7 H386 2021
    (print) | LCC HT169.G7 (ebook) |
    DDC 307.1/2160941 – dc23
LC record available at https://lccn.loc.gov/2021001634
LC ebook record available at https://lccn.loc.gov/2021001635

Typeset in Sabon by MJ & N Gavan, Truro, Cornwall
Printed and bound by CPI Group (UK) Ltd, Croydon CR0 4YY

'Nowadays', complained Mr K, 'there are innumerable people who boast in public that they are able to write great books all by themselves, and this meets with general approval. When he was already in the prime of life the Chinese philosopher Chuang-tzu composed a book of one hundred thousand words, nine-tenths of which consisted of quotations. Such books can no longer be written here and now, because the wit is lacking. As a result, ideas are only produced in one's own workshop, and anyone who does not manage enough of them thinks himself lazy. Admittedly, there is not then a single idea that could be adopted or a single formulation of an idea that could be quoted. How little all of them need for their activity! A pen and some paper are the only things they are able to show! And without any help, with only the scant material that anyone can carry in his hands, they erect their cottages! The largest buildings they know are those a single man is capable of constructing!'

Bertolt Brecht, 'Originality', from *Stories of Mr Keuner* (trans. Martin Chalmers)

Contents

CONTENTS

Introduction

Two Thousand and Five

In the spring of 2005, I began to self-publish a blog, about modern architecture, modern design, cities, music, TV, film, politics – whatever interested me at the time. When I started it, I was hiding from various things and various people at my mother's flat in Northam Estate, a public housing scheme near the centre of the city of Southampton, a port on the South Coast of England. This was the first time, at the age of twenty-three, that I had ever lived in housing that could clearly be described as 'modernist'. Growing up in a city whose centre was flattened in the Second World War, I had always been surrounded by, and fascinated with, high-rises, glass office blocks, concrete walkways – but I had until then lived in Victorian terraces or early twentieth-century suburbs. Northam Estate was a little worn out and had a few tacky little signs and fences added, but its clarity as a design was unaffected.

It was built in the late 1950s by Southampton Corporation Architects' Department, then one of the most powerful and prolific in Britain. The estate replaced an area of Victorian

York House, Northam Estate

and Georgian slums, a dense dockside district mainly inhabited by dockers and the crew of White Star Line ships; 350
people from Northam lost their lives when the Titanic sank.
Like most of Southampton, the area was heavily bombed in
1940, with that damage compounding the poor quality of the
housing. Belatedly, it was all suddenly swept away fifteen years
later, and replaced with around twenty four-storey blocks and
one sixteen-storey tower, placed in irregular arrangements,
oriented to the sun, surrounded by trees, but close enough to
the river to hear foghorns. The buildings themselves were spacious, bright, with polychrome brickwork, big windows and
balconies, and secluded from the main roads. A sanctuary.

Our circumstances were not quite so drastic as those of the
people who first moved into these blocks, but they are easily
described as 'difficult'. The route that took me there, with my
mother, my brother James and my sister Frances, was circuitous. In the 1990s my mother, who had left school at sixteen,
trained as a teacher, taking night classes to get A-levels, a
degree and a PGCE. To pay her way through this, she sold her
house in Eastleigh, a railway town just outside Southampton,

and rented an ex–local authority house in the suburban Flower Estate, a low-density 1920s 'garden suburb' of houses and large gardens, laid out in the hope that dockers would grow their own vegetables. After a while she found teaching and single-motherhood an impossible combination and quit her job at the estate's primary school. After a spell of unemployment, she was put on something called the *New Deal*, which entailed working for her dole at a local cancer charity. Unable to pay the rent, she was evicted. Southampton City Council – who I could fault for all manner of other things – rehoused her, first in temporary accommodation for a few months, then in a flat in Northam Estate. Council housing was once supposedly for everyone – from the doctor to the milkman to the miner, in Aneurin Bevan's phrase – but even in 2000, one could rely on the council to house a one-parent family that had been made homeless, and house them well. After what felt like years of struggle – different rented houses, temporary jobs – getting this flat allowed Mum the space and time to put her life back together.

My path there had been a little different. A year before Mum, James and Frances were evicted, I had already left for university – specifically, Goldsmiths College. Starting in 1999, I was in the first cohort to receive no maintenance grant and to have to pay tuition fees. My fees were being paid for me – again, by Southampton City Council, thanks comrades – but I had fully expected, my mind addled with books about 1968, to arrive at a hotbed of student occupations and marches. Blur, alumni of the college, had even played at an occupation in protest at the introduction of fees the year before! It did not work out like this. I don't think there was a generation between 1945 and the present day that was so politically quietist as that born in the 1970s and early 1980s, yet somehow I hadn't realised this: not only were both my parents card-carrying Marxists (who had for some decades also been card-carrying members of the Labour Party); also various coincidences meant my friends at school had parents who were more often socialists than not. So, intoxicated by the delusion that I'd be entering the Sorbonne in May '68, or at least Hornsey Art College, I was brought quickly down to earth as I realised that most people I was studying with were not there to build a new society out of the ashes of the old, or even to experiment with new lifestyles or ideas; instead, they were attending out of a peculiar kind of middle-class obligation, taking part in a rite of passage of cider and absinthe, virginity-loss, food fights, Gomez records, 'socs' and 'ents'. I viewed this with corrosive inverted snobbery, which I suspect made me quite insufferable. Given that my immediate family were being made homeless at the time, perhaps some of my scorn can be forgiven.

Five years later, I had failed to do anything particularly interesting with my life. I drifted between different rented houses in south-east London, received a mediocre degree in English and History, and took various temporary jobs; these ranged from working in a call centre that cold-called trade union members to sell them insurance – particularly shameful, as my father had spent decades as a shop steward and convener – to working in a Chinese takeaway in Stockwell as a 'personal reader' for its blind and litigious owner. One of the more interesting jobs entailed doing surveys of car parking in the London Borough of Westminster, which gave a neophyte an extraordinary crash course in the capital's impossibly complex geography, and the way that stuccoed neoclassical terraces are thrown hard up against brutalist housing estates. From 2003 I started a part-time Master's degree – an amalgam of English lit, philosophy and cultural studies called Contemporary Approaches to English Studies, again at Goldsmiths. I funded this with a bank loan that I had obtained by working for a week at the British Gas call centre in Southampton – enough of a proper job to convince The Man. But the second year of this was marred by gruelling ill-health, with a full-time job as a filing clerk leaving me little time to study.

But probably the most frustrating problem was housing. After the obligatory year in halls of residence I moved to a flat above the passageway to an MOT depot in Peckham, in a tense flatshare with a Goldsmiths dropout. When I left for good I found every single rubbish bag I had put out for collection over the previous year piled up in a darkened corner, so as to be out of the way of the cars' path to the depot. I moved from there first to another flatshare on Coldharbour Lane, and then, when I started the MA, to a bedsit in Deptford High Street, above Pizza Vesuvio. I loved the area – an endlessly fascinating riverside township, with grand Hanseatic blocks of thirties council flats, macabre churchyards, baroque terraces and a freakish statue of one-time resident Peter the Great, Tsar of all the Russias – but the building I lived in should have been demolished decades before. Skirting boards had been eaten away so comprehensively that there was a continuous raised level for the mice. At least six people used what one tenant, a Scouse woman in her sixties, called 'the smallest kitchen in Christendom'. The kitchen wasn't really the issue, though; it was the toilet. At the weekends, when guests would spill into the bedsits, coming back from the evangelical churches, there could be as many as fifteen people using it. I was, by 2004, very sick – regular violent cramps, diarrhoea, fatigue and, at one point, a case of uveitis so severe that, so I was told by the doctors, I was lucky not to have been blinded in one eye. Finally, in January 2005, after various tests, I was diagnosed with Crohn's disease, which was no great surprise. The local cafes and pubs came to know my needs well, given that my own toilet was so frequently occupied.

The illness was one thing, but after what could politely be called a 'romantic disappointment' with a friend at Goldsmiths who had moved to Berlin, I was fed up. I quit the filing job at T Brown and Sons Heating Engineers and took myself and a large number of books on the Megabus down to Southampton. As my life dissolved into chaos, classes were missed and rent arrears mounted; as I learned to instantly switch off the daily, sometimes hourly, phone calls from my landlord; and as an application for Income Support was stalled for several months – I tried to concentrate just on my surroundings. I was, to be honest, surprised at how warm and pleasant I found the estate. My previous experience of council housing was three years on the aforementioned Flower Estate, as a teenager – probably the most alienating place I ever lived. That sort of close-knit 'traditional working-class community' (here, with the traditional architecture to match) can deal roughly with outsiders, especially young outsiders. In retrospect, we were out of place from the moment we moved into the Right to Buy house, which the owners had painted white in the middle of a row of grey pebbledashed cottages, as if to single it out. A large National Front skinhead contingent managed to survive there as late as the mid-1990s. After a few apparently random beatings for being *fucking faggots* (we would turn out to be tediously straight, but the phrase was expansive), my brother and I had started taking the bus rather than a ten-minute walk to school. The reason Mum ended up defaulting on her rent was because her two sons had *insisted* she take us out of the Flower Estate; the Victorian terrace we moved to as an alternative quickly proved to be beyond her means.

Northam didn't feel like this at all. Partly that's because we were all adults, or nearly; the vicious policing of even mild difference in the Flower Estate had been enforced by other teenagers. But it was also clear we were somewhere urban – multicultural, modern, walkable from town, round the corner from the Saints stadium: the kind of dockland place where people had become used, over many generations, to living next to people who were different from them. On my trips home from London, I could see how much Mum, James and Frances had made themselves at home in Northam. After watching *Changing Rooms*, they had gone all in for stencilling, screen-printing – with three home-made Warhol-style Che Guevaras framed in the living room – and the walls were painted in reds and ochres (there is an idea that council tenants are not allowed to touch their homes, but this certainly didn't apply for Southampton City Council in the early 2000s). There was underfloor heating, which, though it could warp records if you weren't careful, was a delight to lie down upon on February mornings, as the cold light streamed through the wide, wide windows. I would go on long walks around my hometown, a place I had generally avoided if I could – gradually trying to understand it, and how somewhere that had built something like this had lost its civic pride so completely.

I also suddenly had unlimited time to use the internet. I had not been able to afford a computer or a modem in Deptford, but my mum had a cheap version of each. With the low rents of a council tenancy, she was financially stable for the first time since she was in her twenties. She was now working for the NHS, in an X-ray department, and was studying to become a radiographer; she had remarried with a genial Trotskyist cabbie, an old comrade from her 'tendency'. So she could afford a cheap computer and a dial-up connection, which I exploited extensively. I had discovered in Goldsmiths library what was usually then just called 'the blogs'. Freaky Trigger, Blissblog, Infinite Thought, Poetix, above all K-Punk – fireworks of intellectual excitement and rage in this period of quietism and compulsory mateyness. I could now, rather than printing them out in the library or paying £1 an hour to read them in the internet cafe, read the blogs all night, and I did.

Looking back on this moment, I'm struck by how the re-election of the Labour government in spring 2005 was simply a non-event for us – especially as I write this still shaken by the election of December 2019. In 2005 I don't think I actually voted, the only time this has ever happened at a general election. Though a self-professed Leninist, Mum was always insistent that *people had died for the right to vote*, so there was a moral imperative to do so, no matter how little choice there was. She loathed Tony Blair, and would shout at the television when he appeared. Both she and I remembered well how one of the first acts of the Labour government in 1997 – by the 'feminist' DHSS minister Harriet Harman – was to slash lone-parent benefit, which at the time she relied upon; but in 2005 she still voted for John Denham, the local Labour MP who had resigned from the cabinet two years before, over the Iraq war. A comrade from her days in the Party, she had written Denham a letter to congratulate him on this principled stand, which she found deeply unexpected given she remembered him as a vacillating centrist. But if I'm honest, much better than I remember the election, I remember the K-Punk post – 'JOKER HYSTERICAL FACE' – that came with it. It described the prime minister, elected with fewer votes than Jeremy Corbyn would win in the disastrous rout of 2019, as follows: 'That ashen carnival mask, its grim cheerless Joker grin flashing with ritual efficiency, its blank eyes illuminated by empty evange-lism, darkened by perpetual irritation – the PM's being run by Videodrome'.

But there was more going on in our hatred of this man and what he represented than just straightforward loathing of his queasy religiosity and his wars. It was also about what his gov-ernment had done to our lives and our hopes. I guess we were the kind of people – a precarious working-class family – that certain commentators like to say *need a Labour govern-ment*. But for Mum, it had meant having her benefits slashed, working for her dole, and then being chucked out of her home. For me it was not so bad – much of what happened was my own fault – but the abolition of maintenance grants and the appalling state of London housing had made things more diffi-cult than they might otherwise have been. What kept us going, by contrast – what offered respite – were the remnants of the welfare state that Blair and his giggling coterie of think-tank twats were preparing for means-testing, part-privatisation and dismantlement. The National Health Service that finally gave Mum a decent skilled job. Council housing, which finally gave her a decent place to live. It might have become by then a residuum for the dirt poor, those who couldn't 'get on the ladder', but fortunately it had often been built to the highest standards, something which the neglect caused by the crippling of local government couldn't quite erase. As for me, on my walks into town I'd spend hours in the municipal library and the art gallery, with its collections of communal riches.

Mum knew how the welfare state worked, and how to get it to work. As I prepared to return to London, hoping that I wouldn't find my possessions thrown out on Deptford High Street, she insisted I do two things: appeal against the non-payment of Income Support that had left me without any income for several months; and go on the council's housing waiting list. The first worked beautifully. Summoned to a tribunal in Bexleyheath, I was told immediately that I'd won the case and was awarded the arrears. The second did not. I recall very well going to the Lewisham Housing Office on the Pepys Estate in Deptford to hand in my application. The Pepys was bigger than Northam – three towers rather than just the one – but had a similar mix of mid-rise blocks, green space, clear and monumental design, and riverside views – a flat here would have been just the ticket. As I walked round, I noticed that the open spaces were being filled in by new, non-council flats, the walkway connecting the estate to the park was being demolished and one of the three towers (the one closest to the river, obviously) was being turned into *luxury flats*. Naturally, I was applying for the 'priority band', given my toilet-sharing situation, but called into a short interview about my circumstances, I was told I had no chance. 'My own sister has Crohn's,' said the housing officer; 'if it was my choice, you'd be on Band A. But it's not on the list, so I'm afraid you're going to be on Band C.' Me, tens of thousands of others and a likely decade on the waiting list.

But it is *places like this* that made me fascinated with that period in the recent past where *places like this* were constructed for ordinary people, where the most noble and important task for an architect was the construction of housing, outside of the free market, for everyone. I began to read up in Deptford library, which was then a small space shoved in at the side of a 1980s swimming pool, about what had happened here: about how the modern movement in architecture had emerged out of the German and Russian revolutions, the Bauhaus and Soviet Constructivism; about how these ideas were brought to England by the continental exiles, Lubetkin, Goldfinger, Pevsner; and about how this had directly resulted in the creation of places like Northam Estate and the Pepys Estate. I graduated from my MA, was treated for my condition by being put on a cosmonaut-style liquid-only diet, and every week I would make regular trips to that library or to the local internet cafe, to 'update my blog'.

Now that I was writing it, I had all kinds of resentments to expiate, and I had, as will be obvious from a reading of this introduction, various things for which I desired revenge – and of course various enthusiasms I wanted to communicate. A lot of it was trying out different modes, imitations of the writers and bloggers I admired (and very little of it is publishable today). But what I found myself doing most was filtering all of the above through an advocacy of *modernism*. I meant that in various different senses, but most of all I meant it in the sense that the Who's manager, Peter Meaden, meant in 1975 when he was asked for a retrospective definition of mod, short for modernism. 'Modism, mod living, is an aphorism for *clean living under difficult circumstances.*' For the Mods, working-class London aesthetes of the sixties boom, that meant dressing up in Italian clothes, listening to American jazz and soul and watching French films, but beyond that it meant an ethos of modernity as a consciously chosen *way of life*. As I'd interpret the aphorism, this modernism means a declaration of faith in the idea that human problems can be solved, politically, practically, aesthetically; that communal rather than private property can be useful and beautiful; that anybody can understand and take hold of radical ideas in art, architecture, music, design; that human beings can be social and rational, not just selfish and atavistic; and that it is these impulses that should govern how society is run. Almost everything I have written since then has been based on that belief, but I first arrived at it in that flat in the spring that Tony Blair was re-elected.

This book collects pieces that span fifteen years of writing, from the final re-election of Blair to the election of Boris Johnson. What ties them together is this belief in modernism – very obviously combined with, and inextricable from, a belief in socialism – but the emphasis changes across the texts, and so do the places where they were published. The earlier pieces here, from approximately 2005 to 2008, were self-published on blogs. Blogging has mostly disappeared by now, killed off by the social networks which introduced into self-publishing and self-broadcast strong strains of immediacy, outrage, paranoia and mass cruelty that certainly existed in the blogs in embryo but are now mobilised for an economy of clicks and 'engagements' – something which is very novel to those of us who had to use comment boxes or Technorati to find out whether anybody was actually reading. I owe blogging, and bloggers, an incalculable debt, as the essay that closes this collection should make clear. Not long after I started self-publishing, I was noticed by Mark K-Punk himself, and after meeting him at the launch of a book by one of our music press idols, we became friends IRL, as we'd now say, but which Mark in his touchingly naff 1980s William Gibson way called *meatspace*. One of the eventual effects of this was the emergence of what seemed to those outside to be a coherent group of bloggers, sharing interests – Mark Fisher himself, Nina Power, Dominic Fox, Alberto Toscano, Richard Seymour, Ivor Southwood, Anwen Crawford, and a bit later Carl Neville, Rhian E. Jones, Benjamin Noys, Alex Williams. Some of these became close friends (some still are, others very much not), some had never met (and still haven't); but the launch of Zero Books, set up by Tariq Goddard as a specialised imprint, paid for by a ridiculous Mind Body Spirit publisher and run from a barn in Hampshire, launched this as something like a coherent group of writers grandly aiming to be 'public intellectuals'. Yet all of our first books were based, sometimes to the point of simple cut and paste, on the blogs that we wrote. Mine was written at the end of 2007 and in the first weeks of 2008 – when I was finishing it, the financial system started to totter, which I managed to crowbar into the conclusion.

The book was called, right up until it was nearly ready to go to print, *Another Effort, Comrades, If You Would Be Modernists*, which focused it as a polemic against, variously, Alain de Botton, home-improvement TV programmes and New Labour regeneration schemes, all as travesties of that ideal of clean living under difficult circumstances. A last-minute switch of title to *Militant Modernism* refocused it as something else – advocacy for that modern movement whose remnants and leftovers I had come to live and thrive in. The blog had already brought me a little bit of attention – writers with bylines in newspapers, namely Sukhdev Sandhu and Jonathan Meades, had noticed it, and because of them I had started to get sporadic work in freelance journalism, which I combined with equally sporadic work as a typist and occasional returns to the dole. But from the book's publication in April 2009 onwards, I lived solely on writing, and the skills you learn as a blogger – brevity, eccentricity and, let's be honest, 'brand-building' – easily lent themselves to the way that the new comment sections of legacy media tried to build audiences on outrage, cults of personality and urban boosterism.

In 2006, I began a part-time PhD in the evenings at Birkbeck, supervised by the brilliant militant aesthetician Esther Leslie, but by the time I completed it in 2011 it was obvious I had become a journalist, and would not become an academic.

The journalism I did, my *beat* so to speak, was housing and architecture. I combined this with a gradual mapping of twentieth-century modernism, writing articles and several topographical books that expanded out from Britain to Europe to the former Soviet Union and China. The intensity of the assault on the 'modern movement' and all that it stood for seemed to be constantly increasing, with dozens of important buildings and places under threat of destruction and/or privatisation. This gave me plenty of material, but along with that came a parallel movement of nostalgia for modernism, something which it's fair to say I did my best to cash in on, though it eventually became so inescapable and so grossly kitsch that I wrote a book of self-criticism, published in 2015 as *The Ministry of Nostalgia*, to try to disassociate myself from estate agents marketing modernist ex–local authority flats to young professionals.

What we most wanted to do in 'the blogs' was set ourselves irrevocably against the cultural and political status quo of the 2000s, particularly the New Labour settlement in Britain. That status quo was in some ways, compared with the present day, rather lavish. The National Health Service and schools received plenty of money (at the price of letting in private capital and private providers, through the Private Finance Initiative, City Academies and Foundation Hospitals). Money was thrown at new cultural buildings (where staid old municipal art galleries and youth clubs were replaced with centres for this and that or libraries with 'idea stores', always surrounded by clusters of luxury flats, and the old cultural TV channels shifted from Tarkovsky seasons to *Big Brother*). One could see this as *modernisation*, but I found it hard to see it as *modernism* – it was based on the explicit denial of the public good, while the demonisation by those think-tank twats of 'bog-standard comprehensives' and 'sink estates' came out of a disgust at the very notion of equality or universalism. The architecture that came with this was designed to be gawped at rather than used – designed from the outside in, rather than, as with the housing at Northam Estate, from the inside out. Rather than being in any way planned or sustainable, the entire thing was kept going by what was, however computerised and digitised, a classic credit bubble, one that burst in 2008.

What alienated us from it even at the time was being at the other end; it's quite possible none of this would have happened if we'd lucked into good jobs, circa 2002. Most bloggers worked casually or, in particular, taught in FE colleges, which were dilapidated and starved of money. Between 2005 and 2009 I shifted between casual work and benefits. None of us owned property, so the benefits of the boom were essentially meaningless to us. But the financial crash, followed first by the sadistic bonfire of public goods known as austerity – followed more recently by a nationalistic, ostentatiously cruel and proudly ignorant gerontocracy – has made some people of my generation rather nostalgic for that age. I do not share this. Rather than feeling nostalgia for the world of 2005, I look at it as a period of waste and idiocy. From the first moment in 2010–11 when I saw people younger than me protesting, vehemently, en masse, about the trebling of tuition fees, it was obvious to me they were trying to clean up the mess we had made. That effort is still ongoing.

1

Soundscapes

If I ever imagined myself writing about anything while I was growing up, it was music. As a professional writer, it is the art form most important to me that I write about least. As a music journalist *manqué*, the approach I took to writing about places and buildings owes at least as much to Simon Reynolds or Jon Savage as it does to Ian Nairn and Reyner Banham. What 'modernism' means to me – an excitement for novelty and transformation, a dissolving of the divides between high and low art forms, a meeting point between pulp and trash, the avant-garde and experimental – comes much more from popular music than it does from a reading of twentieth-century literature or art. When I first visited the city of Sheffield, I read it through Pulp or Forgemasters; Bristol through Tricky and Massive Attack; Glasgow through Orange Juice; Manchester through Joy Division and New Order; South Wales through the Manic Street Preachers. The reason why I only ever wrote at length about the first of these – in *Uncommon*, published in 2011 – is that in every other case, other people were doing it better, and I had nothing to say that hadn't already been said by Simon Reynolds, Ian Penman, Kodwo Eshun or Rhian E. Jones.

Another reason why I never wrote systematically about music is that it no longer seems to have this role, at least in Anglo-America (this is why the first essay here is on pop music from the decades before Little Richard invented rock and roll). But most of all, it's because I ought to be too old for it. After publishing the essay here on the Pet Shop Boys in the German magazine *Electronic Beats*, an editor there asked me to contribute a monthly column along these lines – I very reluctantly said no, because I knew there was no way I would find it in myself to write about any *new* music, and I knew I would end up being, therefore, *that guy*. Now that I'm closer to middle age, I am less bothered about being him, and accordingly have recently published a literal obituary for Florian Schneider on the LRB blog, included here, and a moral obituary for Morrissey, in Grace Blakeley's anthology *Futures of Socialism*. This collection also includes fragments of the two blogs I wrote in the second half of the 2000s: 'The Measures Taken', for longform writing, intended at first as a sort of academic CV; and 'Sit Down Man, You're a Bloody Tragedy', personal writing aimed mostly at my own and my internet friends' amusement. Both posts are I think fairly representative of what 'the blog scene of the 2000s' – K-Punk, Blissblog, Poetix, Entschwindet und Vergeht, Infinite Thought, the House at World's End, Woebot, the Original Soundtrack, the Pill Box, Fangirl, the Impostume, Velvet Coalmine, the End Times, the Fantastic Hope, Beyond the Implode, Pere Lebrun, Voyou Desoeuvre, to name the greats – were about. That is, political despair, cultural obsession, and OTT writing – crammed with adjectives, sub-clauses, ten references per sentence, misappropriated terminology from theory and psychoanalysis – all applied to whatever you'd just found in the charity shop, the library, the remainder bookshop or the bargain bin. The critique of 'youth' in the first post, written though it was by a twenty-four-year-old, reads quite oddly in 2020, when Anglo-American politics is polarised so acutely between overgrown teenagers in their sixties and responsible, civic-minded twentysomethings.

Want to Buy Some Illusions?

Pop, Pre-Teen

Go into a remainder bookshop and look at the CDs, or go into the contrived fustiness of an HMV basement, and investigate the pre-history of an artform. The Ink Spots, Al Bowlly, Anne Shelton, the Andrews Sisters, the odd name that somehow survived history – Frank Sinatra, Mae West, Marlene Dietrich. There are people called 'Ethel', lacquered singers lumbered with un-pop names like 'Vera' or 'Alma'. The scratchiness and tinniness, eerie and out of place on the cheaply packaged CDs, carries the odd power of extreme anachronism. An unsettling primness, the shoddy recording technology acting like a layer of dust. The music has an alien adultness, an effeminate formalism. This is the distant past, and they do things differently here.

Critique of Teenage Reason

LOGIC

> I was brought up on Immanuel Kant, on the categorical imperative, and his teachings. ('The logical form of all judgement consists in the objective unity of the apperception of the concept which they contain.') Logic was demanded at all times. If there was no logic in my deductions, I was ruled out of any conversation. To this day I cannot get away from this strict adherence to logic, and I demand it of others as it was demanded then of me.
>
> Marlene Dietrich, *Marlene Dietrich's ABC*

The ideal consumer, first of pop music and subsequently of everything else, from coffee to washing powder, has, since 1956, been the teenager. This figure of illusory radicalism has presided over post-welfarist capital like a petulant despot. Capital's administrators all aim to incarnate this figure, which is perpetually obsessed with its own veracity, like the teenage fetish for 'realness', for 'meaning it'. A public schoolboy for PM, or the fratboy presidents Clinton and Bush. The teenager – a demographic created in the 1950s to define those who heard the thrill of the carnal in Elvis or in Little Richard, obsessed with 'freedom' yet utterly dependent – is the true subject of late capitalism, with its deliberate avoidance of actual adulthood, replacing it with an obsession with innocence's violation and subsequent perpetual regeneration, an ever-present mental state of total ahistoricity. Think of the hundreds of times since 1945 the US has 'lost its innocence'. Capital's self-image is that of Cybill Shepherd in *The Last Picture Show*, a perpetually blonde and baffled self-denying carnality, rather than the Kurtz it more precisely resembles.

I found, for 30p in a bin in Southampton Library, a tragically wrong-headed 1962 book that tries to lock the stable door long after the horse has bolted: Grace and Fred M. Hechinger's *Teen-Age Tyranny* (on the cover a stunningly wholesome couple straight out of Bogdanovich's film). What sinks its critique is an inability to understand rock and roll, a bizarre obsession with ability and proficiency that would subsequently be inherited by rock's own internal hierarchy. After dismissing Elvis and Little Richard, they find a redeeming figure in Pat Boone, as he can 'really sing'. Interestingly though, they place the appeal of pop before pop in the experience of twentieth-century horror, specifically War: 'In the early 40s psychiatrists said that Sinatra came along at just the right time, during the war years when men were scarce and war fears had shattered women's nerves. They called Frankie the "love object" of girls suffering from real or imagined war loneliness.' If the subject for pop after

1956 is male, sexualised, independent, carefree and ideally exists in a car radio on an open road, before Elvis it is female, guilt-ridden and speaks through a radio in a tiny rented room. Listening to Al Bowlly's endless professions of eternal devotion, you imagine its listener to be a seduced typist from an early Eliot poem. The pivotal song for this is 'Lili Marleen'– written in Germany during the war, nearly banned by Goebbels ('trash with the stench of death') and translated into English and Russian. A soldier's lament for his wife (curiously never sung by a man), the song was the only point of unity between the opposing powers – stories abound of German battalions being lured to their death by hearing its strains and assuming those playing it must be German. The song is utter kitsch of the most compelling sort, deeply unnerving in its mingling of lachrymose sentiment with militarism in its later verses.

My Echo, My Shadow and Me

MELANCHOLY

> Having the blues, or weltschmerz. Being in the depths of sadness
> is just as important an experience as being exuberantly happy.
> *Marlene Dietrich's ABC*

While he might have seen world-historical significance in the (post–Ink Spots) Orioles' 'It's Too Soon to Know', Greil Marcus is responsible for the term 'Old, Weird America' – and this is markedly not what we find in these records. This is the manufactured pop of its day – overproduced, slick, utterly commodified, with absolutely nothing of the grass-roots – an abnegation of jazz or ragtime. It would make absolutely no sense played acoustically. The Ink Spots are essentially about the microphone and its possibilities rather than some disguised protest, with their ultra-polished, ostentatiously bourgeois (all piano trills and elegance) de-spiritualisation of gospel. The very model of the vocal group is totally contrary to any notion of autonomous subjectivity, as these five men crowding around the machine all pledge themselves to, presumably, the same girl.

Every Ink Spots song is pretty much identical: the same guitar intro; the strikingly Anglicised, prissy falsetto; and the focal point of each record, where Hoppy Jones recites the song's theme and lyric in a low baritone. The Ink Spots sang, perpetually, of an utterly morbid romanticism in the language of poems on Valentine's cards. They create a kind of massified intimacy – the act of recording via the microphone becomes fetishised by the 'closeness' of the backing singers' hums and burrs, providing a bed of abstract sound that is only made audible by its technologies – the personal serenading that their music promised is impossible outside the studio. The Ink Spots wallow, they luxuriate, in a sentimentality that constantly veers on the sinister. 'Do I Worry', pointedly used in *The Singing Detective*, piles on layers of passive aggression that seems to imply real pain in the silences between words in the obligatory spoken section – a quietly startling combination of anger and stoicism. 'Puttin' and Talkin'', meanwhile, includes an extended dialogue between two of the singers in which they discuss the song itself in slow, low tones, with exquisite attention to the tiniest catch of the voice, the slightest brush of ambivalence.

In his 1980 cash-in book *Blondie*, Lester Bangs included a section advocating a re-mystification of pop's libidinal imaginary, entitled 'On the Merits of Sexual Repression'. Though he explicitly disassociates this demand from 'the wimsy weasly pre-rock popular music our parents lived and loved to', it describes aptly how this music works. Listening to the utterly ridiculous and utterly convincing affectedness of Al Bowlly trilling through the clichéd pledges of 'The Very Thought of You', the main charge is a kind of furtiveness of sound, almost seedy in its resolute unphysicality. The protagonist is never actually able to admit the purpose of these perennial courtings and serenadings – instead the pleasure is deferred, leaving behind a purposeless languor.

You Take Art, I'll Take Spam

STANISLAVSKI, KONSTANTIN

Any ideas I might have had about the importance of an actor's approach to a part were extinguished for good when Max Reinhardt, sitting in the empty theatre, listened to my prayer of Gretschen in Faust. When I got up from my knees embarrassedly brushing off the dust from my skirt, his voice rang out, 'you did not make me cry.' I lifted my tear-stained face and said, 'But, Professor, I am crying!' The answer was 'I do not care if you cry or laugh or what emotion you harbour, your task is to make me cry, me, the spectator. I couldn't care less what you feel! Make me feel!'

Marlene Dietrich's ABC

When the very idea of writing your own songs is inherently ridiculous, and when interpretation is more important than authorship, something interesting happens with singing. The singer can slip in and out of character, comment on the song while singing it rather than having somehow to incarnate it. Mostly this is played out over extremely traditionalist songs, but these potentialities can let in a similar approach to the song itself. Friedrich Hollaender, another Weimar relocation, shows this perfectly in his songs for Marlene Dietrich. His lyrics, with their deflating sardonic twists, evoke a kind of bargain-basement Brecht, a premonition perhaps of the turn of the twenty-first century's use of irony as an ideological confidence trick; though lacking the contempt that his attitude usually necessitates, an essential seriousness remains. Suddenly though, both singer and song are in every way knowing.

This knowingness is not, however, demystifying; instead it is a pose of world-weary elegance and sensuality. This accords with the odd status, vis-à-vis male fantasy, of figures like Dietrich or Mae West, and with the stunning variety of (often untrained) female voices in pre-pop pop. A compilation called, with an eye to its most-likely pensionable audience, *Those Wonderful Girls of Stage, Screen and Radio* gathers together some of this 1930s multiplicity (so much in contrast with the one-dimensional lovelorn male singers). The derisive snarl of Ethel Merman, Dietrich's semi-spoken purrs, Helen Forrest's bored, seen-it-all denunciations of man's perfidy, or a barely in-tune Mae West barking a series of barely disguised innuendos on 'I Wonder Where My Easy Rider's Gone'. West ('a milestone, a catchword, sex with its tongue in its cheeks', says Dietrich's invaluable *ABC*) was a kind of self-created fantasy figure, achieving fame when already into middle age as a symbol of cartoonish carnality – not to be desired necessarily, but constantly desiring. This is very much before the prizing of youth above all else.

Kenneth Tynan wrote in the seventies of trying to convince someone post-pop of what is interesting in a performance by Ethel Merman: 'audiences nowadays expect strain and sweat, as provided by pop stars ... she keeps her distance. What she sells is not the song, not herself – you never miss a syllable.' This carefulness is precisely what makes attempts to revive this so incredibly irksome: think of Robbie Williams' grotesque *Swing when You're Winning*. Though these recordings are often riven with self-reflexivity, they are never ironic. They might step back from the song, but they'll never wink at you. Recreating them for a supposedly less credulous age falls utterly short. Pop pre-pop does, however, represent a kind of group of alternate strategies, and a parallel world with its own attendant rules, strictures and kinks. It is an alternate history, whose illusions have 'a touch of paradise, a spell you can't explain'.

October 2005

Hurrah for the Black Box Recorder

New Labour's liberal apologists like to claim that they've somehow established a 'progressive consensus' in Britain. Perhaps the best answer to this absurdity is the unstoppable rise of the *Daily Mail* under their watch, to the point where it leaves the *Mirror* (once the nearest thing there was to a truly 'left' paper, and unassailable) trailing. Sure, pointing out that the *Daily Mail* is rather right-wing is banal, the province of *Have I Got News for You* guests. But that doesn't change the fact that the paper that once cried 'HURRAH FOR THE BLACKSHIRTS' would undoubtedly do so again, were a similar force for order and barbarity to emerge again on British streets. The *Mail* would love a new Mosley, one they could truly get behind, the British Union of Fascists leader being too obviously a narcissistic, opportunist aristocrat – a product of the stately home rather than the semi – and suspiciously intelligent, not instinctive enough to convince as a potential dictator. The new Mosley would listen to Aretha Franklin at home perhaps, and would make quite clear that expulsions of migrants weren't *racist*, much as did Rothermere's editorials in the thirties.

This latent and not-so-latent evil at the heart of England, where *Brimstone and Treacle* could easily be restaged – but certainly not commissioned – without changing a line (except the Irish would become the Muslims), seems barely to leave an obvious trace on pop culture – a matter upon which, as Robin Carmody has ceaselessly pointed out, the *Mail* now proclaims its normality, dishing out free Prince CDs and all. The first Black Box Recorder album is a rare instance of the land of Rothermere put consciously onto record: *Mail*-type values pervade everywhere, but are musically cloaked in an inoffensive Americanism. BBR, meanwhile, expressed all that brutality, emotional atrophy and banal, weary fascism as a (kind of) pop.

The cover of *England Made Me* was originally to have been a photograph from the 1936 Berlin Olympics, in which the

England football team give the Nazi salute. The record might, with that cover, have truly encapsulated British fascism by adding sport to the litany of untrustworthy outsiders, single mothers (see 'New Baby Boom'), lurking paedos and pinched petit-bourgeois malevolence. So in the midst of (cough) cool Britannia, in 1998, a voice that spoke in purest Selsdon curtly declared, 'we don't like you, go away – we're *swinging*': Britpop's politics of racial exclusion in a pithy phrase. 'Ideal Home' sets the cut-glass vowels on a sparse, freeze-dried evocation of the joys of property, wherein there is 'never an awkward silence ...' The evocation of *Mail*-land here is always elided with, and slipping into, an earlier, inter-war, blackshirt-admiring incarnation. The *Mail* of today, the *Daily Hell* as Julie Burchill christened it, is hysterical, at a constant pitch of screaming neurosis in a way that its forbears were not, so BBR deliberately excise this edge of mania.

The blankness and poise evoke an earlier version of middle-class psychosis: 'England Made Me' was apparently based on the dispassionate self-hatred, seediness and moral turpitude of Graham Greene himself (rather than his novel of that title). The inextricable horror of Englishness is impossible to erase or escape: 'I travelled all my life, / But never got away from the killing jar, / And the garden shed.' By 'It's Only the End of the World' a total fatalism takes over, like a British seaside version of 'Is that All There Is?', where the apocalypse is welcomed, but with none of the glorying in destruction of Morrissey's 'Everyday Is like Sunday' or John Betjeman's 'Slough'. And one wonders what to make of the stripping of 'Uptown Top Ranking' into an anaemic, poker-faced march.

Luke Haines is always balancing crassness and egotism with flashes of genius: for every 'Unsolved Child Murder', there might be some blustery, Steve Albini–produced mess. He had made very enjoyable records: the blaxploitation/Red Army Faction concept album *Baader-Meinhof*, or *The Oliver Twist Manifesto*, where Tesco Destiny's Child arrangements back tales of the Gordon Riots and the much-anticipated assassination of Sarah Lucas. But crucial to why *England Made Me* (written with John Moore) is in a different league entirely is the replacement of Haines's perpetually irritated rasp with the perfect vowels of Sarah Nixey. There's never a slippage, never a moment where the facade might fall; she sounds like several husbands and suicide attempts couldn't shake her hauteur. The songs – of surveillance, boredom, suburban idylls and 'cars found parked at Beachy Head' – have to be sung calm and blank, leaving cold spaces between the phrases. *England Made Me* is full of the sheer spatiality of suburbia, the sparseness – often just a drum machine and shards of guitar and keyboard, like Young Marble Giants stripped of all naivete and charm – transliterating the physical emptiness of the cul-de-sacs, arterial roads and tennis courts. The psychoses are occasionally reversed: BBR knew where the Angry Brigade were brought up, as can be heard on 'Kidnapping an Heiress'.

England Made Me's perfection was almost equalled on *The Facts of Life*, where it occasionally seems the sinister idyll is taken seriously, embraced. The sound is bright, seductive, aiming at some sort of unlikely *CD:UK* dominance, apparently inspired by the production on Billie singles, and by far the nearest thing to a convincing pop record Luke Haines has ever made. Here, the chilling net-curtain narratives are exchanged for a peculiar semi-pagan Surrey sexuality, evocative of the Betjeman fetish for the starched, jolly tennis girl. You have to read the lyric sheet for it to be clear that in 'Gift Horse' the alluring voice insisting 'I just want to be loved' is singing in the character of John Christie. Elsewhere, banality becomes transcendent. 'The English Motorway System' channels endless repetition and featurelessness into a placid, Kraftwerkian romanticism of smoothly running infrastructure. The two modes were combined in the last album, *Passionoia*, where anti-nostalgia too often turns into celebration of the past. However, it's ambiguity that makes these two records such rare and precise anatomisations of British psychosis. Obsessed with the petty brutality in the miserable hearts of the Brit bourgeoisie, but capable of finding in it something 'beautiful and strange': aware of the cruelty it is so clearly capable of, the polite smile before it puts the boot in.

November 2007

From Revolution to Revelation: The Politics of the Pet Shop Boys

'Now I'm digging through my student paperbacks,' sings Neil Tennant. 'Flicking through Karl Marx again / Searching for the soul of England / Drinking tea like Tony Benn.' This is 'Love Is a Bourgeois Construct', from the Pet Shop Boys' twelfth album, *Electric*. The song is, as always, tongue-in-cheek – the narrator decides that love is a bourgeois construct after being dumped, and then reaches for the Marx. But for a long time, the Pet Shop Boys have been making records that are alternately about politics and intimacy, or rather the politics of intimacy, writing relationships together with economics. *Electric* has few surprises – like a lot of late Pet Shop Boys, it sounds like Tennant singing liberal truisms over discarded Michael Mayer tracks. But this little couplet is a reminder that there is something in the Pet Shop Boys' songs that seldom gets noticed – a red, or at least reddish thread that traces a route from the parodic Thatcherism of their early years to the satires on Blairism in 2006's *Fundamental*.

The Pet Shop Boys were hardly the first to combine condensed critiques of capitalism with bitter love songs to the point where the two were interchangeable – you can find that in Marvin Gaye's *Here, My Dear*, or in a starker form all over the Gang of Four's first two albums, or on songs like 'Date Stamp' on ABC's *Lexicon of Love* – but Tennant honed it to a fine art on the group's first two albums. The era when they were authentic teen pop stars was also the time that they were the most sharply, slyly politicised. The obvious example of this is 'Opportunities', a song which quickly became a Thatcherite anthem, where 'looking for a partner' is both come-on and business deal: the least romantic invitation imaginable, where apparently 'I've got the brains / You've got the looks' is a compliment rather than an insult. It's there too in the study of place 'Suburbia' – somewhere so tedious that petty vandalism, 'and in the distance a police car / to break the suburban spell', is the only way to make it bearable.

1987's *Actually* was nothing less than a concept album about Thatcherite London. Throughout, it's impossible to tell relationships from politics. In 'Rent', notoriously, the narrator's declarations of fealty are indistinguishable from the financial arrangement that made them possible, blended elegantly together: 'Words mean so little, and money less'; 'we never, ever argue, we never calculate / the currency we've spent'. Yet it's sung in a warm, pleading tone, never degenerating into the cynical and diagrammatic, both sympathetic and deeply unnerving. 'Shopping' drops the ambiguity altogether and goes for a depiction of utterly ruthless City boys and privatisation – 'We're buying and selling your history … It's easy when you've got all the information / Inside help, no investigation'. 'King's Cross' darkened this even further – into an image of the station where the north meets the capital as an apocalyptic city of the dead. Surely one reason why the Pet Shop Boys never went back to this exact territory – a London of endemic poverty and conspicuous consumption, bankers stepping over the homeless – is that so little has changed since. *Actually* describes London in 2013 as much as it does 1987.

After this, the anger drains out of Tennant's lyrics somewhat, and when they do touch on politics and history it's in a post-'89, 'End of History' fashion, as if the optimism of that year, and the deposing of Thatcher in 1990 defanged him. There's a peculiar sideline in laments for the Russian Revolution – in 'My October Symphony', on *Behaviour*, he imagines Shostakovich 'changing the dedication' of the titular symphony 'from revolution to revelation'; while in 'The End of the World' on the same record, there's not much left but a disinterested, hedonistic wait for the apocalypse – 'if it all came to pass now, you'd feel we'd all deserved it somehow'.

It comes back, however, in *Fundamental*. On the one hand, there's more liberal wisdom on the folly of radical change – on the yearning techno of 'Twentieth Century' he tells us he's learnt the lesson that 'sometimes the solution is worse than the problem', but elsewhere the anger returns. 'I'm with Stupid' brings back the personal-is-political metaphors for a vignette on the relationship between Tony Blair and George W. Bush, rendered as a disco farce by Trevor Horn's overwrought production. The eye for using quasi-romantic language as political parody is rendered in the broad brushes of a placard – 'Before we ever met / I thought like everybody did / you were just a moron / a billion-dollar kid … I have to ask myself / like any lover might: / Have you made a fool of me?' 'Integral' borrows the language of Yevgeny Zamyatin's dystopian novel *We* for a potted critique of Blair's ID card scheme (which led to Tennant publicly disavowing his support of the Labour Party); and elsewhere, there are various mordant commentaries on Simon Cowell–issue showbiz. The subsequent *Yes*, though it lacked the same intensity of focus, had similar moments: on 'Building a Wall', the singer complains that there's 'nowhere left to defect to'. On *Electric*, the most damning words are actually someone else's – in addition to an incongruous medley of U2 and Frankie Valli, they cover Bruce Springsteen's ferocious anti-Iraq war polemic 'The Last to Die'.

At one point in the mid-eighties, it might have seemed that nothing was more polarised than the glorious sincerity of Springsteen and the synthetic ironies of the Pet Shop Boys. At this distance, both seem to have been doing the same

28

thing – registering the destruction of the society they knew, and trying to smuggle that into the charts. In electronic music, increasingly as mute and technocratic as a fiscal policy meeting, registering what might be happening in the world outside is now limited to a duo well into their fifties. It's as if the shock of the 1980s was so sudden and overwhelming that it had to provoke a response – but now, the lives lived as transactions that run through *Actually* are considered so normal they're hardly worthy of comment.

July 2013

Dancing to Numbers

After the death of Florian Schneider-Esleben was announced on Wednesday, one of the most shared video clips on social media was of a group of young black Americans dancing to Kraftwerk's 1981 track 'Numbers'. It had been broadcast on the BBC last year, as part of Jeremy Deller's lecture to an ethnically mixed school in London on dance music and politics in Britain, 'Everybody in the Place'. Deller said that whenever he feels sad about the state of the world, he watches this clip. Snipped from a 1991 episode of the Detroit-area cable TV programme *The New Dance Show*, it appears to present a utopian moment, a dissolving of all the boundaries, usually so carefully policed, of race, class, technology and authenticity. It points to the conjunction that made Kraftwerk so important: their forging of a link between the two most revolutionary things that happened in the arts in the twentieth century, the two movements that transformed most people's everyday lives – Central European Modernist design and African American music.

Florian Schneider (he dropped the double-barrel in the mid-1970s) formed Kraftwerk in 1970 with Ralf Hütter, an architecture student and classically trained avant-garde musician. Schneider's father, Paul Schneider-Esleben, was one of the leading West German architects of the 1960s. Kraftwerk are often compared to the Beatles, but in class terms this is a little as if John Lennon had been the son of James Stirling or Robert Matthew, rather than a merchant seaman. Born in 1915, Schneider-Esleben was among the first West German architects to rediscover, in the 1950s, the modernist design that had thrived in the Weimar Republic, all but forgotten by the end of the Nazi era. Schneider-Esleben's major projects, such as the sleek Commerzbank tower in Düsseldorf, show a heavy Weimar influence: clear, linear and rational.

His daughter, Claudia, became a gallerist in Cologne, and his son spent the late 1960s on the fringes of the Rhineland avant-garde scene. Among the exhibits in a recent show of West German Pop Art, 'Singular / Plural', at the Kunsthalle Düsseldorf, was a photograph of the young Florian, naked beside a swimming pool, already mastering an utterly deadpan look. When Kraftwerk moved towards a severe, industrial-corporate aesthetic modelled on the Bauhaus and Russian Constructivism, it was under Schneider's influence. On the cover of the group's third album, *Ralf und Florian* (1973), Ralf is still a scruffy hippy, but Florian, with his tailored suit and side parting, looks like a member of Kraftwerk.

Hütter and Schneider used to tell interviewers that their project was to reopen the constructivist/functionalist/futurist movements interrupted in the early 1930s by Hitler and Stalin; in this, they were retro-futurist from the start. On the back of *The Man-Machine* (1978) there are two interesting acknowledgements. One is El Lissitzky, from whom the group lifted the colour scheme and typography for the album cover; the other is Leanard Jackson, an African American sound engineer who had worked with Norman Whitfield and Rose Royce, apparently hired by Kraftwerk to make the record sound ready for dancefloors. The group had presumably heard that their previous album, *Trans-Europe Express*, had been a hit at parties in the South Bronx. It is often said that Jackson was surprised on meeting Kraftwerk to find that they were white.

Kraftwerk's influence on English synth-pop is patent, but their effect on the overwhelmingly black scenes of hip hop and electro, which came out of the Bronx, as well as on Chicago house, Miami bass and Detroit techno, has been enduringly controversial. It would be absurd to suggest Kraftwerk were the sole influence on these genres (and Kraftwerk's emulation of the mechanised sounds of trains and roads can be easily traced to the J.B.s or Duke Ellington) but links aren't hard to spot. The first electro track, released in 1982, was Afrika Bambaataa's 'Planet Rock', which plays the melody of 'Trans-Europe Express' (it isn't a sample) over an approximation of the beat from 'Numbers', which also formed the basis for nearly every Miami bass track, and has resonated through hip hop and R&B from the US South well into the twenty-first century. The cover of the first widely distributed Chicago house record, Jamie Principle's 'Your Love', was a tribute to *The Man-Machine*. 'Sharivari' by A Number of Names (1981), the first Detroit techno track, is in serious hock to 'It's More Fun to Compute', which had come out months earlier; 'Technicolor' by Juan Atkins, aka Channel One (1986) is as obvious a Kraftwerk tribute as Oasis's most shameless Beatles references.

As to why this should be controversial – well, to call Kraftwerk Eurocentric would be putting it extremely mildly. A vision of 'Europe Endless', as one of the tracks on *Trans-Europe Express* is called, is always going to be chilling for anyone who has seen what European expansion across the globe has meant for those subject to it. To place two upper-middle-class Germans at the centre of African American electronic music may seem suspiciously – offensively, even – neocolonial. But as Kodwo Eshun pointed out in his 1998 treatise on musical Afrofuturism, *More Brilliant Than the Sun*,

> those of Techno's supporters who insist that Detroit brought
> the funk to machine music will always look for Techno's

Af-Am origins to answer these crits. Sun Ra? Herbie Hancock? Kraftwerk's love of James Brown? All of these are routes through Techno – yet none work, because Detroit Techno is always more than happy to give due credit to Kraftwerk as the pioneers of Techno. Kraftwerk are to Techno what Muddy Waters is to the Rolling Stones – the authentic, the origin, the real.

The most militant and politicised of Detroit techno producers have been the keenest to make the connection, whether it's Marc Floyd of Underground Resistance calling an extremely Kraftwerkian track 'Afrogermanic' (1998), or Drexciya imagining an elaborate alternative history in which escapees from slave ships created an advanced, modernist underwater civilisation, 'Aquabahns' and all. Producers from Afrika Bambaataa to Mike Banks have said they didn't see Kraftwerk as white, or as German; Juan Atkins has said he 'had doubts as to whether they were actually human'. Kraftwerk were celebrated for being what they said they were: 'The Robots'.

But why share the *New Dance Show* clip now, of all the dozens of Kraftwerk videos that could be used to celebrate Schneider's life and work? Surely because it seems to capture such a moment of possibility, where all the things that keep people apart, in their segregated sections of society, are suddenly removed. 'Numbers', insofar as it has lyrics, is a series of counts, upwards and downwards, in German, English, Russian, Italian, Japanese, running in syncopated lines above a relentless electronic funk beat. In their astonishing sequence of albums from *Autobahn* in 1974 to *Computer World* in 1981, Kraftwerk seemed to be aiming at a kind of electronic Esperanto, an imaginary universal language that anyone could learn, anyone could speak, anyone could dance to – just as the utopian socialist modern designers of the 1920s had dreamt of universal systems detached from the hierarchies, nationalities and borders of the past. The clip shows that the experiment worked: you could dance to numbers.

May 2020

2

The Island

This is a chapter of essays about cities and landscapes in Britain, a country which, in the period this book covers, went from an apparent success story of 'third way' neoliberal modernisation into the apparently compulsively self-harming nationalistic basket case it is now. That lurch into explicit jingoism, paranoia and dysfunction didn't surprise me particularly, though it has been bleak to watch it unfold, and while it lasted I took part in the major movement to reverse it, the Corbynite movement in the Labour Party. But most of my writing on Britain focuses on trying to work out what exactly it is that went so horrendously wrong with its built environment, given the UK's wealth, geographical position and history. I am firmly of the view that even within the context of European capitalism, Britain has become an outlier: extremely centralised, especially in England, with minimal local democracy and barely existent civic pride, leading to indifferent, cheap and nasty new buildings and suburbs.

Yet I started writing about British cities at the very tail-end of the New Labour project, which in some ways recognised this state of affairs, and attempted measures to alleviate it. The first of these essays describes the early years of the Tory–Liberal coalition government, when the last trickles of New Labour's investment in new libraries were becoming evident in a clutch of delayed new buildings, while scores of branch libraries were being closed as a result of brutal cuts to local government funding. It was written for *Building Design*, an architecture trade paper that had commissioned me to write a city-essay series called 'Urban Trawl', subsequently collected in the books *A Guide to the New Ruins of Great Britain* (2010) and *A New Kind of Bleak* (2012). Editors Amanda Baillieu and Ellis Woodman then tried to set me to work doing national surveys on the state of public buildings under austerity. 'Libraries' and 'Pubs' were published before a failed staff buy-out followed by a managerial clampdown led to *Building Design* becoming little more than an online jobs page. The Libraries essay highlighted the most obvious early consequence of the sadistic cuts to public spending: scores of historic public buildings, well-used and loved, falling empty within the space of a few months.

The other two essays focus on historic landscapes and their present uses. 'Golden Turds' was a response to a commission from the news magazine *Prospect*, on a particularly silly new building in the Scottish capital. There is a post-war Edinburgh tradition of bemoaning any new building whatsoever, and a belief that, to paraphrase Jane Jacobs, the city was 'finished'. I aimed to sidestep this by trying to discover the answer to a different question than the one posed – that is, how conservation and contracting, planning and neoliberalism, conspired together to create new buildings of remarkably poor quality in one of the most beautiful cities on earth. Portsmouth and Southampton are not and have never been among the most beautiful cities on earth, but they have as long and as complex a history as Edinburgh. The essay here on the poet Andrew

Jordan is partly an attempt to draw attention to a writer who would surely be a cult figure were he writing about Spitalfields and Hackney Wick rather than Paulsgrove and Bevois Valley, but also to the way in which his work exemplifies how mundane places can be, in Viktor Shklovsky's phrase, 'made strange' through proper attention to buildings and politics. The Walthamstow piece is the only example in this book of the regular columns I have written for the *Guardian*, *Building Design*, *Architects Journal* and, here, *Dezeen*. It describes one of the sorts of the places I actually like to live in, and some of the ways in which they are misunderstood.

The New and Closed Libraries of Britain

If anyone ever finds themselves wondering what free public libraries are for, they can find an explanation on the facade of Sheffield's Highfield Library, in gold capital letters etched into blue stone: 'That there should one man die ignorant who had capacity for knowledge, this I call a tragedy, were it to happen more than twenty times in the minute, as by some calculations it does.' It emblazons a small free library, designed in 1876 by E. M. Gibbs, for a dense inner-city district to the south of central Sheffield, in close walking distance to a high street, terraces and small steelworks. The quotation, from Thomas Carlyle's *Sartor Resartus*, is a thumping statement of civic gospel – the provision of knowledge, for free, to those whose lives are otherwise dominated by poverty and toil. It's difficult to imagine anything more obviously noble, and, like the NHS, it's something which opponents have to skirt around rather than directly attack. Whether the building's nobility is quite as straightforward might be another matter. It's a small, robust but rather stern baroque box of red brick dressed with ashlar, which suggests the pursuit of knowledge might be a rather arduous practice. Can the purpose of these buildings be continued in a different form?

The Highfield Library was lucky enough to be recently refurbished – its imposing, if staid Victorian exterior houses a typically strange collection, with the usual pile-up of romance novels and bestsellers, an extensive Chinese section and a good corner of local history with some Pevsners. It is small branch libraries like this, however, which have been under greatest attack over the last few years. A startling 450 of them have been scheduled for closure under the Coalition, from Upper Norwood to Calderdale, from Glossop to Gorebridge. Local campaign groups emerged all over the country to defend them, in some cases successfully, as at Friern Barnet in north London, where a campaign culminating in the occupation of the library saved it from demolition. In many similar situations though, a service is just removed, with no hope of replacement – a case in point is the depressing, philistine demolition of Ahrends, Burton and Koralek's Redcar Library, to make way for some vague 'hub' that may never get built. ABK usually specialised in university libraries, which sadly are usually of higher architectural quality than plain old municipal libraries – no post-war municipal effort has ever approached the crystalline serenity of Gollins Melvin Ward's Arts Library in Sheffield. Yet the point of public libraries is to come across knowledge where you're not expecting it.

Local authorities do have a statutory obligation to provide free public libraries, whether the Coalition like it or not; and before the crash, Labour areas saw libraries being closed and opened at a nearly equally rapid rate. Probably the most obvious example is in Birmingham, where John Madin's Birmingham Central Library is scheduled to be closed and replaced with Mecanoo's Library of Birmingham. The latter is nearly finished at the time of writing; and Ken Worpole's *Contemporary Library Architecture*, published last month, is a compendious reminder of the various strategies adopted by councils and architects to address the problems libraries face – reduced numbers, digitisation, cuts. These new library buildings were usually part of PFI (private finance initiative) deals, so had a battle to maintain quality from the very start.

'Knowledge is Power', as the slogan engraved in stone on the (closed) Pill Library in Newport famously has it: a government by the expensively educated has an obvious vested interest in closing spaces where people can learn for free. A typical exchange, scheduled pre-crash and finished recently, saw CZWG's Canada Water Library replace YRM's 1970s Rotherhithe Library, ten minutes' walk up the road. Architecturally, it's no masterpiece – its civic scale and positioning on a former dock are marred by predictably cheap detailing and that typical feature of iconism where one facade (dockside) has been thought about and the other (facing the station) appears as an afterthought. It's an undeniable improvement on YRM's depressing, practically Calvinist red brick cube, however; and inside, especially, it's a vast improvement on the usual branch library dross. A thick spiral staircase from a ground floor entrance/cafe provides both a grand route and acoustic protection to the main library, which is on two floors: essentially, a ground-floor for casual use and for kids, and an upper floor for research and proper reading. The layout, if not the lurid colour scheme of the carpets, is exactly how a library should be – welcoming, intimate and serious without being pompous. But while the old library was at the heart of old Rotherhithe, poor and densely packed with thirties council tenements, the new one is at the heart of the newer, affluent part of the district, ringed with Glenn Howells's and CZWG's contrasting eighties/2000s efforts in executive-spec housing design. Walk round the wrong corner and stark poverty is never far away, but the realignment reflects a wider rebranding of council priorities: attracting the wealthy takes priority over protecting the rights of the poor. As it is, though, Canada Water Library's clientele is a great deal more diverse than the yuppified riverside pubs, and the two Rotherhithes manage, uneasily but visibly, to coexist.

There are several places where a similar process is at work, but with less scrupulousness. In East Greenwich, for instance, the purpose-built baroque Carnegie Library is to be closed and replaced with an afterthought in the ground floor of some Trespa-clad flats by Make. Yet if I think of the two libraries where I spent much of my childhood and youth, neither were stand-alone buildings: one was a wing of E. Berry Webber's twilight-of-empire Southampton Civic Centre, with beautiful materials and an air of high-mindedness; the other was Eastleigh Library, crammed by Colin Stansfield-Smith's Hampshire County Architects Department into the upper level of a shopping mall. So perhaps libraries might actually work better without booming declarations of their status as hallowed sanctuaries of knowledge?

This was the implicit argument behind the most controversial of all these replacements: the exchange of Whitechapel Library, the former 'university of the ghetto' with its unique collection (the building itself would be soon absorbed by the neighbouring Whitechapel Gallery), for the largest of David Adjaye's three Tower Hamlets Idea Stores. Here, even the name 'library' was thought to be off-putting, although the Idea Stores have nothing that most urban libraries don't have – free internet and IT provision have long been the norm in the bigger libraries. The building makes a grand civic gesture, with its escalator from street to (ahem) library, a gesture which has recently been abandoned for fear of vandalism. Its brash green/black/grey barcode facade was the obvious inspiration for BDP's Cardiff Central Library, which has a far better interior, with a sense of flowing space absent in Adjaye's building; but here there's a problem Adjaye didn't have – the co-option of the library space by chain restaurants. A quote on a plaque from the Manic Street Preachers – 'Libraries Gave Us Power' – is far less prominent than the sign for Wagamama. Something similar is taking place at Bennetts' Jubilee Library in Brighton, itself a pretty, thoughtful building fighting against its PFI execution and the signage of Pizza Express. Like the private finance initiative itself, the idea seems to be that a public good must always be offset by a private concession. The libraries in Cardiff and Brighton are at least attempting to be civic buildings, designed for reading in; conversely some of the new PFI libraries, such as Newcastle's (replacing a library-on-walkways by Basil Spence) feel like business park buildings, with big atria and cold surfaces.

Perhaps the only public library built over the last twenty-five years that really feels like a library, in the sense that the great municipal libraries such as Preston, Liverpool or Manchester feel like libraries – buildings unashamedly dedicated to knowledge and power, without a hint of anything ingratiating or patronising – is Colin St John Wilson's British Library, a perennially underrated paragon of public virtue. Its luxurious details and technical complexity are surely as much the reasons why

Birmingham Central Library

The Library of Birmingham

it hasn't been emulated as is the more obvious decline in architectural fashion of Wilson's Aalto-via-Holden civic modernism. Madin's Birmingham Central Library, for all its hard concrete volumes, had a similar approach – that particular sense of rigour and purpose coexisting with comfort and intimacy. It's too soon to say whether Mecanoo can provide something of equal value. Judging from the renders and the unfinished spaces, the approach appears to favour the sublime rather than the intimate, the kind of vast circular space lined with books that runs from Smirke's British Museum Reading Room to Asplund's Stockholm Library, though neither felt the need to clad their building in a screen making 'references' to the city's 'industrial traditions'. The Library of Birmingham promises to have a huge and diverse collection, and whatever the dubious ethics of demolishing Madin's building, the jury is still out. But one thing Mecanoo's building will definitely have is a whacking great big atrium. Apparently a library too needs the 'wow factor'.

June 2013

Edinburgh's Golden Turds

If you go down to the corner of Princes Street in Edinburgh, opposite the symmetrical classical centrepiece of Waterloo Place, where a view of the National Monument is framed by two sandstone porticos, you'll find a construction site on a very worn 1960s building. The building in question – the St James Centre, a widely disliked shopping and hotel complex – is being gradually demolished in favour of the thing envisaged in a pair of renders. A routine glass and stone-cladding mall, around a new hotel wrapped in a coil of orangey-gold fabric in a style which can only be described as excremental. This is in the centre of a UNESCO World Heritage Site, one of the most photographed, most admired and most protected urban ensembles in the world. And it's the tip of an iceberg of poor-quality architecture and planning in the Scottish capital, which extends from substandard new residential districts, lumpen office complexes and unsympathetic renovations of older buildings. How has this been allowed to happen in a city which, fifteen years after devolution and a couple of years after a narrow independence referendum, one might think would be full of the sort of confident, well-designed architecture that is normal in most European capitals?

Of course, one reason why the new St James Centre is being allowed to go ahead based on the questionable designs of Jestico + Whiles is that nobody (aside from a few concrete fetishists with Instagram accounts) has ever had a good word to say about the old one. 'Well, at least it's better than' is a common shrugged-shoulders complaint when a new building is proposed in, say, Southampton, or Bradford, or Swansea; it is setting the bar extremely low for Edinburgh. Perhaps because of this, there have been many attacks on the new scheme, and on what it represents. The writer David Black recently argued in the *Guardian* that the city should be stripped of its UNESCO status, because of the St James Centre redesign, the indifferent

Out with the Old...

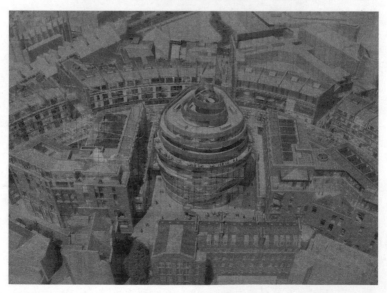

...In with the New

'New Waverley' development being planned nearby and the building of a hotel next to Thomas Hamilton's Athenian-style Old Royal High School. UNESCO did in fact send a strongly worded communiqué on the latter, and the plan was then dropped in favour of retrofitting the building as a music school. But in Black's argument, you can find the heart of the problem. He describes the city, with approval, as an 'unrivalled stage set for a festival of arts and culture'. That's only one of the many things Edinburgh is about: it's a capital; a bureaucratic, administrative city; and it is also – as it has been for centuries – one of the major financial centres in Europe, and its delinquent banks were at the centre of the 2008–9 financial crisis. These have had at least as much influence on its architecture and planning as UNESCO and the Festival. What Edinburgh has achieved, with some aplomb, is to sustain a large amount of new building, often carefully shrouded from the skyline views, given the shrill stylistic debate when anything that might change the city's profile is mooted – as Edinburgh University architecture professor Richard Williams has pointed out, 'Edinburgh being Edinburgh, any sort of change does produce a sort of neurotic reaction'. The results, especially in large-scale projects, have been poor for some considerable time. The real problem might lie elsewhere.

The worst things that have happened to Edinburgh's architecture in the last twenty years have been well out of the tourist view. One of these is the scandal of the seventeen schools built in the city using the private finance initiative, which had to be closed because of safety concerns: not only drab and miserable as architecture, these schools have proven incompetently built, the result of a procurement system where quality is relentlessly driven down through an enforced system of subcontracting and 'value engineering'. Another is the redevelopment of the docklands at Leith – the Western Harbour and Granton Harbour – that were filled, especially in the years before the financial crash of 2008, with an indifferent landscape of speculative apartment buildings, miserable pseudo-public spaces, introverted shopping malls and, again, poor materials which have worn appallingly in the harsh North Sea climate. But neither of these interrupts anybody's view of Calton Hill, the Castle or Arthur's Seat, so they've been much less publicly criticised than anything which creeps into the vista established 110 years ago, when the clocktower of the Balmoral Hotel completed the postcard view.

What makes this specially strange is that in the 1990s and early 2000s Edinburgh had managed to create a strong, and strongly independent, architectural culture. Richard Murphy, Benson & Forsyth and Malcolm Fraser, among others, had distinguished themselves with usually small-scale interventions into the fabric of the historic city, modern without being aggressive, contextual without being sentimental. Two late-nineties designs by Fraser – the Poetry Library, off the Royal Mile, and Dance Base, off Grassmarket – were especially notable for their subtlety and skill. Fraser, who is also a prolific commentator on the city's architecture, had to liquidate his practice last year as it was hit by the impact of the recession. Asked about the effects of the UNESCO listing, he argues that 'it's mostly been business-as-usual. Edinburgh's innate conservatism has saved it from major destruction in the past, but now rubs horribly against the normal open-for-business ethos that politicians and planners embrace. You could say that the UNESCO listing has made development more risk averse but there is, in any case, a general tendency to avoid risk, innovation and beauty by making proposals as bland as possible.' One way this can be seen is in PFI and public–private partnerships, and their effects on the public architecture of the city. 'We have set aside the ideal of public service and common good which once drove public architecture, handing leadership to construction conglomerates and the bankers who direct them. We are saddled with enormous debt and shoddy buildings as a result.'

The Scottish government abolished PFI with some fanfare, but replaced it with something similar: 'the Scottish Futures Trust model and contractor "hub" monopolies that succeeded PFI are not sufficiently better.' Architects are still mostly 'seen as "supply-chain components", whose costs need driving down'. And whereas the debates over independence might be thought to have had a beneficent effect, 'the SNP has failed, so far, to deliver much new and radical, though there are hopeful initiatives in land, planning and tax reform edging forward.' Independence might still offer ways out of this, Fraser suggests: 'an independent Scotland might have the gumption to promote enterprise and equality through a national bank of reconstruction, massive public investment into innovative housing finance and models and renewable industries. A general focus on the craft of making things would be nice.'

That has been one of the things most obviously absent in the city's recent projects – the hideously cheap and nasty renovation of Waverley Station, with its Trespa-clad stairways up to Princes Street or the Old Town, is a particularly horrible case in point. Planning, as much as craft, has also been a persistent problem. This is a city which, in theory, should be one of the great exemplars of town planning in the UK, with the development of the New Town from the eighteenth century onwards as a rationalist series of grids and circuses standing as one of Europe's great consciously created architectural setpieces. Every new scheme in the last couple of decades has held it up as a model, from the grim waterside yuppiescape of Leith Docks, to the sleek business district at Edinburgh Park (whose exurban location was justified by the prospect of a new tram line, which finally emerged fifteen years later), or, most questionably of all, the bumptious, heavy, overbearing office blocks that crowd round Tollcross and Exchange Square, based on a late-nineties plan by Terry Farrell. These latter two projects are what Edinburgh's financial sector has instead of Canary Wharf – they can't build high, so instead they have built long, low 'groundscrapers', which are largely horrible as townscape, but at least don't intrude onto any views. Much contemporary architecture in the city is judged not by what it does, but by what it doesn't do – if it's in keeping, if it's not in the way of any of the sightlines, then wave it through. If it does break those golden rules, then expect a fiercely fought campaign. In a way, it's laudable – there are a few historic cities, like St Petersburg or Krakow, that could do with some of that dogged focus – but because all the energy is dragged into that act of self-defence, positive proposals for what sort of city, and what sort of architecture, might be worth fighting for now are few and far between. And if you're out of the heritage zone, nobody much cares.

One of the planners who worked on Leith Docks is the neoclassicist Robert Adam, who was hired late in the day to try to make sense of the mess that speculative development had made of the place. 'I was the masterplanner for Western Harbour in Leith and Granton Harbour,' he tells me. 'Both had already been masterplanned and the first parts had been built. These were thought to be unsatisfactory, and both plans went on ice in 2008. Nothing of our work came to anything in Granton but some was done according to our codes and layout at Western Harbour – more recently key aspects of our codes, such as enhanced ground-floor ceiling heights, have been forgotten.' Their eventual failure he puts down to 'bad planning that was too simplistic. Even in economic terms there was oversupply of one type which saturated the market. They said, as they always do, that it all related to local character but I think tower blocks on a grid is stretching the point.' In this, relentless cost-cutting plays a major role. 'Design and Build and novation of architects, now the norm, are a disaster, everything gets cheapened – in both senses of the word – and the architect, paid by the cheapener, is powerless and compromised.'

Some of the more intelligent projects in the city since devolution have, of course, been hugely expensive. The Scottish

Parliament, designed by the Catalan architects Enric Miralles and Benedetta Tagliabue, eventually brought to completion by RMJM, has its supporters, but was vastly more expensive than originally advertised. The trams that were meant to link Edinburgh Park to the centre went way over budget when the tracks laid had to be dismantled after a fault was discovered. Yet one might ask whether building schools so cheaply that parts of them fall off is a solution to cost overruns. In the same time that Edinburgh went through this farrago, Nottingham and Manchester – not to mention Leipzig or Le Havre – built much more extensive and complex tram and light-rail lines with little fanfare.

A less trumpeted town-planning tradition than that of the New Town is the 'conservative surgery' advocated by the academic and planner Patrick Geddes at the start of the twentieth century. Geddes's anti-moralistic approach to historic architecture makes him either a great social reformer or a prophet of gentrification (or both). Believing that 'slum clearance' unnecessarily put the focus on buildings as the cause of dilapidation and blight, rather than overcrowding and poor maintenance, in the late nineteenth century he was one of the first middle-class people to move to the then decidedly slummy Old Town, and would convince many of his students to do the same. His developments, such as Ramsay Garden, display neatly these ideas about rehabilitating older buildings and stitching them together with the new. Whereas the New Town tradition is stone dead in Edinburgh – a city that can't even build a tramway properly has no business talking about its great culture of grand planning – the Geddes legacy has been behind most of the interesting new buildings in the city over the last twenty years, following a pattern of large-scale disasters and small-scale triumphs: the vast site of Leith Docks was ruined, but the miniature townscape of Leith Shore, with unfussy infill of the holes between older buildings, was a great success of its kind. Even now, in what is surely a fallow period for Edinburgh architecture, you can find things like the new St Albert the Great Chapel in George Square, a sensitive modern building almost invisibly slotted into the townscape.

According to architecture historian Miles Glendinning, one way that this legacy might be continued is by reappraising some of the architecture of the 1960s. An example he gives is Cables Wynd House, better known as the 'banana block', a brutalist council block which snakes through central Leith, a building 'dictated by its site' rather than imposed as if on a tabula rasa. Preserving this building rather than demolishing it (doubtless for some more Leith Docks–style speculative flats) would be genuine 'conservative surgery' in Geddes's terms. In some respects, the 1960s projects were the last time Edinburgh did planning on a remotely impressive scale. There were sensitive infill projects, such as Basil Spence's work in Canongate, but there were also confident public buildings, including RMJM's sublime Royal Commonwealth Pool, and large council estates near the centre, like Dumbiedykes. The most controversial projects were central – the partial rebuilding of Princes Street, the much loathed (but at this distance, rather decent) redevelopment of George Square by the university, and the (always awful) building of the St James Centre. The experience of fighting against these emboldened one of the most stringent conservation movements in Britain. But there was another consequence of keeping the centre mostly intact: a ring of poverty around Edinburgh, with places like Sighthill and Niddrie seldom visited by anyone from the New Town or the Old Town, and mired in a seemingly permanent limbo between demolition of 1960s towers, 1930s tenements and promised redevelopment schemes. Alone among UK cities, except perhaps Oxford, Edinburgh is a deeply spatially segregated city.

A UNESCO listing for a postcard in lieu of an overall idea for the city can 'stop some quite offensive projects', in Glendinning's words – he mentions Richard Murphy's cancelled

Haymarket Tower, and the original plan for a 'Gherkin'-style tower on the site of the St James Centre as two examples. But it has led to a 'sterile debate', polarised between heritage fundamentalism and growth at any cost. One possible escape from this deadlock could be offered by independence, not necessarily because it would give a boost to new building, but perhaps because of the opposite. 'Politically, I'm in favour,' says Glendinning, 'though the consequences would be a recession and less building; but independence in Ireland led to a lot of serious architectural debate in the 1920s and 1930s, so there's a possibility it might stimulate architectural quality', if not necessarily quantity. One explanation, he argues, for the vitality of Scottish architecture in the 1990s and its relative drabness today is that, then, architectural expression was caused partly by a political blockage. 'When John Major wouldn't allow any devolution, it encouraged a lot of energy to go into culture; since then, it's been directed into politics.' But more than anything else, Edinburgh's architectural problems are British problems. Its inability to plan coherently, its chaotic, hobbled attempts to bolster public transport, its willingness to let the market do what it likes as long as it's in certain places (Leith or Edinburgh Park, yes; Calton or Haymarket, no), its neglect of social housing, its hulking speculative office blocks, the ever-present dominance of the financial services industry, the baleful effects of PFI ... these are all specific to the UK and the grim reluctance with which it faces architecture and urbanism.

'Edinburgh', according to Muriel Spark's fascist school-teacher Miss Jean Brodie, 'is a European city'. Unlike Glasgow – which, architecturally, culturally and politically has been the livelier city for some considerable time – it did not shift towards support for independence in the 2014 referendum. However, it did vote overwhelmingly to stay in the European Union. And Edinburgh, historically, is most definitely a European capital, for better and worse: a middle-class population living in the centre in flats rather than on the outskirts in houses;

dense and tightly planned inner-city districts; a disciplined classical architecture; and – like Paris, but unlike London – it has a *banlieue* around the city where poverty and dereliction are concentrated. That 'European' identity has actually lessened since devolution in many respects, largely because of the particularly British procurement methods it has, in tandem with the rest of the UK, enforced upon itself, and a belief that public goods are worth little, except, perhaps, when they can be classed as 'heritage'. What it hasn't managed to acquire during the same time is what architects, commentators and politicians frequently spoke about – having new architecture and infrastructure on the level of European capital cities. Worthwhile architecture of recent years in the Scottish capital has often borrowed from European models, from the interventions in historic cityscapes by the Italian architect Carlo Scarpa, to the Catalan modernism of Josep Antoni Coderch or Miralles (the latter, not coincidentally, hired to design the Scottish Parliament, with devolved Catalonia an obvious parallel for Scotland).

Compared with Birmingham, Edinburgh was not too disfigured by the construction boom of 1997–2008, and not too devastated by its collapse; compared with Barcelona, Berlin, Hamburg, Aarhus, Porto, Rotterdam, Vienna, Ljubljana, Helsinki, the legacy is far poorer. For Edinburgh to attempt a plan that would finally stitch this city – one part typical shabby British town, one part straggling council estate and one part obsessively maintained heritage site – into a coherent, egalitarian capital city may or may not involve a break with the British state. But it would most definitely need a total divorce from a culture which regards architecture and planning as an optional afterthought following the protection of historic views and paying off of building contractors. As it is, Edinburgh today is built with one eye to UNESCO and the other to Serco.

March 2017

False Landscape Syndrome: The Poetry
and Propaganda of Andrew Jordan

A Machine for Revolution

Unlikely as it may seem, there was a local preservation campaign to save the Tricorn Centre in Portsmouth from the demolition that eventually came to it in the mid-2000s. Once ritually voted 'worst building in Britain' and seen as a sort of national joke, the Tricorn had nevertheless been praised by critics including Ian Nairn as an example of avant-garde ideas applied to the apparently commercial and mundane function of a shopping mall. There was a campaign to save it when, after years of plotting and promising, its owners began to make serious attempts to redevelop the site. This led to the distribution of a leaflet – 'URGENT CALL TO ACTION! SAVE OUR TRICORN' – handed out in 1997 by an organisation that went by the name PROLES 4 MODERNISM.

The leaflet featured a grainy black and white photograph of the building's photogenic, sculptural car park, a slogan in bold and a text which took the building to be symbolic of considerably more than the aesthetics of *béton brut*. The Tricorn, it said, 'up ends the aspect of denial that is a function of the architectures of consumerism and militarism that suffocate the city, its civic life. The Tricorn stands for a consciousness of what is, rather than repression in what seems, and the memories lost in that.' This was more than an architectural conservation campaign. What is much more interesting about the leaflet is what it demands, and what it promises. 'We shall complete the modernist project', say Proles 4 Modernism, 'in its social aspect, and express the non-identity which we have found within "our" class (that to which we were assigned). No more enclosure. The Tricorn is an open field, an urban commons, which we have walked upon, and imagined. We spit on "Prince" Charles, and on the scum who execute his wishes.' What is the importance of the Tricorn here? It's as a building that disrupts the city, ideologically as well as visually. It is a 'machine for revolution. It negates bourgeois culture. It puts people off shopping.'

This is in fact a very astute explanation of why the Tricorn Centre was going to be demolished. It is one of three brutalist structures designed by Owen Luder Partnership (and largely designed by the young partner Rodney Gordon) for the developer Alec Gordon, the others being Eros House in Catford, London, and the Trinity Square development in Gateshead, also now demolished, and most famous for its use in *Get Carter*. These were experiments, in which hugely complex, multifunctional megastructures were designed in a monumental concrete manner of aggressive forms, gesturing skylines and rough surfaces. Their complexity and strangeness were far from conducive to their major function – as shopping centres – and in the Portsmouth case, at least, the building became instead a centre for the city's relatively marginalised, with record shops, goth clubs and the like. Alec Gordon's bankruptcy was directly connected with the failure of these buildings as conventional shopping malls. Proles 4 Modernism had hit on the real reason why this building was in trouble – not a question of 'ugliness', but of ground rent.

Later communiqués developed these ideas into an increasingly baroque melange of neo-communist sloganeering and historical myth-making: delirious, hilarious but deadly serious. Another handbill, from 2000, 'SAVE OUR TRICORN!', asserts that

> The **fascists** want to destroy the Tricorn as a bulwark against placelessness.
> The **capitalists** want to destroy the Tricorn as it discourages consumption.
> Both of these is a form of demolition.
> **Proles for modernism** will realise the Tricorn as a 'machine for revolution', for which it was designed.

Below these demands, the flyer descends into the realm of historical speculation, and the following concoction, written in the stone-faced tone of a guide to ley lines: 'according to local tradition, the Tricorn was constructed on the site of an ancient "Druid" temple', a Portsea Island equivalent of Stonehenge. Far from destroying the henge site, the Tricorn – a building which embodies notions of social progression and (holy) trinity – is seen as protecting the hidden 'temple'. Local lore would apparently warn against the demolition of the building. 'It is considered bad luck to disturb the Tricorn site. Ill-fortune will visit the city if it is knocked down.' That's because the Tricorn's own architectural manner is actually deeply ancient, connected with a primordial, pre-historic idea about architecture. Citing Le Corbusier, Proles 4 Modernism claimed that 'the henges and stone circles of the Neolithic period were designed as "machines for living". They "simultaneously" negated the class differences inherent in society and consolidated – in massive blocks of stone – the social power of a tiny elite of architects, poets and shaman-priests.' The relevance of this to the Tricorn is as follows:

> in post-industrial Portsmouth, with the translation of cosmopolitan values into insularity, the modernists fought a rearguard action, attempting to create – at the heart of Portsea Island's sacred landscape – a single, architectural structure that channelled the unity of being envisaged by the Neolithic hierarchs into an image that simultaneously represented the identity of Portsmouth and the cosmopolitan or internationalist ideology that had been all but destroyed and (as Ludor [*sic*] pointed out) ironically emphasised by the second world war.

Accompanying a short poem, 'Tricorn', with a similar interpretation of the building, is the date of a demonstration on the site of the Tricorn that will 'fight art with art'. This also tells you what pub Proles 4 Modernism will be meeting in prior. There is then an explanation of who exactly has produced the leaflet, with a correspondence address in nearby Southampton. 'Proles 4 Modernism is an edgeless organisation working towards quantum proletarian revolution.' A slogan in bold sans serifs at the bottom of the page: 'REVOLUTION WITHOUT CO-ORDINATES'.

This, I realised some time later, was my first introduction to the work of the poet Andrew Jordan, who was, it became clear, the main voice of Proles 4 Modernism – the designer and writer of its leaflets, although not, apparently, its only member. It is also an introduction to the preoccupations that run through his small but violently powerful published corpus of poetry: the built environment of two almost interlinked South Coast cities, Portsmouth and Southampton; the falsification of heritage; the sexual properties of landscape; and the manner in which life in both cities is determined and haunted by the presence of the British imperial past (and present), of the military, of a massive carceral complex, and by the overwhelming interests of capital. In the process, he has created some of the strangest, most personal and most moving work on what the built environment does to people written in the last couple of decades in Britain. The fact that these works are not more widely known is probably connected with the undeniable fact that these two cities are, or so stereotype would assert, unlikely subjects for such an endeavour.

Although both are historic cities, with stories as long and as complex as anywhere in the UK, they are seldom visited (except to pass through, given their principal function as ports) and are as frequently mocked as ignored. They are also remarkably unlike each other, although as the combined South Hampshire conurbation, they form one of the largest urban areas in Britain, larger than Greater Glasgow; for a time in the 1960s, the government considered merging them into one 'Solent City'. Southampton is sprawling and suburban, filled with parks and with a huge wedge of common land in the middle of it; although there is an attractive old town bound by surprisingly intact medieval walls, there are no views of the port in the centre. Atypically for the south-east of England, it has mostly been a Labour-voting city since the 1920s. Its port is for commercial and cruise traffic, with some mundane passenger travel on a little ferry to the Isle of Wight. Portsmouth is concentrated on Portsea Island, and within that is starkly urban and unforgiving, its borders demarcated by the ends of the island, which give remarkable views of the busy, heavily defended harbour. To the north is a landscape of nineteenth-century fortresses on Portsdown Hill, nicknamed 'Palmerston's Follies' after their prime ministerial sponsor, who anachronistically feared a French invasion. It is dense, the densest city in the country outside of London. The historic architecture of the city is concentrated in the Dockyard, a chilling and hard-line showcase of the eighteenth-century 'Functional Tradition'. For all its poverty, Portsmouth is traditionally Conservative-voting, something often explained by the industrial dominance of the army and its later offshoots, such as BAE Systems, who operate, among other things, a large shipyard in Gosport, an even bleaker town opposite Portsea Island. In Jordan's work, these two cities become the site for utopian imaginings, scenes of sudden and apocalyptic revolt.

The Red Button That Would Turn Place Off

Jordan's volumes of poetry are usually focused on a particular subject or obsession, which is portrayed from a variety of angles and perspectives, pieced together through oblique rants and descriptive sketches. *Ha Ha* (2007) is relatively rural for Jordan's work, mostly concentrating on the landscapes between and around Southampton and Portsmouth, only occasionally returning to the cities themselves. Its subject is heritage and archaeology as subterfuge, an elaborate joke being played by the ruling class upon the ruled. In the opening 'Giggle', spotting the titular landscape feature – an artificial slope, often

used in the gardens of stately homes for game-playing – makes
Jordan and a friend realise

> these places
> are taking
> the piss
> out of us.

The piss is taken by the manner in which heritage is produced, not so much in terms of the writing of history, but in its
actual physical production. 'Heritage, Southampton' is from a
three-part cycle, 'The Antiquarians'. It begins:

> Someone was executed near the reservoir.
> That's good. Near the A33.
> A butler killed for stealing *plate*.

This atrocity, this moment of horrific class oppression, becomes
an interesting little tale, a story of the bad old days with no
continuation into the present.

> Meanwhile, in Lord's Wood, archaeologists
> dig banks and ditches that did not
> exist before they came to make
> a cold prosthetic history. Quaint,
> how they make the ground look old.

This is not necessarily a conspiracy theory about archaeology,
a sort of moon-landings-were-faked aversion to *Time Team*,
but a reaction to the prosaic, spineless manner in which these
remnants are presented – a production of attractive pasts which
has the additional function of hiding the nature of another sort
of production, where these landscapes are still very much used,
and by malevolent and punitive forces which still very much
exist. Jordan's own wanderings through these picturesque
Hampshire locations try to leave in the sites of production
that exist. In part three of 'The Antiquarians', 'Kore':

I sang the field edge, bloody minded,
lyrical – the nameless row of cottages
along from the silos, the grain depot

An encounter with 'a schoolgirl in a ditch' (many of Jordan's poems return to teenage memories of the South Hampshire landscape) leads to him trying to rediscover some sort of personal experience of the landscape through sex:

and, as a symbol, she overwhelmed the loss
of place in me, by grounding it in flesh.

Landscape here begins to come into focus when it becomes carnal. Jordan's poetry has a Wilhelm Reich–influenced, somewhat touching belief in the liberating power of untrammelled sexuality, as an alternative to the 'cold prosthetic history' produced by the heritage industry. This is not, however, a matter of the rediscovery of 'authenticity'. For Jordan there are no authentic landscapes, no real and true place that is otherwise reified. In 'Topiary Landscapes',

The synthesis remains there mystified,
its artifice, a real ground, concealed
within the countryside that we'd invented.

Specific spaces explored here include 'A Southampton Stone Circle' and 'On Bevois Mount', referring to a dilapidated inner-city district of Southampton; but the most extensive exploration of an urban space in *Ha Ha* is of Owen Luder's failed shopping centre. Midway through *Ha Ha*, this time credited to Jordan rather than Proles 4 Modernism, is the 'Tricorn' poem, which describes the building as

A cold war cathedral, built to be buried
under a mound, as at Silbury.

The South Hampshire conurbation's western, outer-suburban edges fade into the neolithic landscapes around Salisbury Plain and into Wiltshire and Dorset – the stone circles at Avebury, Silbury Hill and Stonehenge, and the priapic chalk figure at Cerne Abbas. Here, they're conflated with the much more recent artificial mounds and forts of Portsdown Hill, still extensively used by Britain's military-industrial complex. The Tricorn here is between these two and pointing towards the sea, with its own concrete and stone forts embedded in the bay. The Tricorn's triangular ground plan unifies them, and gives the city of Portsmouth a coherence and grandeur that it would otherwise lack.

> Being aligned with the fort at Hilsea –
> and echoing of the Lump Forts in the swell,
> and the muniments on Portsdown Hill,
> at their centre, measured easily –
> it guards its groves and maidens, although fallen,
> and holds the platform of the city up
> above the rising waves, unconsciously.

This conflation of the accepted heritage landscape of rolling hills and ancient stone circles with the more sinister and (apparently) modern hilltop sites of fortresses and military bases continues in 'Looking Down', one of several poems Jordan has written about Portsdown Hill. This one focuses on ASWE, an acronym for the facility known as the Admiralty Service Weapons Establishment. A note at the start of the poem tells us that it 'dominates the skyline of Portsmouth, like a basilica or Kremlin, shaping the lives below'. Or, as Jordan describes it, the building is 'a prominent secret', constantly seen but never discussed. Jordan and a companion explore what they can of ASWE, and its secrecy and inscrutability begin to infect their relation to each other, separated by the vertiginous space of this 'Establishment':

From a centre of conspiracy, you looked down
to watch me as I walked below – my image
broken in the glare – as if you did not know me, or
had never thought, before, of what was there.

In the title poem, largely on the club-wielding, tumescent chalk figure at Cerne Abbas, the ancient, green hill on which the figure was outlined has underneath it another military base, which again Jordan and an unnamed partner explore. The hill is actually a bunker, 'yoked to Nato',

an image of a commonwealth denied
in borders and centres, a fused grove
... you lifted the lid of the tomb so I could see
the machinery, intact – the engines called
Reliant and *Victory* – the greasy undersides of hills
thick with asbestos.

Inside it, they find a 'red button that would turn place off'. At the end of the poem, Jordan, in language much clearer than the oblique, sometimes cryptic lines he uses elsewhere, outlines their findings from this journey into the dark heart of heritage:

A new technology installed
on ancient battlefields;
the progress of enclosure;
not power dispersed, but
power disguised; an abdication.

The figure of the phallic Giant also features in Jordan's subsequent book, *Josian in Ermonie – a Poem Writ Over,* published in 2009, a work so full of innuendo and silliness that it sits a little strangely alongside the horrors of the two subsequent, deadly serious books, *Bonehead's Utopia* (2011) and *Hegemonick* (2012). It is mainly of interest for the obsessive way in which it makes a work of literary-archaeological forgery into a fantastical scattering of fragmentary information on a particularly mundane area of Southampton. It is based on an actual medieval poem of the fourteenth century, the *Romance of Sir Bevis of Hampton*, montaged, paraphrased, rewritten and overlaid with maps, history, anecdote, sex-obsessed rants and a phallic theory about Eilís O'Connell's abstract sculpture *Shear*, which was installed in Bevois Valley, Southampton as part of an urban regeneration project in 2001. Sir Bevis of Hampton was a knight and (of course) a giant, who lived in Southampton at some point in the dark ages; Josian was his wife, and his sparring partner, Ascupart, also features heavily in both the 'real' poem and in Jordan's 'writ over' version.

The area in which he allegedly lived and that has been named after him since the Middle Ages is a somewhat scuzzy, working-class and multi-ethnic area around a long-established hippy pub called the Hobbit, the city's red light district and a riverscape of light industry; cutting it off from the river is a bypass, Thomas Lewis Way, driven through in the 1980s and named after the city's first Labour MP. Opposite its high street of pubs, repair shops and supermarkets there existed until recently a surface car park and a mound of waste. Since 2001, it has been faced with a large billboard of two tall local youths, captioned with the legend 'BEVIS AND ASCUPART'. In among the speculation about giants' penises in the poem are notes and references to things left by Sir Bevis in the area: the alleged stones with which he played marbles, displayed in 1866 'in the courtyard of the Hartley Institute' and a 'huge skeleton' exhibited in the eighteenth century, and then buried – 'the decorative tomb was on a site now covered by a car park opposite the Aldi supermarket'. In response to the invented histories in *Ha Ha*, Jordan invented one himself, but left in the joins and signs of construction, the mediocrity of the place as is, as compared with what was.

Many of these themes run through another photocopied journal Jordan has issued, sometimes running parallel to the Proles 4 Modernism texts – *The Listening Voice*, which describes itself as 'the Newsletter of the Equi Phallic Alliance and Poetry Field Club'. With dating that follows the French revolutionary calendar, it promotes organised walks and has had special issues on the alleged need for children to massacre adults on Portsdown Hill, and on the construction of 'Wessex'. The journal often works as somewhat more legible notes on the poetry – *The Listening Voice* 4, in 1999, is a pre-emptive gloss on *Ha Ha*:

> Comrades, there is no such thing as 'nature' nor 'authenticity'. The 'archaeology' was put in place by those we think are paid to dig it up! When you look through those panels which are erected around an archaeological dig – when you see a glimpse of the site – you are looking at *construction*, the raising of the nation state.

Issue 9 relates to *Josian in Ermonie*, being rather more specific about the area in which it is set:

> Bevois Mount and Bevois Valley, once the locus of pleasure for the few, now abuts Bevois Park, an industrial area built on reclaimed land. By night it serves the pleasures of the many. The prostitutes, displaced from the brothels of Derby Road by local authority action, provide a similar range of thrills to those found in the early 18th century English landscape garden. During a walk down Empress Road at night you will be amazed by Variety, moved by Beauty Ruinous and filled with the Horror of the Sublime. The transitory nature of the prospect, with its shifting lights, its variety of mood and scene, its gloomy shades, will fill your heart with sentiments not available elsewhere in the city.

The same issue features an attack on the 'Cultural Quarter' intended to offset the city's dominance by big-box retail: 'Southampton', it asserts, has

> suffered a material amnesia; with its symbolic centre so hurriedly rebuilt, a commercial rather than a modernist architecture

created a malign enchantment that has proved remarkably persistent. It informed the development at Ocean Village and it is aggressively present in West Quay ... Southampton, city of destroyed beauty, has beauty's absence as its inverse 'unique selling point' and civic leaders have made it their business to ensure that there are no flames from which a Phoenix might ascend. Repeatedly, in renewal after renewal, the city has predicted the retail park.

He would seem to be vindicated by the fact that the Quarter's first tenants were Nando's.

Sirens Whisper at the Top of the Fence

The shift in tone from the cryptic prurience of *Josian in Ermonie* to the subsequent *Bonehead's Utopia*, published two years later, is sharp. The volume is the result of a writer's residency, funded by the Arts Council and local arts organisations on the South Coast, in Her Majesty's Prison Haslar, a placing which, judging by the afterword appended to the book, Jordan seems to regret. HMP Haslar, as it was called then, is a Victorian prison in Gosport. In 1989 it was repurposed to hold foreign nationals, in most cases people who had been rejected for asylum. Around the time Jordan's poem was published, it was being turned into an immigration removal centre, dedicated to processing people being thrown out of the country. HMP Haslar is a reminder that the carceral, punitive built landscape of the South Coast is not merely historical, but something that actually exists, and has consequences. The note at the end of Jordan's book is specific on what sort of space Haslar is: 'The detainees at Haslar live in dormitories. Within each dorm were live-in cubicles – each cubicle has two beds, two lockers and little else. The partitions stop well short of the ceiling, so although only your cubicle-mate can see you, everyone can hear you.' He notes that these punitive conditions

elicit little in the way of protest from the local community –
quite the reverse.

> Some people were pleased at the harsh treatment endured by the
> refugees in detention. I'd see their faces light up with pleasure
> when I told them where I worked and what it was like there
> ... 'Oh good,' one woman said in a Gosport cafe, 'I thought we
> were soft on them.'

In January 2003, the Ukrainian asylum seeker Mikhail
Bodnarchuk killed himself on the 'day he was to be removed.
Despite the regular stories about asylum seekers, I don't recall
seeing it mentioned in the local news media.'

Bonehead's Utopia takes place in an imaginary version of
HMP Haslar, one which has undergone a drastic transformation. The Haslar buildings, and the space around them,
as described in the poem, are a more vicious iteration of the
southern subtopia described elsewhere in Jordan's work. In
'Minaev's Ghost', a spectre-like prisoner reappears at a site
described as

> ... a homeless breeze, a gale
> backing and backing. A solitary officer crosses
> from the admin building – a low hut, a bungalow,
> an outbuilding from a suburban concentration camp.

'Waterlights' describes the horror of an imagined prison on
the Solent, melancholy in its cold beauty, where one of the
worst things that can happen is your being let out: 'Men have
been known to cry when released/ from this endless day of
light over the sea', and 'sirens whisper at the top of the fence'.
There are also vignettes from the exercises that come with
a writer's residency in a prison. 'Disclaimer' is inspired by a
workshop where inmates discuss the irony and meaning of the
phrase *economic migrant*, presumably on Jordan's prompting:
'Hello', says one prisoner, 'my name is Vermin.' Haslar here is
just one outpost of

A gulag or concentration camp, dispersed
over the globe, it has no fixed point, no centre
or periphery, except in these legitimated fences.
Everything is in disguise. Discretely, reality is maimed.

Yet in *Bonehead's Utopia*, this camp where people who have committed no crime are held in brutal conditions is gradually changed by a prisoners' uprising into a state, one which is in the midst of trying to create a new society, with new rules and rituals. The titular Bonehead is one of the prison guards, who play an ambiguous role in the new society. In the opening 'A Celebration',

... the guards
(that is, the ones who didn't go home)
perform a folk dance for the new regime.
In the past the officers would pace
from door to door, along the corridors,
lifting their feet at intervals to show
a nimble step, a sensitivity,
like Morris dancers, uniformed, with keys.
Now they form the core of the command
of the People's Liberation Militia.

Much unlike the pinched, mean, enclosed world described in the factual essay at the end of the book, this is a place which is created by the people who have to live in it, and for that, they are grateful: 'We sing a citadel in which we're safe', and

Loneliness makes statesmen of the weak
Who dared to dream – or worse – who dared to speak
of this unity, of this strange republic.

The guards lurk in Bonehead's Utopia as a sort of Committee of Public Safety, apparently patrolling now on behalf of the prisoners, rather than as their jailers.

As with so many attempts to create revolutionary societies run on rational and egalitarian grounds, the Haslar commune

64

has been cut off from the rest of the world, seemingly block-aded and starving, penned into its fenced-off space in the outskirts of a grim industrial town on the South Coast. In 'The Hunger Strike', the inmates/communards imagine what a 'popular bureaucracy of food' could distribute, and dream of an abundance created by mass production, to which they do not, currently, have access. That lack is reimagined as a fullness, where

> In my memory I can see
> the giant machines working
> fields of light where hunger
> fills you up like nothing else.

Like a Soviet or Jacobin republic, embattled and with a gulf between its heroic rhetoric and a clearly completely ruined state, the HMP Haslar Utopia is horribly limited by its small size and its confinement in the space of the old prison. In 'A Map of the Republic', 'our geography' is

> a prison yard, a set of vague abstractions
> no-one understands – is too small for the role
> we have assigned.
> [...] our land does not exist
> except within the mad map on the wall,
> it is buried or imprisoned now, caught outside,
> in an envelope of light, 'behind the wire'.
> We are an unnamed nation you do not believe in.

Those who live there are occasionally noticed by the world outside, as they try to create artworks or artefacts of their new society; one inmate's efforts are as follows:

> He is shown in the Portsmouth News
> fixing the last tile to the Tree of Life
> Which was made by the detainees –
> it depicts the creatures of the earth.

65

The anomalous attempt at creating this new society at an outpost of the British imperial state at its most cruel is left unresolved: a moment of possibility, circumscribed by the forces around it. The considerable conviction and concentration with which this scenario is visualised also run through Jordan's most recent book, another political fantasy set in the securitised spaces of the South Hampshire conurbation, this time in the form of a violent insurrection.

The Portsdown Hill Apocalypse

Hegemonick, published in 2012, is set entirely on Portsdown Hill. It is useful to have some knowledge of the place before reading it. Portsdown Hill is a chalk ridge that overlooks Portsmouth from the north, and has been used as a fortress for centuries; this was a military site even during the Roman Empire, and the mostly Roman Portchester Castle still stands below. The hill is lined by the early nineteenth-century fortresses which were extensively used during the Second World War, including by the US Army: Fort Nelson, Fort Southwick, Fort Widley, Fort Wallington, Fort Fareham. Alongside these are currently operational military and industrial-technological facilities, such as the IBM headquarters at the foot of the hill in Cosham, and the Defence Science and Technology Laboratory (DSTL), which originally occupied the domineering 1950s classical headquarters of the aforementioned ASWE. Alongside it QinetiQ occupies a dramatic, white-towered privatised military-research installation that is just along James Callaghan Drive from Paulsgrove, a sprawling low-rise council estate that became notorious in 2000, when a series of riots erupted after the *News of the World* revealed that a convicted paedophile was living in the area. These all feature in a poem-cycle dense with overlapping narratives, verses in the footnotes and explanations which often pose further questions. The book is also about the place Jordan lived as a teenager, and

chronicles 'the war against children' as it took place in one
apparently mundane and bland suburb, which is, if even cur-
sorily explored, full of secrets, intrigues and horrors.

The air of paranoia that often seeps through Jordan's poetry
appears to be especially acute in *Hegemonick*, given that it has
so much empirical justification. 'The Paulsgrove Experiment'
sets out his stall:

> A test rig, canvas draped on scaffolding,
> about it many obsolete fortifications,
> buttress and bastion, a bulwark built for the defence of the
>   past. I had it in my mind
> to walk up to the tower, to look down
> into the gardens, to see the houses below,
> the shops and flats a colossus bends to inspect.
> Paedophile thoughts were beamed into the estate.

The links, physical and mental, running through the embattled,
paranoid council estate that lashed out in 2000 in a sudden
and shocking jacquerie, make up much of the subject matter.
In 'Hypnophrenia',

> The lines I followed led me to Portsdown Hill
> past the house where I had lived as a teenager
> the location of despair, and up into the dazzling light
> that extraordinary view, where the insights began

that place being, in 'Equus',

> Paulsgrove, a vast
> betrayed estate – like an otherworld –
> surrounding it

In 'Fort Nelson', the most picturesque of the fortresses, and
the most often visited (I remember vividly being taken there
on a school trip, into its labyrinths of corridors and tunnels),
creates, through its placement above the estate,

> An impression of gloom above
> exposed gardens – the lines of sodden washing
> and fields of Wimpey Homes. Suffocation.

Jordan imagines the 'Paedophile Riots' of 2000 as an eruption of popular anger that was wholly justified, if partly misdirected towards only one facet of an elaborate complex of subterfuge and cruelty:

> Paedophile, they cannot spell it,
> but they know it's wrong

The *News of the World* scandal is one part of a history which also includes the Hampshire 'horse ripper', who castrated horses on Portsdown Hill and was never caught, and a burning Ku Klux Klan cross that was erected on the hill in the late 1970s. From the vantage point of Portsdown Hill, however, all of these things go from being opaque to visible, the elevated point creating a panorama where it is possible for the narrator

> to look back safely, and admire
> Portchester's keep, the twin towers
> at Gosport (an optical illusion)
> light tilted off the Solent, the Isle of Wight
> and the 'visored mask' of Portsmouth

These all refer to actual landmarks. The keep is at the castle in Portchester; the twin towers of Gosport are two council tower blocks, with abstract murals running down their sides; the north coast of the Isle of Wight is visible from Portsdown Hill; and the 'visored mask' may or may not refer to the gigantic Spinnaker Tower, a Dubai-like observation tower that now dominates the estuary.

The sheer complexity of Portsdown Hill as a built structure, encompassing industrial, residential and infrastructural spaces weaving in and out of the chalk cliff and piled on top of each other, leads to sudden shocking images where its different lives interpenetrate: in 'Research, Hillsley Road, 1978', we find that in Paulsgrove,

> One resident said she knocked on the floor
> and heard someone or something reply

This is, in the poem dedicated to one of the military structures, 'Farlington Redoubt', a place where

> There is a sphere of power – the centre is beneath the ground –
> like a bubble over Portsmouth and the harbour,
> its hinterland and marine approaches. It has an edge,
> it forms a dome, and everything is washed and rewashed
> by radar, the endless monitoring and the chatter within.
> A tradition that overlays the land, radiating out, spread
> by missionaries of war, foreign aid, free trade

It is all laid out for inspection, with all of the spaces that are usually secret and heavily guarded left exposed, next door to a large and sprawling council estate. The results haunt the memory of the narrator, as he realises how comprehensively his childhood has been determined by these spaces, lurking over and above the places where he lived and played in his youth. Of crucial importance in this narrative is a photograph of Jordan and other teenage Pompey punks and hippies in the late 1970s, sitting placidly on a grassy hill. He later realises that this is the ridge of the fuel oil reservoir, built by the navy in the 1930s, used extensively in the Second World War, and a site for contingency planning in the Cold War.

> Behind the bank of earth, on the left of the photograph,
> the low bulk of Fort Southwick can be seen.
> It looks like a scab on the horizon, within
> which the NATO COMMCEN was operating
> and beneath which the UGHQ was waiting
> for the future emergency, the apocalyptic war that
> has long been visualised.

> In the far background, where the ridge of Portsdown Hill
> is capped by the edge of the picture
> the back of the military research establishment
> that was ASWE and became DERA,
> and then Distl and Qinetiq, can be seen.
> This is the facility called Portsdown Main.

They sit there in the photograph as if blissfully unaware that underneath them is part of the infrastructure of nuclear warfare. The puzzlement created by the succession of name changes, as these government facilities are outsourced, privatised and proliferated, belies their physical inescapability. They are visible everywhere, although landscaped into what the untrained eye might perceive as pretty, historic, south of England semi-rural landscapes. What could possibly be sinister about a green hill in Hampshire?

Alternatives to the total environment of *Hegemonick* come in two forms, one of them through the Reichian revolutionary sexuality that is such an intrinsic part of Jordan's peculiar cosmology – and here, the major role is played by a mostly forgotten 1970s porn star. 'Inside Mary Millington' imagines the actress, who died in suspicious circumstances in 1979, merging, on her death, with Fort Southwick, conflating

> [...] The outcrop
> of her pretty cunt – a hooded mound –
> with the long building
> of the Vosper Shipyard visible way off below

This poem, apparently inspired by a porn mag the teenage Jordan carried with him on his walks through Fort Southwick in the 1970s, sees the landscape transformed as she herself becomes the fortress's infrastructure, her promise of the free sexuality that, citing Reich, he calls 'orgastic potency', locked up in the British state. This, at any rate, provides some of the humour that leavens the otherwise exceptionally sinister world of *Hegemonick*, though it also reveals a certain mock pagan mother goddess mysticism that creeps into Jordan's world of neolithic brutalism and phallic giants.

> The architecture of her colossal cunt
> leading into a network of tunnels. Murky
> doorways opened into offices, switchboards
> and rooms with dials. Workshops
> and machine rooms. Everywhere
> cables and pipes. Looted transformers.
> [...]
> On the casing of her clitoris, a sign:
> DANGER
> NO UNAUTHORISED PERSON TO
> TOUCH THIS SWITCHBOARD

The concluding poems of *Hegemonick* chart the progress of a brutally fought insurrection on Portsdown Hill, as the proletariat of Paulsgrove come to consciousness, through 'the most strong urge to communism'. Here

> the young though bewildered
> and greatly abused will throw off the notion
> of the bourgeois centred subject to express
> personhood through the narratives of the tribe.

The long poem that ends the book, 'How the Light Was Held', is a sweeping narrative of the eventual children's revolt at Paulsgrove. It begins with the official enemies, the paedophiles conveniently rehabilitated by local authorities on peripheral council estates, where

> the Paedophile riots in Paulsgrove erupted
> via a deep underground fault which vented
> directly into the national media. Qinetiq operatives
> were on bonus payments for weeks. Journalists
> with dodgy images on their laptops
> bought drinks for vigilantes, suggested scenarios

Thus far, so familiar. But what happens next, is that

> later we learned that this was not the home
> of a Paedophile, but of a Qinetiq operative,
> the house had been identified by youths who discovered
> and explored the tunnels that connected
> the house of the Qinetiq operatives with the research
> complex on the hilltop above. It didn't take long
> for the teenagers to work out what was going on.

This is not an unconscious outbreak of mindless violence, but a planned rising, the workers imagined in the Proles 4 Modernism leaflets organising themselves and reacting, ferociously, against all the things that run through Jordan's poems, all of which suddenly have a focus: centuries of enclosure, the use of working-class youth as cannon fodder, the construction of a fake historical landscape to mask HMP Haslar and the fortresses that lie beneath their mothers' kitchens.

> So they gathered for a meeting of their parliament
> in the park, by the swings, as is the custom
> and then they moved in procession around the estate,
> going from door to door, collecting money, weapons
> and recruiting volunteers, and then they went
> to the houses of the state operatives
> and they dragged the occupants outside
> to interrogate them, and then to execute
> revenge for what had been done to them over the years

The Portsdown Hill panorama, which has featured throughout the book as a site for contemplation and analysis, is now the scene of an apocalyptic revolt, one where capital old and new is swept away by a relentless push from the teenagers of Paulsgrove.

> The flames leapt high
> about the IBM complex creating stunning visual effects
> as they were reflected in the landscaped lagoon that had once
> reflected corporate domination, an unassailable system

The book ends with the results of this uprising unclear and unresolved. It has instead a series of notes, explaining – or not – the apparently unclear aspects of the narrative and the places that feature in it. Inside there is a definition of a term, which explains exactly what Andrew Jordan's project is. 'False Landscape Syndrome (FLS), a condition in which the subject's identity and relationships are affected by beliefs pertaining to the nature of landscapes and the construction of "places" in terms of their histories, physical structure and social, economic and political functions'. One of these false landscapes is a created and curated England, that of the National Trust and English Heritage, where power and its ruthless exercise are softened into sweetness and light. The other false landscape is the one Jordan tries to create to counter them: a working-class revolt to save the Tricorn Centre; an immigration detention centre creating its own communist state; the people of Paulsgrove exchanging the *News of the World* for World Revolution. These are exactly the same landscapes, and neither is 'true' – but one involves inhabitants taking control, and in doing so, taking control of their destiny.

2018

The Shop Signs of Walthamstow High Street

One of London's great secret virtues is its ability to make a street that in many other cities in Britain would be a grim parade of chain stores and empty units into an endlessly interesting global microcosm. One such place is Walthamstow High Street. If you're looking for architecture, don't bother – aside from a decent municipal library and the rather piquant Festival of Britain–style clocktower on the junction of Hoe Street, this is a parade of Victorian, Edwardian and modern buildings of minor aesthetic value, which could probably be demolished from end to end without offending all but the most zealous Victorian preservationists. That's not the point of this place. What is the point is the assemblage of Lithuanian and West African grocers, Bulgarian restaurants alongside eel and pie, a plethora of charity shops, a busy street market mostly full of tat with the odd bit of gold – an exhilarating, warm and convivial fragment of a world where borders are irrelevant and nationalism a joke, laid out in what is, in terms of actual buildings, a normal boring street that could just as easily be in Southampton, Kidderminster or Barrow-in-Furness. It's no exaggeration to say that it is places like this, as much as better employment opportunities and the underfunding of the north, that make people move to London. But something strange is happening here. All the street signs at the corner of St James Street and the High Street have suddenly been replaced with neat, upper-case sans serif on muted colours. Suddenly, it looks like Harrogate or Bath – except the old shops are still there. It's a surreal experience.

This is part of a £3 million makeover by Waltham Forest Council, a process which is intended to begin at the St James Street 'gateway' and then creep up the High Street. It also includes new signs for directions, new paving and new street furniture. Most of this is uncontroversial and welcome. The Victorian buildings have been given a sprucing up – so their plaster griffins and gables are a little more apparent to the eye – and the new stone facings look hard-wearing and elegant. That's all to the good. The problem is the notion that the best thing to do with a street like this – with its audacious combination of Vilnius, Accra, Nicosia, Varna and the old East End – is to make everything look the same, with all those messy and strange shops all having exactly the same typeface. Some have

Beste …

or Best

taken the opportunity to rename themselves slightly. The handmade bubble lettering of 'Beste – French Crop Undercut Colouring Highlights Shave (Hot Towel Massage)' has become the sans serif of 'Best Hair and Beauty'. Costa and Lituanica now have the same look, at least on the outside. The makeover was of course optional, but only one hairdresser has kept its old cheap glam sign of the Mona Lisa.

Where has all this come from? Although the impulse to tidy up in this manner often comes from Victorianists and conservationists, the early twentieth-century High Street looked absolutely nothing like this. In fact, in terms of signage, it would have been messier than the street is now, with signs upon signs, devoid of even the slightest input by a designer. A little taster of the Edwardian horror of empty space is imparted by the painted advertisements that still exist on the sides of some of Walthamstow's buildings, which are now delightfully nostalgic but would at the time have been among many shouty voices imploring you to buy potted meats, jellied eels, penny-farthings and suchlike. So what exactly is it Waltham Forest and its design team think they're doing here?

In a post on his blog Fantastic Journal a few years ago, Charles Holland called this process 'Farrow and Ballification', after the good-taste paint and wallpaper company. This particular approach to 'conservation' is, in his words, a 'sanitised version of the urban streetscape, with its heritage paint shades and expensive bread shops', which is 'as historically suspect as any other era's vision of the past'. Holland argues that 'for all its assumed sensitivity, it is ultimately more about a certain kind of pervasive middle-class aspiration than it is about conserving the past.' It's certainly hard to talk about what is happening here without using the term 'gentrification', and perhaps here it's a misnomer – none of these shops are being forced out, yet. Instead, what is happening is that ordinary nail bars and kebab shops are being made to look like branches of Labour and Wait, on a principle of 'if you can't remove them, redesign them'. It's not hard to imagine that they'll be followed soon enough by the sourdough bakeries and artisanal stovemakers. Many of the old signs were and are naff, some of them very enjoyably so (the black-painted B.A.D Warehouse, perennially having a 'BAD SALE'). Of those that survive a few are very fine, like the gorgeous embossed frontage of Saeed's Fabrics, or the pink fifties-eighties retromania extravaganza of Jesse's Cafe (whose owner is perturbed by the programme, mostly because she's only recently paid for the current sign), though neither conform to the current nouveau Eric Gill canon. What they do, though, is display to the pedestrian that they're in a place where people from every continent live without discord. Today, that means a lot.

Urban coherence is a good thing. Nobody in Walthamstow will complain about better paving, cleaner buildings and nicer benches. The standardisation of road signs, Tube stations and maps, street information and suchlike are all progressive measures that only the kookiest Ayn Rand fan could object to. But the remodelling of the shop signs of Walthamstow is an anal-retentive mistake, driven by a total misunderstanding of what makes London interesting. Inner-city London streets don't need to look like a historically illiterate retcon of a 1940s that never happened – they're fine looking like what they are: hugely successful experiments in multiculturalism, whether in Deptford, Peckham, Haringey, Wembley or Walthamstow. Let's hope the sans-serif 'gateway' stops here.

November 2017

3

Elsewhere

These three essays, though written over a decade apart, are closely linked, geographically and politically – all of them focus on the Central European crucible in which modern architecture, in the sense of a 'modern movement', was formed. It should be clear by now that I see this movement as a renaissance of enormous importance, and as a movement with ideas to live by in the present rather than as a failed past experiment. The concentration on this particular region, though, is an outgrowth of the other obsessions listed already. An interest in the history of socialism leads to Eastern Europe and its failed experiments in non-capitalist systems; getting very into Kraftwerk can lead you alternatively to constructivism, to West Germany or to the Bauhaus; becoming fascinated by post-war reconstruction in your English hometown can be a gateway drug to the much harder stuff you'll find east of the Rhine and the Danube. The modern movement here, in the first modern industrialised capitalist country, consisted initially of shockwaves from the earthquakes that happened between Cologne and Moscow.

The essays here on German expressionism (written for the *London Review of Books* and spiked), and on the divergent architectures of the two capitals of the Hapsburg Empire (published in a drastically truncated form by *Places Journal*), begin with the emergence of a distinct modern*ist* architecture in the aftermath of the First World War. What they focus on in particular is the way in which, in its Central European birthplace, an internationalist modern movement was ranged explicitly against a rival nationalist architecture, which has taken various (sometimes highly experimental) forms ever since. The essay on Israel–Palestine was written fairly soon after I'd finished rewriting several blogposts on the modern movement into my first book, *Militant Modernism*. It emerges partly from a need to acknowledge some of the less comfortable outgrowths of Central European modernism as a school of thought and a practice of building. An obvious place to see this would be Mandate Palestine, where the enormous apparatus of repression and exploitation that was the British Empire worked with enthusiastic socialists, trade unionists and modernists who were driven to emigrate from Central and Eastern Europe, to build a settler colony in the Levant. Originally conceived on the occasion of Israel's sixtieth anniversary as a review of the picture book *Bauhaus Tel Aviv*, it grew, via the non-existence of wordcounts on architecture websites in the 2000s, into an essay drawing heavily on the critical research of the Israeli radicals Eyal Weizman and Sharon Rotbard. The piece was uncontroversial at the time – whether it remains so today, I'm not so sure. As in chapter two of this book, I end with somewhere I like, Warsaw, where I had the pleasure of staying on and off between 2010 and 2015, in the flat of the writer Agata Pyzik. It was written for *Architecture Today*'s 'My Kind of Town' column, and is about probably the most extensively destroyed – and extensively rebuilt – capital in Europe: a true city of the twentieth century.

Arab Villages

Architecture and War in Israel–Palestine, Sixty Years On

NOMADIC ARCHITECTURE

Arab architecture has a precious lesson for us. You appreciate it on foot, walking. Only on foot, in movement, can you see the developing articulation of the architecture. It's the opposite principle to that of Baroque architecture, which is conceived on paper, from a theoretical standpoint. I prefer the lesson of Arab architecture.

Le Corbusier

Let's start, then, with the Arabs. Except here they aren't real Arabs; they're fictional, photomontaged out of place. An infamous postcard distributed by the Nazis of Stuttgart in 1934 depicts the Weissenhofsiedlung, at that time the most famous single statement of modernist architecture, as a destination for another kind of tourism – the exotic picture-postcard urbanism of a North African casbah. Using that most modernist of techniques, photomontage, the anonymous Nazi designer fills the frame with camels, women in veils, etc. – designating modernism not just as un-German, not just as Semitic, but also as

'Arab Village, Stuttgart'

81

Arabic. This was common on both sides of an ideological and aesthetic divide. Le Corbusier evidently approved of a certain idea of 'Arab' aesthetics, and pointedly retained the Casbah in his fantasy plan for Algiers, regardless of what he described as 'bad boys' at large. Meanwhile, conservative German architects such as Paul Schultze-Naumburg considered flat roofs and all they represented as a Middle Eastern imposition, deriving from the Jewish roots of modernism, seemingly as some kind of folk memory.

Any German reader in the early 1930s would have known exactly who Schultze-Naumburg was talking about when he wrote of the 'face' of Nordic art and architecture being defaced by those with 'a different spiritual principle and probably different physical ones as well' and would have known exactly who the nomads were when he wrote of 'nomadic' architecture. Perhaps more innocently, inter-war modernist developments were frequently given North African nicknames by those who lived nearby. Workers' estates like Le Corbusier's in Pessac and J. J. P. Oud's at the Hook of Holland were, according to Paul Overy's study *Light, Air and Openness*, dubbed the 'casbah' and 'the Moroccan district'. In Berlin, one could see the nomadic architecture and the Volkish literally facing off against each other: the modernist *Siedlungen* of Bruno Taut and Martin Wagner, designed for working-class trade unions, usually elicited immediate pitched-roofed responses from conservative architects and the white-collar unions they built for.

If this had remained at the level of a semiotic slanging match it would have been fairly harmless. It can't be stressed enough that it did not. Pentagram's new pamphlet *Forgotten Architects*, based on researches by the late Myra Warhaftig, is a stark reminder of just how serious this was. It profiles forty-three Jewish modernists at work in Germany before 1933, and their subsequent fate. The photographs, all black and white, with even the recent ones having the haunting clarity of photogravure, depict not so much the famous monuments of the

82

Neue Sachlichkeit as the many more low-key blocks of flats, schools, private homes and shops by those who didn't get the chance to make up the post-war modernist canon of Corbusier–Gropius–Mies. After 1933, these architects were incrementally stopped from practising legally. Some would emigrate to the US or UK, and many others, though by no means the majority – Alexander Klein, Wilhelm Haller, Leopold Lustig, Kurt Pick – would set up practice in Palestine. Not all of the architects who left Central Europe for the Middle East were exactly kitted out for the change. Harry Rosenthal, for instance, 'suffered from the sub-tropical climate' and opted for London instead. Bruno Ahrends, co-designer of Berlin's Weisse Stadt *Siedlung*, would eventually move to South Africa.

All were at least lucky enough not to become one of the many listed in this booklet as 'fate is unknown', or to have ended their lives in places like Theresienstadt, the final destination of Alexander Beer; or, like Mortiz Hadda, to have been 'deported to an unknown location'.

White Mythologies

It's with these two points in mind – the fetish for a certain 'Middle Eastern' approach to elevations and planning in modernism, and the stylistic and physical obliteration of modernism and modernists in Nazi Germany – that one should try to appraise Nahoum Cohen's gazetteer *Bauhaus Tel Aviv*, recently published by Batsford. This is the most complete profile in English of the 'White City' period of (proto-)Israeli architecture, at least in this city. The number of people taking the *aliyah*, the journey from Europe to Palestine, then run as a colonial 'mandate' by the UK, had unsurprisingly increased in the 1930s. In that decade, Tel Aviv, a settler appendage to the Arab port of Jaffa, grew exponentially in an impressively bold and modernist form. Here, the style that was being rejected as 'nomadic', racially impure and alien to the *Volk*, was putting down roots and becoming something close to an orthodoxy. According to Cohen it never quite formed an architectural majority, but nonetheless a statement was being made of unashamed modernity and cosmopolitanism in the face of a Europe that was determinedly returning to barbarism.

Tel Aviv has thousands of what it (imprecisely) terms 'Bauhaus buildings', the largest concentration in the world, something acknowledged by a UNESCO World Heritage listing. It bears repeating that in so doing it didn't warp people's consciousness, nor create a technocratic dystopia – in fact it appears in Cohen's book as decidedly idyllic, if a tad shabby. The scuffed and battered buildings have a certain charm, although the archive photographs of urban set pieces such as Dizengoff Square show a fidelity to the ex nihilo ethos. This circular plaza, planned and mostly executed by Genia Averbuch, had the distinction of being one of the largest and most impressive works by a female architect at that date.

Yet this carries more than an undercurrent of one of the most ambiguous elements of the modernist and Zionist projects, the desire to set up a *tabula rasa*, starting from scratch as

Dizengoff Square in Tel Aviv, 1940. Public domain

if nobody else had ever inhabited the spot you're building on. Tel Aviv, and Mandate Palestine in general, was treated as a test-bed, a laboratory, for ideas that would be employed on a much larger scale elsewhere. In particular, the town planning ideas that would become prominent after the Second World War were rehearsed in this disputed colony, especially for the adherents of the urban Fabianism of the garden cities. Patrick Geddes planned Tel Aviv in a manner which limited congestion and provided space and air, and at the same time deliberately cut it off from the Palestinian city of Jaffa; while Patrick Abercrombie's qualifications for planning a new London in the 1940s derived in part from his experience of planning new areas of Haifa. The problem with this is that a *tabula rasa* rarely exists – and certainly didn't in these settlements. Jaffa and Haifa were well-established cities, thousands of years old, not the nondescript farmlands and villages on which the UK's garden cities had been built. Regardless, this wouldn't be the first nor the last time that this tiny area took on a significance belying its size.

There was much debate over whether local references should be allowed to creep into modernism as applied in Palestine. In Jerusalem the 'local stone' was made compulsory, but not in Tel Aviv. Nahoum Cohen's book details quite extensively how particular motifs were transformed to fit with the far from Central European climate. Erich Mendelsohn–style ribbon windows were in many cases referenced, rather than replicated, by long, curved balconies; large areas of glass were generally left out, replaced by screens and brise-soleils, although many of the buildings had glazed 'thermometer' staircases, as if to make clear that there was still some sort of allegiance to 'the new glass culture', as Paul Scheerbart called it.

Erich Mendelsohn himself was decidedly unimpressed by what his former students and disciples had created when he settled in Palestine in the mid-thirties. His own architecture for the colony used a formal vocabulary which referenced the

Arab architecture all around, using domes and stone while avoiding the stylised chic of the 'Bauhaus style'. In amongst this is a strange political paradox. Mendelsohn, a 'spiritual' rather than socialist Zionist, was at pains to make clear the need to unite with, or at the very least live peacefully beside, the local Arab population as fellow 'Semites'. Conversely, the leftist modernists of the Tel Aviv 'Chug' (circle) had no interest whatsoever in making any such concessions. Julius Posener wrote in their house journal that 'here, there is no past or experience'. In another context this might seem a purely aesthetic preference for not replicating or patronising an idealised past, but in this environment – especially with the Arab revolt that began in 1936 – it took on a rather more colonialist character. One of the most photogenic modernist buildings of the period is the Talpiot Market in Haifa, designed by Moshe Gerstel in 1937 to replace the earlier multiracial market after tensions between Palestinian Arabs and Jewish settlers had spilled over into violence. One archive photograph shows its spectacular flowing lines towering above a block of 'indigenous' stone-built

Hadassah University Hospital, Jerusalem,
Erich Mendelsohn, 1939. Public domain.

dwellings. More straightforwardly, many 'tower and stockade' villages were designed after 1936 as semi-military outposts.

Nahoum Cohen writes in *Bauhaus Tel Aviv* that these buildings often look like stage sets or models, 'too good to be true'. The cleanness and austere geometry are difficult to maintain in the local climate, yet the restoration programmes established since the area was declared a World Heritage Site seem determined to wipe away the grime of history. Tel Aviv, he writes, 'is a showcase of the way town planning is an expression of beliefs and social practices', and this principle extends into his own book. Within this collection of images and plans are two buildings not designed for the new settlements, both in Jaffa itself. One is stone built, and is favourably contrasted with the staginess of 'Bauhaus style', enabling 'integration' into an existing urban fabric. The other, more impressive, with an ornamental motif that recalls the work of Oskar Schlemmer, was designed by one Ahmed Damiaty ('not the only Arab architect to adopt the style, but very little is known of these architects as a group'). Although Damiaty's block, with its alignment of stylisation and *Sachlichkeit*, is very close in appearance to those of his counterparts to the north in Tel Aviv, Cohen's language becomes rather loaded: 'it has to be remembered that oriental architecture is more decorative by nature than that of the west', a statement that both Le Corbusier and the Nazi designers of satirical postcards would have disagreed with. Jaffa, he notes, was 'deserted by most of its inhabitants in 1948', which is a rather polite way of describing the results of what many historians have considered a systematic policy of expulsion (or 'transfer').

The Israeli architect Sharon Rotbard has written prolifically about the myths of the 'White City' of Tel Aviv, as occlusions of the 'black city' to its south. And as he points out, the very idea of a 'Bauhaus style' is misleading. The only major Bauhaus-trained architect to have worked in Palestine was the Chug's Arieh Sharon (though three less illustrious students were at large), who had worked closely with the Bauhaus's most controversial director, the committed Marxist Hannes Meyer. Sharon's work appears to have been one of the few real outgrowths of Meyer's teaching, with its emphasis on collectivity and rejection of pure aesthetics. In particular, Sharon was, as the title of his autobiography *Kibbutz + Bauhaus* suggests, keen to employ Meyer's ideas for the purpose of the collectivist, workerist forms of living developed by 'Labour Zionism', the socialist movements which largely supplanted the religious or straightforwardly colonial Zionism of Theodor Herzl. Arieh Sharon masterminded kibbutzim such as the Kibbutz Ein Hashofet of 1938; and with a series of four collective housing blocks in Tel Aviv these principles were transferred to an urban environment. Meanwhile, the first *moshav ovdim*, or workers' collective farm, was planned by Richard Kauffmann, who would become known in the thirties as a modernist architect in his own right.

Michael Sorkin wrote that Labour Zionism was remarkably appropriate for the aims of socialist modernism, not only in providing the ideal light, airy, whitewashed setting, but also because its 'workers' housing cooperatives, kibbutz dining halls, and hospitals represented the kind of programs modern architecture always wanted for itself'. Labour Zionism developed its own specific aesthetic of noble labour and modernity, something which can be seen in the graphic design of the 1930s and 1940s as a less kitschy variant on Socialist Realism. A concrete statue originally erected in 1934 as part of an international exhibition – *The Hebrew Worker*, designed by Arieh El Hanani – would become the iconic, constructivist emblem of early socialist 'Central European' Zionism, a nostalgia for which, according to Rotbard, lies behind the mythology of the White City: an Ashkenazi elite's desire to Europeanise its far-from-Western (even in the Israeli context) environment. As socialists, these architects should have been sensitive to the implications of treating an existing country as if it were virgin territory; yet in its confidence modernism might have provided a visual alibi for an effacement of the majority of the population. The perception of the 'Bauhaus' and its outgrowths as a colonial imposition would be a major influence on perhaps the most famous Israeli architect, Moshe Safdie.

Systems for Refugees

Expo 67, held in Montreal, became best known for an enormous structure called Habitat. This complex was made up of a tangle of boxes – 'houses', according to its architect, Moshe Safdie – interconnected by walkways. This description might sound like any other post-CIAM (Congrès internationaux d'architecture moderne), International Style plan, but anyone who has seen a photograph of Habitat could attest that this is the diametric opposite of the windswept plazas and Platonic towers of the Miesian, Functionalist city. In fact, Habitat resembles a 1920s *Siedlung* smashed to pieces and then piled

A Mediterranean Village

up on top of itself. Meanwhile, an order of some description apparently resided in the complex: these boxes each had its own garden.

Moshe Safdie's Habitat 'system' was famous for the first few years of its history, finding its way onto the covers of children's textbooks on architecture in the UK. By participating in that advance guess at the future, the International Expo, it appeared on stamps and on all kinds of ephemera. It now perhaps best exemplifies what Peter Eisenman and his journal *Oppositions* dismissed in the 1970s as 'Revisionist Functionalism' – the attempt to hold what had become a 'Bauhaus style' to its original promises of a socially engaged, technologically advanced, mass-produced anti-style. 'The reaction (against Modernism) occurred not because the basis of Functionalism was wrong, but because it didn't go far enough', according to Safdie. Habitat tried to have it both ways – to provide the 'identity', irregularity and individuality that CIAM orthodoxy denied, but at the same time to create 'homes from factories'. Like Weissenhof, Habitat would prove very photogenic, a building more frequently identified than visited and almost bombastically futuristic. This wasn't *just* architecture, which is what Eisenman and his group were intent on returning to. It was a model of ideal social structure, of fundamental unity and equality coexisting with anti-Platonic messiness. It tried to pioneer a new kind of social space with extreme levels of density and collectivity, or at the very least attempted a prototype for such a space. It's no surprise that the New Left held Safdie's work in high esteem, with his system being proposed for student housing by some of the campus radicals of the late 1960s; perhaps, as with the old Viennese 'workers' fortresses', as a means of defence, an urban environment that the police wouldn't know how to explore.

In 1970, after Habitat's success, and its elaboration into further projects for Puerto Rico and New York, Safdie published a book entitled *Beyond Habitat*, which provided biographical and political detail to point to how exactly this image, and this structure, had come about. At the start of the book we find the young Safdie as the son of a small businessman in Haifa, recalling the jubilation in the streets that accompanied David Ben-Gurion's declaration of the State of Israel on 14 May 1948, and the excitement at being caught up in an experiment: 'there was an air of being part of something unique'. The opening chapter centres on the two elements of Israeli life that the likes of Arieh Sharon had based their lives around: 'kibbutz' and 'Bauhaus'. Growing up in one of the few environments with a 'stylistically consistent architecture of the International Style circa 1930', Safdie also felt the pull of the socialist settlements in the countryside – this was after all perhaps the only country in the world where people actually *chose* to form collective farms. The architect was full of praise for the Israeli variant on socialism: 'I still believe that socialism in its co-operative form in Israel is the highest social development reached anywhere in our century ... this is not bureaucratic socialism – it's a much more humane interpretation of Marxism.' Yet the roots of Habitat were based in Israel's bad conscience as much as in its experiments with collective living.

One thing Habitat is not is suburban, any more than it's a Miesian grid. The massing creates peaks, hills, valleys and corners that seem to be more geological than architectural. *Beyond Habitat* is at pains to stress that Habitat (although built in cold, northern Montreal) is Mediterranean: inspired by the hills of Haifa, the close-knit communities that the International Style had aimed to create but had lost in its pursuit of purism and skyscrapers. This was a return, in a singularly strange form, to the Arab village. After moving to the Americas and training as an architect under Louis Kahn, Safdie devised various projects for 'systems' as opposed to buildings. One of them was a hypothetical scheme to rehouse the Palestinians who had been dispossessed and made homeless by the war accompanying the formation of the State of Israel: this became the 'Giza

91

Plan', so-called because Safdie would ideally have wanted it to neighbour the Pyramids. This 'model city, an ideal community' was intended to circumvent the possible accusation of mere charity: 'the political idea was that the refugees, who are in camps and have compensation money coming to them' would be offered material incentives to move to the site, and given the materials and resources to set up their own town. They would not, however, be encouraged to return to the cities and villages they had been exiled from not so long ago.

Nonetheless, the original ideas of circulation (this was, like Corbusier's 'Arab' aesthetic, to be appreciated through walking) and the 'image of a utopian city' that would coalesce into Habitat are all there in the Giza Plan. With the touching geopolitical naivete common among leftist architects, Safdie saw an opportunity for the plan's partial realisation after the Six-Day War, after which Israel found itself occupying the entirety of the former Mandate Palestine (as well as a chunk of Egypt that was later returned), which it continues to dominate forty years later. Now that the areas containing most Palestinian camps were in Israeli hands, he hypothesised, surely the refugees could be properly rehoused in one of his systems – structures which would be nearer in essence, if not in superficial appearance, to their own architecture rather than that of the settlers. Safdie would not be the last Israeli architect to declare that 'the Arabs build so much better than we do', as he recalls telling an IDF soldier. He seems horrified by the modernist architecture imposed on the landscape – blocks which 'do violence to the mountain. They are foreign, as if imported from some rainy, cool European suburb' – in a direct reversal of the Nazi fear of a Middle Eastern 'Nomadic' modernism imposing itself on that same European suburb.

Beyond Habitat exhibited faith in the power of architecture to change lives as much as change space, which shouldn't be dismissed too glibly. Safdie places his hope in the idea that the future 'life of harmony' between Israeli and Palestinian can

Kingsway, Haifa, in the Late 1930s. Public domain.

be brought about through building and living together – if at all possible through building and living in one of his gigantic concrete modules. His 1967 plan, for the resettlement of the refugees after the Six Day War, was entitled 'For and By the Refugees'. What, though, if the refugees wanted their own homes back? And what if this instrumentalisation of architecture and urban space could be appropriated by power?

Simulating and Militarising the Arab Village

Safdie's idea for Israeli–Arab reconciliation via concrete megastructures and collective labour obviously failed to come about. Indeed, the architect has long refused to work in the occupied West Bank, or take any part in designing the settlements which encroach on Palestinian territory. He has, however, been working in Jerusalem since the early seventies. Jerusalem was originally designated a UN protectorate in the 1947 Partition Plan, then partitioned between Israel and Jordan; it has since 1967 been wholly occupied by Israel. After 1967 Jerusalem became an experimental site for postmodernism, where, unlike earlier experiments in this territory, the aim was to blend in as much as possible with the existing landscape, by cladding all new developments in 'Jerusalem stone'. Notwithstanding this return to contextualism, there was still a place for Futurism's destructive side: *Ha'aretz* recently claimed that Safdie had a hand in the design of the Merkava tank in the early 1970s.

This act of 'petrifying the holy city' is one of the 'layers' of occupation charted in Eyal Weizman's *Hollow Land: Israel's Architecture of Occupation*, a stunning, comprehensive and disturbing study of the deliberately complex and contradictory ways in which the occupation of Gaza, the West Bank and East Jerusalem since 1967 have been translated into space. The petrification of Jerusalem as an aesthetic tactic dates from the period of the British Mandate, and local modernist developments in the 1930s (such as Mendelsohn's) were clad in a yellow stone which today usually comes from within the West Bank. Weizman's book outlines how the Arab quarters of the city were subject to expulsions after 1967, then to a programme of urban redesign that was at pains to stress continuity with the existing city, itself an enormously complex palimpsest (something which Weizman explores to absurd effect, in a discussion of 'vertical schizophrenia' around the Temple Mount: the fight over territorial rights to earth and thin air). This coincided perfectly with an incoming theoretical orthodoxy. Modernism had effaced the traces of the past, and those traces should be both excavated and extended. The postmodernists at work in Jerusalem were creating a style where 'the disciplines of archaeology and architecture merged', and 'the upper storeys of new homes would become literal extensions of their archaeological footprints, while other buildings would be built using older stones for the lower floors and newer stones at higher levels: others were simply built to appear old.' Among the new developments was Safdie's David's Village, a grouping of little cubic houses and domes, shying away from the

David's Village, Mamilla, Jerusalem. Creative Commons.

grandiose futurism of Habitat. 'To build in Jerusalem', wrote the architect, 'is almost an act of arrogance.'

Behind much of this was the belief that 'they build better than us', something reinforced by Bernard Rudofsky's MoMA exhibition and book *Architecture without Architects* (1964) – a study of the hill towns, casbahs and Arab villages which modernists, from Corbusier to Safdie, saw as a dense, angular and ornament-free alternative to sterility and eclecticism. The employment of these faintly patronising, Orientalist eulogies to the unchanging Arab vernacular would specifically aid in the continued immiseration of the Palestinians themselves, who were expelled from their picturesque habitats. Weizman details how the influence of this MoMA project supplanted that of MoMA's earlier *International Style: Architecture since 1922* (1932), to the point where the most fashionable architecture no longer considered it necessary to distinguish itself from its surroundings. In the process it formed perhaps a regression to a previous mode of colonial style – that of Lutyens's

New Delhi and its contemporaries under British rule, where a version of the architecture of the colonised peoples is developed into the architecture of the settler and ruler. Needless to say, this hasn't brought about a new affinity between the two groups; although one irony is that some Palestinian districts of Jerusalem started to resemble a bastard version of 1930s Tel Aviv, with low-rise concrete modernist blocks raised on piloti contrasting with the idealised Arabism of the Israeli settlements that – literally, given that settlements are deliberately built on high ground – overlook them. Nonetheless, the majority of settlements in the West Bank, at least outside Jerusalem, prefer the instant identification provided by a suburban red pitched roof to a chameleonic postmodernism.

Hollow Land is full of examples of the tortuous intricacy of the borders, crossing points and obstructions that the occupation imposes on this small territory. Weizman's illustrations include a diagram of the 'separation wall' as it makes its way through a massively expanded Jerusalem. Rem Koolhaas once quipped that the Berlin Wall, with its blunt monumentality and bizarre, snaking contours, was the most remarkable built structure in that city. The separation wall takes this to bizarre lengths – curving, starting, stopping, transforming from wall to checkpoint to barrier, becoming almost fractal in its illogicality. Rather than a line of straight demarcation, the wall is 'more redolent of Scandinavian coastlines, where fjords, islands and lakes make an inconclusive separation between water and land.' The parts of *Hollow Land* that have, quite rightly, made it an architectural talking point in the last year centre on the use of another wave of architectural and urbanist theory, quite distinct from the Heideggerian *Heimat* of the 1970s planners. After the start of the Second Intifada, the Palestinian uprising against the occupation, a wing of the Israeli Defence Forces has taken an interest in the work of a remarkable list of theorists and architects. Specifically, the syllabus of the IDF's Military Operational Theory Research Institute (MOTRI) featured such architecture school favourites as Gilles Deleuze and Félix Guattari, Bernard Tschumi, Paul Virilio and Manuel DeLanda, alongside lectures on 'the generalship of Ariel Sharon'.

Here we are, back with another conception of 'nomadic architecture', with the identity of the 'nomads' having switched again. Deleuze and Guattari's 'nomadic thought' developed from an interest in the possible forms of organisation that might be more effectively able to resist power, a kind of philosophical guerrilla strategy. Study of this then provided the IDF with what it thought was an insight into the organisation of urban space thrown up by the Intifada, where the small armed groups would expect the larger army to use overwhelming brute force. To upset this expectation, the MOTRI, under its directors Shimon Naveh and Dov Tamari, encouraged the IDF to think of itself as a non-state, nomadic force, and to attack Palestinian refugee camps and towns by dividing itself into small, decentralised, 'deterritorialised' entities. One strategy was to 'walk through walls', by blowing holes through civilian dwellings, and avoiding whenever possible the actual street plan. This was the method used in the attack on Jenin in 2002, under the command of Aviv Kochavi, where 'most fighting took place in private homes'. This could be applied to the asymmetric street patterns so admired by generations of architects: after a battle in the Nablus Casbah, a Palestinian architect surveying the area found that 'more than half the buildings had routes forced through them'. Although severely tested in the Lebanon war of 2006, where it was found ineffective against the more sophisticated military machine of Hezbollah, this 'becoming-nomadic' military strategy has apparently had some influence on the practice of the US Army in Iraq.

Perhaps the last word in the tortured affair with the vernacular of Arab Palestine is a city constructed in the Negev desert at the Tze'elim military base. Known as 'Chicago', this city was first designed in the mid-1980s as a simulation of a Lebanese village. Weizman writes of it expanding to the point where it can 'simulate all different types of Palestinian environment', with its own historic casbah, a refugee camp and so forth. It can morph itself into any kind of structure that the Israeli Army might be operating, and was even able to mutate part of itself into a Jewish settlement in preparation for the expulsion of settlers from Gaza. Finally, the Israeli government managed to design its own Arab village, with details replicated not for the purpose of urban edification, nor for community reconciliation, nor even for the production of urban continuity, but for war games, with the Arabs being similarly impersonated and simulated. Now Arab architecture could best be appreciated by walking – or blasting – through its walls. While one wing of 'radical' architecture designs fantasy cities in the United Arab Emirates, its ideas form part of an apparatus of control and collective punishment on the other side of the Middle East. In the process, the promise of modernist architecture – that it might, by itself, innocent of politics, bridge an idealised vernacular past and a technological, collectivist future – has never looked so much like a desert mirage.

May 2008

Socialism and Nationalism on the Danube

Architecture and Politics in Budapest and Vienna

If there are two cities that most exemplify the possibilities and the limitations of European urbanism and architecture, they might be Vienna and Budapest. These two cities were the former co-capitals of the Hapsburg dual monarchy, the Austro-Hungarian Empire, that lasted from 1867 to 1918. Their coffee house culture, twentieth-century intelligentsia and attractive eclectic architecture have been praised practically ever since the Empire dissolved. Both sit on the river Danube, and have both been at the centre of some of the most turbulent events

98

of the twentieth century before becoming apparent backwaters. Both have experienced some kind of fascism, and some kind of socialism. Both are proportionately oversized capitals dominating small countries: ever since Austria and Hungary became independent states in the aftermath of the First World War, they have often seemed parochial despite the imperial scale of their metropolises. Today, both cities are dominated by the service industry, but have a significant industrial past. Both have been multicultural, historically, but in the twenty-first century Vienna is considerably the more so of the two, with 34 per cent of the population born abroad, compared with 7 per cent in Budapest. The two cities are of a similar size, however, and accommodate a similar total population: Budapest, 1.76 million; Vienna, 1.87 million. Most of all, both are the sort of cities where a British – or American – observer might be inclined to sigh, 'Ah, this is Europe. And this is better.'

'Europe' in this context is a vague thing – a matter of post-card views, pavement cafes and historical monuments – and also something concrete: the fact that both cities are visually very homogeneous. In the centre of each, poorly designed modern buildings are rare, and bourgeois urban planning in the nineteenth century was clearly very extensive. Insofar as both cities are visited by tourists, it is for their efforts at civic and commercial grandeur in the nineteenth and early twentieth centuries. Both cities demolished their city walls in the mid-nineteenth century, and built grand boulevards along their former outlines. Their status meant that lavish attention was bestowed on the cities' surfaces, producing an urban display befitting the administrative capitals of an enormous continental empire: a contiguous area encompassing the fringes of Italy, the Czech lands, Slovenia, Croatia, Slovakia, a swathe of what is now Romania and much of western Ukraine – an improbable state whose major cities, outside of these dual capitals, were Prague, Trieste and Lviv, and which built miniature Viennas and Budapests as far afield as Salzburg and Chernivtsi.

That need to *impress* the resident, visitor, pedestrian or tourist, led the Viennese architect Adolf Loos, in a text of 1898, to condemn the Austrian city as a 'Potemkinstadt', whose open spaces, grand axes and ornamented plaster facades hid dire poverty. Much of what has happened to Vienna since 1918 has been a response to this problem, as the city has embarked on arguably the most impressive and certainly the most sustained and consistent public housing programme in Europe. Budapest, though built on a similar scale and in a very similar style, has not the same social legacy to display.

On the face of it, this would belie the Cold War interpretation of both cities. Budapest and Hungary were in the 'East', Vienna and Austria in the 'West'; and accordingly, the former was communist – now 'post-communist' – the latter, capitalist. This distinction, when applied to the development of the two cities in the last hundred years, may obscure more than it reveals. Even under the system alternately described as 'real socialism', 'Stalinism' or 'state capitalism', depending on your politics, Budapest did not build public housing on the same scale as Vienna, and in many respects, left its bourgeois centre relatively untouched. Since 1989, what socialist legacy may have been left by the old system has been dismantled at a far greater rate than Vienna's less dramatic legacy of moderate, reformist socialism.

Today, however, both cities – and both countries – are increasingly associated with the continent's dramatic rightward shift. In 2016 Austria very nearly elected as president a member of the 'post-fascist' Freedom Party (a group which was founded after the war by former SS officers). Since winning a supermajority in the elections of 2010, Hungary's Fidesz party, founded in the late 1980s as a centrist liberal group, has shifted towards what Prime Minister Viktor Orbán openly describes as an 'illiberal democracy', which claims to defend a 'Christian' Europe against contemporary multiculturalism, Muslim refugees and any remaining traces of twentieth-century socialism.

Through this, both cities – attractive, even sleepy and quiet in comparison with the noise and visual chaos of London, Berlin or Moscow – are at the heart of a crisis about what 'Europe' is today. To discover if that crisis can be read at the level of architecture and planning, we need to be very clear about the trajectory these two cities have taken over the last century, and where that has left them.

Potemkinstadt *Today*

Budapest was, until recently, the larger of the two cities. In 1990 its population was 2 million, Vienna's 1.5 million; and although numbers are going up, it hasn't recovered from the sharp declines of the 1990s, whereas the former Hapsburg co-capital has continued to grow. It is, as it has always been, poorer, with an average monthly income of approximately €400, compared to around €1,800 per month in the Austrian capital; the post-communist hope that the West and East of Central Europe would converge has proven illusory. However, in many respects, Budapest is the more impressive city, something reflected in the much higher levels of tourism it attracts – according to the most recent figures, Budapest's 15 million is triple the number of annual visitors to visit Vienna. The slightly larger and distinctly richer city boasts the imperial showcase of the Hofburg; the Art Historical and Natural History Museums, designed as one symmetrical entity by Gottfried Semper in the 1880s; the Ringstrasse; the flamboyant baroque Karlskirche; and a much photographed Ferris wheel. Yet it wastes the Danube, which has been left either undeveloped or lined by forgettable office buildings. The waterfront in Budapest, however, was built up in the 1890s as a consciously romantic spectacle, with sublime suspension bridges arching from flat Pest to hilly Buda, and with the composite gothic-baroque Parliament appearing as a sort of summation of all nineteenth-century architecture in its imperial grandeur and historical fantasy. Pest was developed as a city of tall baroque and classical tenement buildings, with ornament fashioned cheaply out of stucco, and shabby brick courtyards behind, best seen on the Korut, the Ringstrasse that is the twin of the one in Vienna. The older Buda, dominated by the neo-classical National Museum, was gradually turned into a free improvisation on speculative historical themes, exemplified by its late Victorian castle, whose fanciful turrets and battlements prove that Disneyland was anticipated in Central Europe some decades before it made its way to California.

The experience of walking the streets of Pest today is akin to walking the nineteenth-century districts of Vienna – there are relatively few chain stores outside of the main tourist centre, with H&M and the like present, but crowded out by cafes, bars and a lot of preserved 1970s neon shop signs. Picturesquely crumbling 'ruin bars' are carved out of the basements and courtyards; and, unlike over-restored Vienna, where the facades are obsessively spick and span, Budapest has a material richness caused by its decay – limbless statuary, melted stucco, crumbling brick, often bullet-riddled. Capitalism is a little more glaring in Budapest, adverts are bigger and crasser and there are more of them. The public transport system, centred around the second underground metro system ever built, is terrific. What you'll miss, however, by comparison with the Austrian capital, is the density of social housing and public spaces, the adventure in housing that Vienna embarked upon in the twenties.

During the Cold War, Vienna, though part of a neutral country outside of NATO and sometimes governed by (increasingly unconvincingly) professed Marxists, was in the capitalist West, and Budapest, the state-socialist East. Given that both elite and popular opinion in Hungary, as with most other former 'communist' countries, ascribes the country's relative poverty to 'communism', this difference matters. But if the difference was decisive, it was in ways that are much more complex than the easy dichotomy would suggest. In theory, the legacy of 'communism' should have left all over the Hungarian capital evidence of its ideology and its social programme. Yet of the two cities, if you want to find large-scale housing projects in the city centre or Socialist Realist sculptures in public space, it's Vienna you need to visit. Not uncoincidentally, it is by far the more egalitarian of the two cities. Given how much cheaper Budapest is – one obvious reason, other than its visually superior riverside, for that far larger volume of tourism – this is easily missed, as Vienna's wealth, visible in the impeccable state of preservation of most of its historic buildings, can lead one to assume that underneath the pretty facades is a city dominated by its well-heeled bourgeoisie. It certainly *looks* bourgeois, but the city's development has been significantly affected since 1918 by non-capitalist actors.

Viennese housing comes in four types: council housing, cooperative housing, private rental housing and owner-occupied housing, and is divided roughly equally between these four. I asked Andreas Rumpfhuber, an architect and historian of Vienna's architectural history, about the relative low cost of housing compared with other West European capitals. 'I think it is also important to make clear (on an international level) that Vienna still is a rental city and that the municipal housing stock is around 21 per cent and the publicly funded housing stock (mostly built by co-operatives) own another 20 per cent', but he points out that these levels have declined in the last couple of years, as private investors are building fast, 'flooding the market'. Municipal housing construction virtually stopped for ten years in the 2000s and early 2010s, and has only been resumed since 2015 – though co-operative construction remains high. In Budapest, the situation is much more polarised. The Budapest-based historian and filmmaker Carl Rowlands pointed out to me that while 'there have been some very limited efforts by one or two municipalities in Budapest to build new flats, I believe the numbers of new, socially owned flats since 1989 to be in three figures'. There was significant state-directed housing in the communist era, of course – but much of what had been built between 1945 and 1989 was subject to an 'instant privatisation' in the 1990s that let residents buy flats at a discount from the municipality. 'That said, there remain large numbers of socially owned flats in Budapest, as not everyone has been in a situation to buy from the local authority. The approach of the first Fidesz government was to subside mortgages for families to buy from the private sector. This scheme continues in one form or another.' The results are predictable: 'high levels of homelessness, resulting from either low or non-existing wages, or personal circumstances which the social system isn't able to mitigate'.

But these are bare numbers. What puts flesh on these statistical bones is the enormous qualitative difference in the building programmes of the two cities, and the sense of pride and collective endeavour that their architecture and planning has aimed – with some success – to convey. So we need to look at their very different legacies in detail, as monuments that are not static or confined to architectural history, but are lived in, and exist in an increasingly unsympathetic political and economic context.

Housing or Revolution

Politically speaking, both cities were, a hundred years ago, urban, multicultural, left-leaning islands in conservative, underdeveloped, rural countries; both underwent revolutionary turmoil in 1918–19 as the Austro-Hungarian Empire collapsed. An attempt at a revolutionary communist Republic of Workers Councils in Budapest collapsed after less than a year, when Hungary was invaded from all sides and dismembered. The subsequent, violently antisemitic White Terror, followed by two decades of right-wing dictatorship, provided a good counter-example for the Austro-Marxists, so-called, who dominated the Socialist Party of Austria. They aimed to follow a path distinct from the political conformism of the British Labour Party or the German Social Democrats, with a determined attempt from 1919 onwards to create a sort of socialism within one city – and also, distinct from the violent class conflict of the Bolsheviks in Soviet Russia, preferring to achieve their aims through legal and peaceful means, something in which they had some success, until they faced their own quietus in 1934.

What is distinctive in Budapest's twentieth-century architecture – what can't be found in Vienna to anything like the same degree in the same period – is its engagement with the major competitor to socialism in the twentieth century: nationalism. There was an international modernist Budapest, of course. There are many fascinating early modernist office blocks and apartments from the years just before the First World War, experiments in rationalised exoticism similar to the work of Viennese designers such as Otto Wagner; and in

On the Eve – Organic Proto-Modernism in Pest

CIAM-Designed Modernist 1930s Flats in Pest

the thirties there were private houses designed in the Buda hills by Bauhaus-trained émigré architects after they came home, and one large-scale private housing complex by the Hungarian CIAM group, in Pest. From the sixties on, there were attractive, often decorative co-operative blocks of flats inserted into infill in Buda, usually for the more-favoured groups in the allegedly classless society. What is more characteristic, perhaps, is the ongoing attempt to create a specifically Hungarian architecture.

The earliest examples of this came from the designer Ödön Lechner, who tried in the first decades of the century to achieve a 'Hungarian language of form', reflective of the fact that, historically, Hungarians, who do not speak an Indo-European language, were not 'Europeans', despite having managed to create in Budapest one of the most impressive bourgeois cities of the late nineteenth century. Inspired by the patterns of folk embroidery and a great deal of personal speculation, Lechner's buildings used richly coloured ceramics moulded into exotic skylines, dripping over rational steel or concrete framed structures, an attempt to supply the 'real Hungarian' architecture that may never actually have existed. As architecture, this is often thrilling to experience – the bizarre skyline of Lechner's Postal Savings Bank poking out above the security grilles of the US Embassy, so different to the proto-modernist clear lines and machine-made surfaces of Otto Wagner's Postal Savings Bank in Vienna. The peak of Lechner's career was the magnificent Museum of Applied Arts, with its spiky, mosaic encrusted dome and stained-glass lightwells shaped like imaginary starfish – Edwin Heathcote describes it as the first public museum ever to have been built in a non-historicist style.

However, the first of the two capitals to embark on a serious municipal housing experiment was actually Budapest, and using a similar language to that of Lechner. Under the influence of the British garden city and the work of the Arts and Crafts movement, the Wekerle estate, built between 1907 and 1914, was intended as both a response to the profit-driven development of the city centre and to the pressure of demands for reform – particularly from Budapest's large Social Democratic

Gothic-Islamic-Magyar – the Dome of the Museum of Applied Arts

Social-National Dreamworld – the Wekerle Estate

Party and a restive trade union movement. The streets that are admired by tourists today were dominated, as in Vienna and elsewhere, by dense filling in of private plots with tall tenements and courtyards (with grand plaster facades, of course) – and, more unusually, as an attempt to house the urban working class in attractive housing set in green space. Rather than being noted for its social aims, the estate is perhaps best known for its piquant and dreamlike architecture, a Transylvanian style of turrets, organic and biomorphic doorways and archways, designed by a large team that included the celebrated Károly Kós, after whom the main square was later named. Like many garden city estates, the popularity of the design and the indeterminacy of ownership has made it hard to preserve the original political aims – particularly after privatisation – and Wekerle is no longer public housing today. It is, however, the only housing estate in Hungary to be placed on a preservation list. Its integration of social purpose and nationalistic architectural speculation would not be repeated.

Vienna's experiment begins later, and first, it had to defeat some much more radical proposals which questioned the accepted ways of building in cities altogether. Informal 'squatters' settlements' had risen up on the outskirts of the city in response to the housing crisis caused by the upheavals of the First World War. There was no system of ownership, housing was self-built, and people were growing their own food – something close to the dream of contemporary anarchists and left-wing environmentalists. Architects such as Adolf Loos, Josef Frank and Margarete Schütte-Lihotsky, and the sociologist and philosopher Otto Neurath looked at these areas, in 1919 and 1920, and saw in the self-organised spaces the possibility of building a new kind of city, in which the people would build their own spaces as they chose – low-rise, homely but modern, with a closeness to nature and an anarchic independence that were hard to achieve in an inner-urban tenement. This would very quickly be rejected by the Social Democratic city government, in favour of a new generation of dense and

The Marxist Founders of the Republic of Austria

strongly urban tenements, on a different spatial model to those of the nineteenth century. Taking power at the end of the war, the Austro-Marxist government ran Vienna practically as a city-state until it was overthrown in 1934 by a military coup organised by the clerical-fascist Christian Social Party. From the start, the administration was embattled, to put it mildly. Social Democratic leaders, such as the Mayor Karl Renner, suspicious of anarchic experiments such as the promotion of self-building and informality, and keen to rehouse people as quickly, reliably and cleanly as possible, opted for what they regarded as the more pragmatic solution of building in 'infill' sites in the city centre, rather than starting anew. The result was the *Hof*, a type of monumental tenement building, street-facing, with green courtyards, schools, baths, libraries and other social facilities inside. These were interpreted by the Christian Social Party as literal fortresses, and there's little doubt that they were often as ideological as they were practical, and absolutely loaded with rhetoric.

The most famous of Red Vienna's monuments, the Karl Marx-Hof, is the architectural equivalent of a mass demonstration, stepping in line, arm in arm, to the glorious future. Immensely long and broken up with wide entrance arches, it is not massively far from the Wekerle estate's attention to public green space and the creation of grand vistas, but it bulks up the imagery and the scale to operatic proportions. Yet it is only the largest example of a much more general project: smaller estates will frequently have sculptures or reliefs, usually of workers and worker-families, or more occasionally motifs related to the history of the particular area of the capital they were built in. The craftsmanship in bronze, clinker and stone on the facades of these masonry-built structures was a means of keeping as many workers employed as possible, in a city where imperial collapse had caused a profound crisis both of finance and of identity – that is, what was the city for, now that it no longer presided over a gigantic, German-dominated land empire that

Karl Marx-Hof

stretched from the Alps to the Carpathians? One answer was that it would become a city whose reason for existing was the welfare and edification of its residents, particularly its working-class inhabitants, who had hitherto been ignored in one of the definitive bourgeois cities, an administrative capital with little industry compared with, say, Berlin or St Petersburg. Massive taxation of the wealthy and of landlords, and the introduction of a 'luxury tax' made possible this shift from an imperial capital into a socialist capital. In order to do this, the socialist idea is communicated by a heroic, pathos-ridden imagery of collectivism.

Inside, these *Gemeindebau* – municipally built – flats weren't quite so glorious. The need to get people out of the nineteenth-century slums, fast, meant that the innovations enjoyed by other, richer cities – Berlin, London, Amsterdam, where workers could have private gardens, central heating and bathrooms – were brought in much more slowly in Vienna, where much of the effort went into producing an impressive effect, and housing as many people as possible. However, these are still flowing, public, attractive spaces, which it is a pleasure to walk through – and off the Gürtel, the 'Ringstrasse of the Proletariat', you can walk for around a mile just through these courtyards, linking one housing estate to the next, all of them beautifully maintained and well used. And on the entrance to each one, in big red metal letters, is 'BUILT BY THE CITY OF VIENNA'. Vienna Council shouted it proudly, from the rooftops, and that's why these housing estates were literally bombarded by fascists in 1934, in their coup d'état against the socialists. What is surprising today is that these buildings and the city's housing in general still proclaim that sense of pride, although not as loudly as they used to.

I asked Michael Klein, co-writer with Rumpfhuber of the recent *Modelling Vienna* – a proposal for reviving in a new context the ideas of Viennese socialism – about whether these estates are still popular locally. 'I would say so. Even though [Red Viennese apartment blocks] have rather small floorplan layouts, they are considered as good housing. Refurbishing them has been an ongoing issue, particularly since the 1980s', and by now, the municipal housing stock has both been thermally insulated and adapted to the needs of disabled people via lifts, usually not part of these walk-up blocks. Also, he points out, 'the renovation of council housing also became important in terms of a signalling effect. In the 1970s major parts of the historic housing stock was in really bad condition, poorly maintained – the downside of strong rent-control: the owners did not maintain the buildings – and poorly equipped, with no built-in central heating, toilets outside the flat, etc. Because of its large shares of the housing stock, renovating the *Gemeindebau* took the role of an incentive in urban renewal.' This was partly possible because, although they are easily identifiable, *Gemeidebauten* are contiguous with the existing city in terms of their street plans. Unlike the housing estates of the post-war era, their block structure is not much different to the street-facing grid of the imperial city; the main difference is in the interior courtyards, which are open, green and filled with bathhouses, schools, sports centres, libraries, nurseries and polyclinics, whereas in the nineteenth-century city they were filled simply by more, darker flats.

You can, in bookshops in the city, buy glossy albums on the *Gemeidebau*, postcards and trinkets. There is nothing to compare in the housing of inter-war Budapest, which is unsurprising given that housing was a very low priority for Admiral Miklós Horthy's dictatorship; the most impressive housing project in the city centre, the nearest thing to a Karl Marx-Hof, is the Madach Apartment block, a brick colossus built in 1938. Its archways have some connection to those of the Karl Marx-Hof – but it was intended as elite housing. Slightly earlier, on Miklós Horthy Square (now Móricz Zsigmond Square), a large-scale block of flats around a circular plaza was built that also slightly resembles Viennese precedent – but, again, these were middle-class flats. The pre-war experience of socialism in Budapest was brief, violent and quickly extinguished, so of course it has left little trace. But the counter-revolution against it didn't lead to particularly widespread construction either, with a few villa settlements, some bourgeois apartment blocks and a few new factories being about the extent of new construction during the Horthy years; the regime survived on repression and nationalism rather than on a social contract with its citizens. Needless to say, after Red Vienna was suppressed, both cities now avoided large-scale construction of workers' housing. Official politics was rooted in nationalism and antisemitism, with both communists and Jews seen as an alien – and linked – presence in the city. But curiously, the nationalist architectural experiments of Lechner were not developed. Budapest architecture of the 1920s and 1930s, and the very little 'planning' that happened at the same time, appears oddly aloof from the bleak and violent politics of the era. The nineteenth-century city was maintained, almost in its entirety, with all its inequalities.

After 1945, the Red Army occupied both cities. Vienna – half of it occupied by the Red Army until the late fifties – only slowly re-embarked on its social programme. Next to many of the grandiose estates of the 1930s, you can find little extensions from the 1950s and 1960s, where the graphic programme continues – near the Karl Marx-Hof, a block of tenements features a mosaic postman, next to the letterbox. At the end of the fifties, belatedly compared to most neighbouring countries, Vienna built its first high-rise. It is a single-point block in a park off a side street. There is an abstract mural in the entrance, and cutesy murals of Old Vienna in the lift lobbies. Some drab high-rise estates were built soon after. Michael Klein, who took me around several post-war estates in Vienna, tells me that 'change came above all from an architectural side. Council housing as well as subsidised housing after '45 hardly involved the few leftovers of progressive architecture after fascism.' Some designers who had been closely involved with fascist planning in the city between 1934 and 1945, such as the influential Roland Rainer, became important drivers in the post-war era, in a city now run, again, by the Social Democrats.

The results are not significantly different from those of post-war Budapest. There, peripheral estates were built widely after the suppression of the 1956 uprising against the Soviets, on much the same model as elsewhere in the Eastern Bloc, although compared with the imaginative layouts and surface treatments that were becoming common in, say, Poland or Yugoslavia, the results were monolithic, such as the massive Újpalota development. These were not ghettos; as the sociologist Iván Szelényi pointed out, they were quite the reverse, usually favouring the relatively privileged groups in 'real socialism', such as skilled workers, clerks and bureaucrats, whereas the historic city's crumbling – and still private – housing was more likely to accommodate those on the lower rungs of society, such as unskilled workers and recent rural-to-urban migrants. The peripheral location and homogeneous appearance of these

Prefab Planning in Post-'56 Pest

estates means that modernity and public housing was very much something that happened *outside* of Budapest's historic city centre, which was increasingly being marketed to tourists in both the East and West from the sixties on. This no doubt pleases tourists, who generally prefer not to be reminded of the twentieth century when they're walking around (except when it comes to electricity, clean running water, the internet or the jumbo jet), but it creates a division between the lovely Hapsburg capital and its concrete, industrial outskirts, remnants of a disappeared time when this was one of the foremost manufacturing cities of Central Europe. Another upshot of this was that, during the height of the Cold War in the fifties and sixties, Budapest and Vienna had new housing that was more similar than it had been at any time since the collapse of the empire, with much the same grey, spaced-out blocks, in *Zeilenbau* ('line-building') layouts, all more modern than the *Gemeindebauten*, but, unlike them, breaking with the existing city and dropping the dramatic socialist stylistic rhetoric.

And although Vienna was more democratic, its politics have been dominated by one party to an astonishing degree. Since 1945 it has been semi-autonomous within Austria, so that some degree of power-sharing has existed ever since – the Social Democrats controlling Vienna and a couple of smaller cities, and the Christian Socials maintaining their hold on the countryside. The two parties have frequently been in coalition governments together, although at times, particularly under the leadership of Bruno Kreisky in the 1970s, the Social Democrats have been popular enough to govern the country alone. The result is that Vienna has been governed by the same party after every democratic election it has ever had, since the end of the First World War – only the intervening years of Austrofascism and then Nazism have been exceptions. It is oddly unnerving, when in Vienna, to realise that perhaps the best managed city in Europe is so partly because it is effectively a one-party state, something which helps explain the scale of Austrians' rejection of politics in recent years, with the Social Democrat vote collapsing at much the same rate as that of the Christian Social (renamed after 1945 as the OVP, the People's Party) – the establishment here is very established indeed. But in the urban fabric of Vienna, results are results. As one Viennese architect – whom I would rather not name – put it to me, 'it's corrupt, but it works'. Corrupt, not in the sense that there are backhanders being paid, but because the links between the Social Democrats, the co-operatives, the trade unions and the building industry are so established and closely linked that there is little incentive to change a system which satisfies all parties.

Vienna's housing policy has twice shifted towards something much more unusual, in the 1970s and 1990s, to models which were in no way similar to anything happening in Budapest. In the seventies, two new housing estates were built in the south of the city, along the new U-Bahn that extended the imperial Stadtbahn into a very sexy transport system, with stations clad

From the Swimming Pool at Alt-Erlaa

in a distinctive moulded plastic, now evoking a nostalgic futurism. The first of these, Alt-Erlaa, was designed by one Harry Glück ('Harry Happy', a gift for subeditors) for a housing cooperative. The housing co-ops have often had bigger budgets to play with than the council itself (although they are maintained largely by government subsidy), and at Alt-Erlaa, you can see a rare combination of brutalist aesthetics and spatial opulence. In the way it is laid out, it is, like the estates of the sixties, a classic Radiant City, of the sort planned by Le Corbusier since the 1920s, and increasingly rejected after 1968 by the New Left. Alt-Erlaa's giant towers, on a stepped section that enables most of the storeys to have deep, lushly planted balconies, are spread out on landscaped parkland with artificial hills; a shopping mall by the U-Bahn station provides the neighbourhood centre. The novelty is, first, visual – as architecture, it is tremendously exciting, with a drama and grandeur that had been absent here since 1934. Where Alt-Erlaa is original is in the way that each of the blocks has an interior social structure, built into the blocks. The plans of each tower are deliberately sprawling and deep, so that the spaces in the middle could be turned into social clubs, pool halls, leisure centres or whatever the residents in each block want – and they have been adapted exactly in this way, with each block containing slightly different facilities. On top of each tower is a swimming pool. It's a vision of collective luxury all the more convincing because it never fell into decline.

It was, however, heavily criticised in the architectural press, partly because of its strange plan: you could fit in a pool hall, but you couldn't have dual-aspect flats, and ceilings are low; individual spaces were compromised so as to provide more space for the collective. More importantly, it was criticised on the level of urbanism, for the clear break with the structure of the existing city. Michael Klein notes that 'the rise of architectural critique in Vienna in the sixties came along with the rising critique of the monotonous *Zeilenbau*', and Alt-Erlaa was 'seen as an attempt of following the lines of modernist optimisation'. He continues, 'the Architectural debate ran against the project, as it did not really contribute to the city', but was instead a self-contained utopia. The response of these critics – Am Schöpfwerk, built by the city council – is just round the corner, outside its own U-Bahn station. Council housing is lower rent than co-operative, and Schöpfwerk is a much more multicultural area; it has been considered a 'problem estate' to some degree, although this is in a Viennese context, where housing is far better maintained than is the norm, either in Anglo-Saxon countries or in the former Eastern Bloc. It is an attempt, as in the Vienna of the 1920s, to create social spaces without disrupting the tenement structure built up in the nineteenth century, with a rigid grid of blocks identifiable as 'streets'. Towards the U-Bahn station, there is a massive, monumental tower, but within it, a series of mid-rise courtyards create a sequence of public spaces with plenty of room for bars, cafes and schools; and as with the

Am Schopfwerk

housing of the twenties, everything flows together, nothing is gated or marked off. The interior staircases of the blocks are a little eerie: galleried and top-lit, to a degree that feels one part utopian nineteenth-century philanthropic project, one part model prison, though rather livelier than that comparison might suggest. If this is the closest Vienna has ever got to a 'sink estate' – which, by all accounts, it is – then they've been exceptionally lucky.

Post-Communist Divergence

The market socialism that the Hungarian Communists pioneered as a means of maintaining social peace after the Red Army crushed the 1956 revolution eventually collapsed into debt in the late 1980s. Its cadres managed to become a minor part of a new capitalist class, and the Socialist Party that succeeded them – increasingly not so much social democratic as neoliberal – alternated in power for a couple of decades with

Fidesz, a liberal party reliant on the middle class the regime had fostered, practically if not officially. According to the 'transition theory' that has dominated interpretations of Central Europe over the last twenty-five years, the fall of communism should have led to an increasing similarity between politics and economics on either side of the Iron Curtain that Hungary was the first to open up. The major architectural trend of the 1990s, though, led by a group of organic architects including the feted Imre Makovecz, stressed difference rather than convergence. Starting to practise in the 1960s, but receiving few commissions until the eighties, Makovecz based his tent-like structures on speculation about what the yurts carried by the nomadic Magyars, who moved over a millennium ago from Central Asia into what is now Hungary, might possibly have looked like. Developing this into a school of self-described organic architecture, characterised by swelling, maternal domes, phallic protrusions and anthropomorphic faces, Makovecz and his partners such as Ervin Nagy created a fascinating and deeply odd form of design based on nationalist fancies about Hungarian uniqueness and chthonic specificity. These architects favoured the 'authentic' rural Hungary, rather than urbane, cosmopolitan Budapest, but it can be seen there – in several homes Makovecz designed for the intelligentsia of late 'real socialism', but also for larger works by his collaborators and disciples that try to translate organic ideas into urban terms. One example is the monumental Swan House, a mixed-use commercial building designed in the early 1990s by Ervin Nagy. The articulation evokes mountains, crystals and caves, and the materials – thick limestone, witchy carved wood – are crafted, not mechanically produced. The building embodies a shift right back to the 1900s, and the imagined Hungarian form that can be seen in the Disneyland castle on Buda's hills, or the more serious work of Ödön Lechner or Károly Kós; it belongs to a fantasy city that tries to evoke a past which is impossible to picture, let alone recapture.

Monumental Organic in Buda

Was this so specific to Hungary? There was a lot of fantasy architecture around in the 1980s, and Makovecz's or Nagy's work was often seen in these terms. Vienna, for instance, had the far less talented Friedensreich Hundertwasser, who usually decorated straightforward blocks with a colourful, textured, populist and ostentatiously irrational repertoire of forms, as a reaction against the alleged inhumanity and industrialised interchangeability of modernism. Hundertwasser even got to design a couple of blocks of council housing in the centre of Vienna – something which Makovecz or Nagy, infinitely superior architects and spatial thinkers, never had the chance to do in Budapest, either during 'socialism' or in post-1989 capitalism. The crucial difference here is that, while Hundertwasser's critique of modernism was based on a situationist-sentimentalist disdain for industrial aesthetics as the destroyer of place, informed by 1960s radicalism, Makovecz's dislike of the city and internationalism was premised on something more turn-of-the-century: antisemitism and anti-communism, where the modern city was the result of a rootless, cosmopolitan disease common both to Americanised capitalism and Soviet communism.

Makovecz's unpleasant politics are not a side-issue. The vehemence of the national style's advocates in Budapest, massively outnumbered as they are by practitioners of international beaux-arts and international modernism, was not about a solely stylistic opposition. It was constantly discussed in terms of Europeanness, and the lack thereof. Whereas the centre of Budapest is one of the most quintessentially, stereotypically European cities, organic architecture set out to present an image of difference: we are not truly European, so the architecture that speaks to our souls, that speaks to our blood, must be different. For most of the last few decades, this has been combined interchangeably with the opposite claim: we are true Europe, the heart of Europe, the bastion of Europe, at the gates of Christendom. Occasionally, we are knocked off course by enemies – the Turks, who occupied the country in the early modern era (and introduced one of the most enjoyable things about Budapest, its public bathhouses), or the Austrians, who occupied us for centuries, or the communists, who threw us off our European path and dragged us into an Asiatic, collectivist barbarism. It is incoherent, but nationalism often is. Given that Makovecz was seldom allowed to build under 'socialism', but was treated as a guru in the 1990s, he showed that a certain kind of rhetoric, which could have been expected to die with fascism in 1945, made a reappearance in that decade.

So it should not be a surprise that beautiful, Central European Budapest has been the home for the last few years of the 'illiberal democracy' of Viktor Orbán, which has kept itself in power by constant appeals to fears: of non-existent communists; of migrants (who seldom want to settle in Hungary, although this is Hungary's loss, as it faces a demographic crisis, with a sharply falling birth rate and population); and particularly, of Muslims. Once, these were the Turks at the gates of Vienna; now, they are the Syrians sleeping in the underpass under Budapest's Keleti station, that glorious iron and glass train hall, designed by Gustave Eiffel himself. The appeal to fear has been influential: the Austrian Freedom Party, Law and Justice in Poland, United Russia, the Front National in France, the Freedom Party in the Netherlands, the People's Party in Denmark and UKIP in Britain have all taken inspiration from Orbán.

Many – though not of course Vladimir Putin or UKIP – have drawn on this approach, holding up European values against those who the foolish, multikulti Germans might let into our pristine nation states to destroy our culture. Orbán's party, Fidesz, grew out of a liberal grouping set up by the Budapest intelligentsia as the Communist regime liberalised itself out of existence. It is not an insurgent party, but a group of smart, experienced operators merely changing the emphasis of the 'Europe' they discuss. In the last few years, they have closed opposition newspapers, appointed political like-minds to all relevant media and business positions, and embarked on yet another round of nation-building, this time painting the 'heart of Europe' as the last holdout of sanity and Christianity against the multicultural hordes. It has been a notably successful shift. Vienna, as the increasing Freedom Party vote makes clear, faces the same problems of insecurity, boredom and bigotry as Budapest, but it is in a far better position to oppose them than Budapest, with its marginal, embattled and complicit remnants of liberalism and socialism. Vienna's resilience against populism must reflect a residual loyalty to the social democracy that has delivered a decent life to most – however off-limits it may be to migrants.

It is often argued that Europe became definitively neoliberal in the 1990s and 2000s, with decreasing options for local authorities and national governments in the face of continent-wide pressure to liberalise and privatise. However, Vienna actually continued to innovate in its social housing in that decade, in marked contrast with most other capitals. Another of those Viennese shifts came in the early 1990s, this time away from a preoccupation with amenity, morphology and continuity, into an official policy which foregrounded sexual difference. The (of course, still Social Democrat-dominated) City of Vienna, under the influence of feminist currents both in the Social Democratic Party's left and in the Greens they were often in coalition with, embarked on a programme of 'gender mainstreaming', which in practice meant extensive research into how men and women (and boys and girls) used public space, followed by the design of new spaces to make sure that they didn't discriminate in any way. The results, while explicitly feminist – the first test estate, the Frauen-Werk-Stadt, was for women only – are universal, being based around close connections to public transport, plenty of natural surveillance and abundant childcare facilities. These ideas have fed into the new housing built in the city of Vienna over the last fifteen years or so, to the point where they have become common sense.

One example is the Sonnwendviertel, a housing scheme completed in 2014 near the recently reconstructed Hauptbahnhof, by several different firms of youngish architects, their individual blocks sharing space around a public garden linked by walkways and skyways. One block, designed by StudioVlayStreeruwitz, has within it a farmers' market and a cinema for residents only, which I was greatly struck by when I visited it from London at the start of 2016. 'Gender mainstreaming guidelines were not integrated as such', architect Lina Streeruwitz told me, 'but the competition brief asked for a specific and new approach to the issue of social sustainability. The accessibility of common spaces for different types of uses and users was very important, and that is where the diversity and specificity of proposed uses (swimming, reading, playing, climbing, sitting, hiding, smoking, dancing, cooking,

Twenty-First-Century Social – Sonnwendviertel

eating, grilling, shopping) came into it. Our idea was not to offer open and undefined spaces that can be appropriated and negotiated because in order to do so you need to have time and energy which a lot of people don't have. By proposing specific uses the spaces turn into an invitation rather than a challenge, and in a project of that size (more than 450 apartments) this seemed the right answer in order to involve people of different ages, genders and backgrounds.' The little things, the details that are so often done badly in 'Anglo-Saxon' economies, with their 'value engineering' and their private finance initiatives, are exquisite, such as the smooth, poured-concrete stairwells leading to the flats and the cinema, with seats moulded into the structure. This sort of meticulous detail, like the social facilities here, are usually the preserve of luxury flats, high-end speculative housing. 'One third of the apartments were given out directly through the City of Vienna,' Streeruwitz told me. 'There you can apply for each project and on a certain day you will be offered up to three apartments via an internet platform.

Since there are a lot of people on the list, it is a kind of lottery. The rest of the apartments are allocated through the housing association, in personal meetings and according to waiting lists based on a first come, first served principle – although this process is not very transparent.'

This is essentially the same social state as in the 1960s, with the same potential and the same limitations. 'There was little in the way of public consultation when the flats were built – allocation', Streeruwitz says, 'started about a year before we finished with construction.' The architects were keen to try and help 'people to appreciate the main ideas and understand what we had in mind' in the project, but the residents were eventually 'confronted with these at a meeting organised by some of the inhabitants who were unhappy – mostly with organisational things that had little to do with architecture. We could clarify the different responsibilities of architects, project management and facility management, but it was too late to get rid of a certain mistrust with some of the inhabitants. There was one person who complained about finding out that he has a double-height living room only after signing the contract and being handed the key to the apartment. He was completely annoyed with the fact but did not dare to try for a change of apartment. That was quite sad because it was something we had fought for a lot and it seemed such a waste that the person living there does not appreciate the space.' While sympathetic to her frustration with her inability to communicate with this particular resident, I was somehow pleased that there was still a place in Europe where having too big a flat is something someone is able to complain about. A social housing tenant in Budapest – or, indeed, in London – would be very happy to have such problems.

Similarly, the new city extension at Aspern, still under way at the time of writing, shows influences both from Alt-Erlaa and from the gender mainstreaming techniques of the Frauen-Werk-Stadt. I was taken here by the organisers of a conference on the architecture of the sixties, who, I gathered, wanted to show visitors the place as an exemplar of the limited ambitions of contemporary housing. If that was the intention, it wasn't successful. Partly this was a question of the difference with British examples: public spaces were not gated, chopped up and littered with CCTV cameras, but logically threaded together, both intimate and collective. The estate was three-dimensional, in that walkways and multiple levels constantly created partial views of the estate and vistas of the distant inner-city skyline. Most of the blocks had swimming pools on their roofs. A U-Bahn connection was built before the housing was even occupied. Some of the public spaces were for residents only, and the blocks followed an easily definable 'street' pattern, with shops on the ground floor, but these came alongside abundant and cleverly conceived public spaces to explore. Some of the housing was private, but most of it was for the co-operatives. Aspern has, in social terms, almost all of the things that I wanted in housing, and that at home, I could find most often in post-war architecture. The main divergence was that it lacked visual drama and confidence. That, it became clear, was the extent of the conference organisers' problems with it, as architecture. And it's true – this is an architecture of modest pieces placed together, rather than the collective expression of one overwhelming idea, as is the case with Karl Marx-Hof or Alt-Erlaa.

Yet Aspern had delivered the highest vote in the whole of Vienna for the Freedom Party, a violently anti-immigrant, openly xenophobic party, which had been founded by SS officers as an extension of the banned Nazi party, and whose leader came within reach of winning the presidential election in 2016. When talking to people – both architects and residents – in Vienna, I seldom found much awareness of just how good they have it – all they noticed was that their living standards were falling, slightly, in relation to the recent past, not how astonishingly high they are compared to Britain, never mind neighbouring Hungary. There is one possible explanation. Half of Vienna's housing is in this 'social' system – which is, as Andreas Rumpfhuber explains, allocated in a totally different way to a residual, philanthropic housing for the poor, that is, 'housing for a group in society that is "in need", the ones that cannot afford to live otherwise. It is crucial to understand that the project of housing might be one that is for everyone.' Much of the city's middle class live in municipal or co-operative flats: 'I live in a project that was publicly funded', he reminds me. But as Michael Klein points out, 'from the seventies onwards the city introduced several subsidies also for renovating and equipping the private housing stock (toilets, heating, warm water, etc.). While this seemed necessary, the downside effect was the loss of really cheap flats. Today's housing market has little to no really low-rent offers which some years ago still existed, with more and more people depending on council housing.'

The rental market is unstable and expensive, which makes the non-market parts of the system more important; but the universal principle is now being criticised. 'A few years ago it was commonly accepted, and people were proud of it, that there would be a mixture of different classes that would live in the municipally owned housing schemes – i.e. the shoe-maker, the factory worker, as well as the professor or a member of Parliament would live next to each other,' says Rumpfhuber. 'For some years now there has been a public debate, via daily newspapers like *Krone*, that is upset about the fact that members of Parliament (with his/her income) is allowed to live in such places.' The system has some way to go before reaching the residual level of Budapest, even so. He continues, 'If a nationalist party would win elections it would take some time or years to destroy or substantially change' the city's housing system, so entrenched is it at an institutional level.

Vienna also has strict citizenship laws, and to obtain council or co-operative housing, you must be a citizen. 'If you are not in the game', Klein says, with 'no legal status, not long enough in Vienna, etc.', then 'you are confronted with crazy rents' on the private market. This disenfranchises the city's many immigrants, and helps to create a certain paranoia among the majority who do, still, today, maintain access to what could plausibly be described as the most extensive social provision and the fairest housing system ever established in any city in human history. One could make the argument that the shift towards a paranoid politics of irrational hatreds and passionate insularity has been the result of all that excessive rationality and cleanliness, and of the lack of private, guarded spaces in the overwhelming majority of Vienna's housing. I am not convinced. I think that Austrians *do* know how lucky they are. The growth of a new, slightly rebranded fascism – in a Vienna that, while still Social Democrat–dominated, has a large and growing Freedom Party vote – can only be understood through that fear that they, out there, beyond the 'gates of Vienna', formerly so heavily guarded against 'the Turk', might want to come and get their nice things, an impulse not so much unlike that of Budapest's residents. Vienna is one of those cities that lies on the refugee route from Syria to Germany, and, unlike Budapest, refugees might actually choose to settle there, in a city which is already reasonably multicultural.

There is nothing like Aspern or the Sonnwendviertel in Budapest, and there could not be, given its flat taxes and aversion to social housing. Instead, there are two major developments. The earlier of these is the Millennium City Center, created a decade or so ago along the Pest riverside in Ferencváros. It is a good exemplar of how aggressive nation-building and internationalised capitalism so often go hand in hand, and how 'European' need not mean 'progressive', which was a view held by many people in the field of 'transitionology'. This riverfront redevelopment begins with office blocks for the likes of Morgan Stanley or the local bank K&H, and speculative luxury flats marketed in the English language to an international clientele, all designed in a modern but traditionally street-fronting style that can be found in Vienna, Madrid or Athens (more seldom in Birmingham or Moscow); and there's the Ludwig Museum, a modern art museum in a hard-lined modernist style much like Vienna's MAK, or anything you'd find in a big city in Spain or Scandinavia. These are seamlessly integrated with a new linear park, featuring realist sculptures of Moses holding the tablets aloft, of Hungarian medieval warlords and kings stroking their beards or flexing their muscles, of 'interactive' sculptures children can climb on modelled on the Tower of Babel and the aforementioned yurts. An archway in neoclassical style with a broken pediment is draped with a theatrical curtain, leading to the new National Theatre, designed by Mária Siklós and opened in 2002. This monumental effort in neoclassical kitsch is hard to read – particularly in terms of whether its giant statuary and gimcrack classical details are intended to be funny. It was widely considered as a personal project of Viktor Orbán, a monument to nation-building and indigenous folk culture. Its placement

The National Theatre, Pest

alongside the more modest monuments of international capitalism should not be seen as contradictory: one offsets the
effects of the other.

The other development, still ongoing, is the Corvin Quarter,
in the working-class Eighth District. A large baroque circus
just behind Budapest's radial Haussmannian boulevard is, at
first, a continuous monument to the 1956 uprising against
the Soviets. The big tenement blocks curve around a small
cinema, which is covered with plaques for the revolution that
had one of its main centres exactly here. Insurgents are com-
memorated with dozens of plaques, with biographies that
aren't afraid to make clear how many of the insurgents and
their leaders were communists; in fact, the only communists
to have surviving monuments in the city, after a widespread
purging of any trace of socialist iconography, are Imre Nagy,
Pál Maléter and Sándor Kopácsi, party members who saw no
contradiction between socialism and an insurrection against
Stalinism. A map of the Quarter shows the battles fought there.
Walk around it and you'll realise that these are the only historical buildings left, as you suddenly find yourself in a new,
shiny modernist shopping arcade, and then on a promenade
lined by pristine luxury apartment blocks, exactly the same in
style as any in Western Europe, with Trespa and brick cladding and wan fountains. The way it is all planned, from the
memorial circus leading to the new development, appears to
suggest that the Hungarian revolution against Stalinism and
Russian imperialism has culminated in luxury living solutions
for the new European bourgeoisie. There are few places where
the spatial link between nationalism and capitalism is quite so
obvious, but here the socialist legacy has been well and truly
left behind – far more so than in Vienna.

Carl Rowlands tells me that 'these developments represent
different strands of Fidesz thinking'. While at the Millennium
Center, 'the sort of exhibition they hosted when it first opened –
great Hungarian innovations, that kind of thing – did reflect a

kind of national boosterism. I'm not sure it was more or less than that advocated by New Labour at around the same time. And the first Fidesz government wasn't so far off from the European mainstream at that time, at least in that regard. It was nationalist, in a kind of post-communist way. Now Fidesz are nationalist in a kind of post-democratic way.' Accordingly, 'the Corvin Quarter is a different thing – that is serious money, much more of a pure money grab. Hyper-gentrification of one of the most staunchly working-class and potentially bohemian areas of the city. The flats that are being built there are indicative of the market segment – a small 40 m² flat is 40 million forints – and in Hungarian terms, that is outside the range of all but the very richest. Going by equivalence to salaries, access to credit, etc., this is about the equivalent of half a million pounds for a small apartment, and marks the arrival of London-style housing finance inflation.' Irrespective of the 1956 paraphernalia at its entrance, 'the development is obviously not aimed at Hungarians', exceptionally few of whom can afford these London-level prices. Again, nationalist discourse and openness to globalised business are in no way opposed in practice. The government fulminates against international finance – particularly in the form of the financier and Hungarian-Jewish refugee George Soros, who has funded some of the opposition – but this is not meant to be taken seriously when it comes to making deals.

A quick Google of the Madach Apartments, the huge 1930s development that is Budapest's only comparison with a Karl Marx-Hof, will take you to dozens of flats being offered on Airbnb. Rowlands is careful to temper the impression of the city centre as somewhere that has been decisively transformed into a mere tourist showcase. Inner Budapest 'is still inhabited by a lot of long-time residents, including old ladies and gentlemen who still – just – balance out the burgeoning hipster tourist inclinations, a little. Secondly, there is often in the heart of Pest a feeling of genuine randomness, a universality which encompasses tourists within a wider spectrum of different people from Hungary and surrounding countries. There is still, sometimes, a feeling that Budapest is a capital city for an area beyond the confines of Hungary. This makes the working class visible as they go about daily business.' But whether this can last appears unlikely: 'the cost of living is high compared to relative wages, and house prices are currently surging in Budapest relatively to salaries, which are now, finally increasing, but only at a much slower rate.' There is no safety net, nothing but the free market, with a dressing of nationalist rhetoric.

The 'European' city is not merely the social city that so often appears to the Anglo-Saxon observer: dense, historically rich, egalitarian, clean, walkable and dominated by public transport. It is also the city of the nation state, a European invention which has caused countries all over the world to reshape themselves – or be forcibly reshaped – in its image. Budapest is beautiful, just as it was beautiful in 1944, when the Arrow Cross government was deporting its Jews to Auschwitz. The twentieth-century European city at its best promised something beyond this. In Vienna that still survives – for a lucky few.

May 2017

Fragments of German Expressionism

As German art institutions and museums – some of them newly set up for the purpose – celebrated the hundredth anniversary of the foundation of the Bauhaus, it didn't escape the attention of some critics that the architecture that school came to stand for has been rejected comprehensively in its country of origin. The Neues Bauen, so-called, rebranded as the International Style by American critics, an architecture of clean lines, industrial materials, open space, crystalline purity and refusal of historicism – the true foundation of what came to be called modern architecture – is accepted as heritage, but it is rejected as a contemporary model. When a new Bauhaus Museum was opened in the school's first home, Weimar, its stripped classicism was 'contextual' with the Nazi-era Gauforum around it. The notion that it would be bad manners to insert a modernist building to this thin-lipped ensemble won out over the possibility that there might be something wrong with commemorating a school that was closed by the Nazis within a building that shares the aesthetics favoured by the Nazis. Seeing architecture and politics as intersecting categories is deeply unfashionable everywhere, but perhaps nowhere more so than in German architecture institutes and city halls.

This has been going on for some time, but the Bauhaus anniversary made it especially obvious. In the most famous example, the post-1989 replanning of Berlin by the SPD-affiliated *Baumeister* and classicist Hans Stimmann imposed a mandatory nineteenth-century grid, with architects forced to use stone facades, regular windows and proportions, and to follow the historic street lines that had been smashed to pieces during the twentieth century thanks to the successive and intersecting efforts of modern architects and planners, the Royal Air Force, the Red Army and the Berlin Wall. This was a break with West Germany's planning both immediately after the war – new buildings roughly to the scale of the old, but in various modern styles, and with East Germany's spacious, Moscow-derived monumental baroque – and much more so, with the 1960s and 1970s, when the Federal Republic and the DDR opted decisively for modernist architecture and planning. In fact, by the seventies, even the most discordant classicism was vehemently rejected by German architectural opinion. When the British architect James Stirling used parodic, decontextualised classical references and a monumental scale in his Stuttgart Neue Staatsgalerie in 1979, modernists like Frei Otto accused the work of evoking Nazi architecture. If that was absurd, by now the notion that aesthetics have no political or historical resonance has won out completely. Stimmann's model – stripped classicism, modelled on the Prussian architecture of Karl Friedrich Schinkel, severe, imposing and travertine-clad – resembled nothing more than Third Reich buildings such as the Luftwaffe Ministry, the Reichsbank or the square at Fehrbelliner Platz. Evidently that's mere coincidence, not worth considering. It's just good building, nothing more.

The resultant model of restorative classicism has spread out from the capital to encompass an enthusiasm for historicism, and increasingly for historical reconstruction. Total reconstruction had previously been limited to Warsaw's post-war Old Town, which had been an anti-Nazi gesture, a reaction to a very real German attempt to wipe Poland and Polish culture off the map by razing its capital to the ground. Seventy years later, Dresden has a new Altstadt, around a new version of its bulbous baroque cathedral, and Frankfurt has supplemented its high-rise 'mini-Manhattan' with a reconstruction of the medieval city. Yet new German architecture since the 1980s, conservative as it is, hasn't necessarily been classical in the literal-minded manner of English postmodern classicists such as Quinlan Terry – it has been minimal, tasteful, stripped down, without swags or pediments; there is even a ghostly modernist presence in its serene regularity and lack of ornamental excess.

In fact, this turn towards classicism emerged out of the radical architecture of the 1980s, where West Berlin was subject to 'critical reconstruction', with new council housing blocks built in the holes and open spaces in districts near the Wall, in buildings that imaginatively both repaired the ravages of the twentieth century and drew attention to change, and to the creation of new space. Under Stimmann, the 'critical' edge in this movement disappeared – yet the apolitical nature of this shift has been almost unquestioningly accepted. In the 1990s, it was occasionally criticised on the grounds of stylistic conservatism, and the occasional daring voice pointed out that Prussian classicism might not be wholly appropriate for the multicultural reality of Berlin; East Berliners in particular protested at the demolition of the modernist Palace of the Republic in favour of a reconstruction of the Palace of the Hohenzollerns. Nonetheless nothing significant has changed in Berlin's architecture and planning since Stimmann's retirement in 2006. So it was unusual when a scandal broke out in the German press this year over probably the most prominent and prolific of these modern classicists, the designer Hans Kollhoff, who originally emerged out of the 1980s critical reconstruction milieu.

Before being picked up by the mainstream press, the controversy began with an article in the journal *Arch+* by the architecture historian Verena Hartbaum, focusing on Kollhoff's 2013 development at Walter-Benjamin-Platz in Charlottenburg, which consists of two arcaded blocks, in a rigorous yet materially rich style. As part of a critique of the nationalistic undertones of the various *Altbau-Neu* developments in German cities, Hartbaum drew attention to a paving stone in the square, into which Kollhoff had cut the following verse (translated into German):

No Usura Here

> With usura hath no man a house of good stone
> each block cut smooth and well fitting
> that design might cover their face.

The verse was not attributed, but the word 'usura' led Hartbaum to Ezra Pound's 'Canto XLV'. The lines are a critique both of capitalism and of modern architecture – the usurers, Pound's usual code for Jews, do not build with well-cut stone, they build with newfangled materials such as concrete and steel that will not last, as in the modernist department stores and housing estates that were relentlessly attacked by the National Socialists on their way to power. Hartbaum, pointing out how uncomfortable it was to cite Pound's openly fascist tirades at 'usura' on a square dedicated to a Jewish Marxist who died fleeing the Gestapo, described the stone as 'an antisemitic message in a bottle' to contemporary Berlin. Naturally, Kollhoff denied antisemitism, somewhat compromised by the fact that he also denied Pound's abundantly attested antisemitism, on the basis of a disavowal several decades after the war in a conversation with Allen Ginsberg. Nonetheless, it does not seem to have harmed Kollhoff's career particularly. In contemporary Germany, supporting a boycott of Israel can get you stripped of an art prize, as happened to the Lebanese artist Walid Raad, but quoting one of European fascism's major exponents on an ostensible memorial to one of its Jewish victims is an esoteric matter, an attempt to politicise an apolitical discipline.

Kollhoff, though an occasional contributor to reconstruction projects such as the Frankfurt Altstadt, is an enthusiast capable of working in a variety of neoclassical styles, best known for his large-scale works in a style developed in Germany and the Netherlands in the 1910s and 1920s: brick expressionism. His most celebrated works are the Piraeus housing complex in Amsterdam and high-rises, such as the Main Plaza in Frankfurt, the Ministry of the Interior and Ministry of

Justice in The Hague and the eponymous Kollhoff Tower at Potsdamer Platz in Berlin; all share an instantly recognisable style, with glinting, precisely cut and glazed clinker brickwork assembled into surging masses, with traditional windows and spiky skylines. What makes Kollhoff an interesting case is that he is a powerful, gifted architect – the combination of drama, scale and craft in his work can be genuinely exciting, especially in bland neo-modern environments such as the Amsterdam docklands or Potsdamer Platz, where their physicality and tactile richness can be a relief from so many tatty and tinny facades. If you know the buildings he's drawing on – the urtext is the Chilehaus office block in Hamburg, designed in the early 1920s by Fritz Höger, its spatially distorted prow surging towards the docks, decorated and embellished with brown brick gargoyles – there will often be a moment where you're not sure whether you're looking at an actual building

A Kollhoff

Not a Kollhoff

dating from the Weimar Republic, or 'a Kollhoff'. In any case, the architect has become so well known in this idiom that the Daimler-Chrysler Tower on Potsdamer Platz was quickly renamed the Kollhoff Tower after its architect, a rare honour for a living designer. Because of this, he was the natural choice to write a foreword for *Fragments of Metropolis – Berlin*, an anthology of photographs of brick expressionist buildings from the 1920s and 1930s, the first in what would become a multi-volume series, a crowdfunded project that has become one of the major successes in architectural publishing in contemporary Germany. Widely read and translated well beyond its original context, the project is gradually widening its remit from the German capital to large swathes of Central Europe.

The cover of *Fragments of Metropolis – Berlin* sets the tone. It's a photomontage of many of the buildings included, their craggy forms and pyramidal surges assembled to look like one gigantic cityscape – a metropolis that never existed, made up of real buildings that did and do, and are in reality spaced out amidst sprawl. Those who know the art of the period will recognise it as a fusion of the original posters for Fritz Lang's *Metropolis* and Walther Ruttmann's *Berlin – Symphony of a Great City*, with the Bauhaus teacher Paul Citroen's 1923 collage of American skyscrapers, also called *Metropolis*. This sets a scene of nostalgia for the drama and irrationalism of the Weimar era, and especially sets it in the context of German expressionist cinema, with its combined revulsion and excitement for the big city, its use of spatial distortion as an analogue for emotional turmoil, its mechanisation of the gothic.

Yet none of this features in Kollhoff's combative introduction. He has other battles to fight altogether. 'These days', he writes, 'everything is expression – leaping at you shamelessly from all sides, in the meantime, rather violently.' This refers, although names are not named, to other architects who draw on certain elements in the expressionist repertoire – the once fashionable, now heavily criticised 1990s generation of Zaha Hadid, Frank Gehry and Daniel Libeskind (whose titanium-clad Jewish Museum in Berlin, with its aggressive response to its Prussian classical neighbour, could only be built because it was begun a year before Stimmann came to be Berlin's chief planner – he told Libeskind that he would have blocked it if he could). Kollhoff speaks nonetheless with a tone of marginality. 'In architecture today, a simple building tectonically derived from that which has gone before stands out as an emphatic gesture of denial'; in the City of London, in Dubai, Manhattan or Shenzhen, this might have some salience, though hardly in Berlin. An expressionism that wanted to 'shatter' reality and 'shatter' capitalism is 'alluring to contemporary architects', Kollhoff contends, but he makes clear that there were really two expressionist architectures. 'If you take the architecture of expressionism not just as a fad, but rather as the hard-worked desire for tectonic expression, then the wheat quite quickly

The Wrong Kind of Expressionism – the Jewish Museum, Berlin

becomes separated from the chaff.' The wholesome and nutritious 'wheat' here is represented by the neo-gothic brick expressionism of Fritz Höger, and the 'chaff' is represented by the organic curves, moulded in plaster and render around a hidden brick structure, of Erich Mendelsohn's Einstein Tower, designed as an observatory and laboratory for the scientist in Potsdam, in which 'the temptation of sculptural effect' is 'pursued at the expense of architectural integrity'. This can 'tip suddenly into the fashionable, time-dependent – into the non-architectural; for architecture is oriented towards perpetuity, both physically and in its conception'. This obsession with authenticity and roots is pure Heidegger: 'what is more natural', Kollhoff asks, than to 'work with the malleable earth; with sculpted loam and fired clay?' It is hard to think of an architect less suited to designing a square named after Walter Benjamin, who devoted his unfinished life's work to an analysis of the utopian potential of machine-made metal and glass shopping malls.

There are two critiques happening at once here: one of contemporary 'starchitecture'; and the other of the modernism of the 1920s, which, in work by the likes of Erich Mendelsohn, began to float free of the gothic and classical heritage. In Mendelsohn's work, at least in the Einstein Tower, the eye-catching form is realised via structural dishonesty. By contrast, 'expressionist construction is construction rooted in craft' – that is, in skilled work, as opposed to the Taylorist machine construction that modernists aspired to, or frequently tried to simulate. In the process, the architects of the Neues Bauen, who often considered themselves socialists, became 'subsumed by the principles of economics'. Moreover, 'the Expressionists' – the brick expressionists – 'were not opposed to the classical language of architecture'. Specifically, they drew on a North German tradition of brick gothic, much as had the German affiliates of the Arts and Crafts movement. A brick expressionist building 'is not designed and knocked together, but rather gains its morphological form from its own inherent order, emerges from the earth, sets itself upright and vanishes towards the sky'.

The *Fragments of Metropolis* books are a collaboration between the photographer Niels Lehmann and a writer-researcher, Christoph Rauhut – who keeps text or explanation to a minimum, as if it would compromise the objectivity and austerity of the images. In his introduction to *Fragments of Metropolis – Berlin*, Rauhut puts the images in the context of the formation of Greater Berlin in 1920, an agglomeration that immediately made the German capital the largest city in Europe outside London; but the book's scope goes some way beyond the city limits established then, encompassing huge swathes of Brandenburg and north-eastern Germany, so this is not metropolis so much as *Metropolis*. Rauhut also makes some attempt to define what expressionism is and what makes it different to the mainstream modern movement, and here the vagueness is a real indictment of how architectural history is currently taught. Expressionism apparently emerged from 'the hope that a new architecture and urbanism could contribute to a better society', where 'people wanted to get away from the political and social formalisms of the nineteenth century, away from the stench of its tenement housing'. Aside from the fact that this was what motivated every strain in early twentieth-century German architecture, from the Neues Bauen in Berlin, Frankfurt and Stuttgart to the various far-right-affiliated Völkisch styles that were especially popular in Bavaria, it also writes out expressionism's specific emergence from a movement in painting, one with profound political ambiguity. Some strains were affiliated with the November Revolution of 1918 – to the point where many expressionists formed themselves into a Novembergruppe – and others, particularly those around the German-Danish painter Emil Nolde, openly fascist. Many in the Novembergruppe shifted in the early 1920s from expressionism to constructivism and the Neues Bauen, a process that also took place at the Bauhaus, as the mystical racist Johannes Itten became replaced as the school's guiding force by the Hungarian-Jewish socialist and technophile László Moholy-Nagy.

Expressionist architecture emerged, according to the architectural history of the 1970s and 1980s – that is, before the current superstition that architecture and politics are wholly separate took hold – from affiliated groups of enthusiasts for the German Revolution and for socialism, particularly in the collaborative work of the Arbeitsrat für Kunst (Workers Council for Art) and the Glass Chain, a letter exchange involving many architects who would later practise in the Neues Bauen, such as Bruno Taut and the Bauhaus director Walter Gropius. The architectural drawings that came out of this were fantastical and barely buildable, crystalline, organic, monumental and seemingly in motion; in the Weimar era, only Mendelsohn's Einstein Tower, Mossehaus printworks in Berlin and Hat Factory in Luckenwalde, or Gropius's Monument to

Paper Architecture in Concrete – Mossehaus, Berlin

the March Dead (i.e. to the workers killed in the successful resistance against the far-right Kapp Putsch of 1920) came even close to emulating these dreams. In her introduction to *Fragments of Metropolis – East*, the historian Beate Störtkuhl quotes the Weimar-era critic Adolf Behne, who argues that for 'the expressionist architect', 'everything must start from scratch; he creates it all from within. Each form must necessarily be something unique, because the specific conditions of each task will never be the same twice.' This describes the paper architecture of the era well, but not the contents of these books.

The actual expressionist architecture that did emerge and that came to dominate North German and Dutch cities in the 1920s came from a different route altogether – from the late Arts and Crafts of the Deutscher Werkbund, particularly the monumental brickwork of Joseph Maria Olbrich's Wedding Tower at the artists' colony in Darmstadt, and from the Amsterdam School founded by H. P. Berlage, where architects in love both with Frank Lloyd Wright and with post-impressionist painting created sinuous social housing blocks using the precise, banded brickwork that had long been part of Dutch tradition. After the First World War, a parallel to this emerged in Hamburg's Kontorhausviertel, a new dockside office district whose mammoth blocks were planned by Fritz Schumacher and mostly designed by Fritz Höger, in a style that then spread from the north to Berlin and the Ruhr. It is fair to call this expressionist, not because of its connection with the shimmering dream-projects of the Workers Council for Art – which had been left permanently shelved, with the failure of the German revolution – but because it exhibits the angst and force, and crucially the regionalism of expressionist painting. This sort of apocalyptic, tortured expressionism was not an objective style that would lend itself naturally to architecture, such as constructivism or purism, but an emotional, subjective one, and it is this spirit that lies behind the gutwrenching roar of Fritz Höger's buildings. The other aspect to it, as with the expressionist painters' love for Albrecht Dürer and Lucas Cranach the Elder, was a deep engagement with German tradition.

In the context of the 1920s, this architecture was a 'middle path' between the two most discussed styles of the Weimar Republic. On the one hand, the clean, mechanistic lines, inorganic colours and new technologies of the Neues Bauen became the aesthetic for department stores and cinemas, largely through the work of Erich Mendelsohn and his many imitators, and for the housing programmes of local authorities, trade unions and building societies, above all in Berlin and Frankfurt. On the other was the Völkisch or Heimatschutzstil (homeland protection style), which like the Neues Bauen emerged out of the Werkbund, but reacted to revolution and metropolitan change through the creation of a nostalgic, folksy, rural style. The polemics between these were ferocious, particularly when the Nazi paper *Völkischer Beobachter* launched a concerted campaign against the Neues Bauen, whose flat roofs were considered a non-German aberration, a sign of these frequently Jewish architects' lack of roots in the German soil (its loam and clay, as Kollhoff would put it). This was reflected, notoriously, in the way the Bauhaus was chased around the country, as it was closed by far-right municipalities in successively Weimar, Dessau and Berlin.

The north German brick style was not cute or quaint, unlike the Völkisch style, and it was not putatively machine-made or abstract, unlike the Neues Bauen. Like the gothic it modelled itself on, it favoured the massive and the imposing. The architect best represented in *Fragments of Metropolis – Berlin* is Hans Heinrich Müller, who was the house designer of BEWAG, Berlin's municipal electric company. In works such as the enormous Wilhelmsruher Stepdown transformer station in Pankow, or the central Substation Buchhändlerhof (which served for a while in the 1990s as the nightclub E-Werk), you

Architecture of (Electric) Power

can see how his patterned and fluted brickwork, round arches and a use of steel framing that nostalgically recalls seventeenth-century wooden beams offers an experience, as Kollhoff suggests, of both historical continuity and massive modernity. These motifs are a metaphorical response to their function in Berlin's electricity network, suggesting power through what is in reality superfluous decoration; here, one could easily compare Müller's work to that of another middle-path architect of the inter-war years, Giles Gilbert Scott, particularly in his power stations at Battersea and Bankside. Another architect well represented is Richard Brademann, whose job at the Berliner Reichsbahn (now the S-Bahn) produced stations such as Eichkamp and Wannsee, and various substations – these are much smaller-scale examples of the same style, showing that it could be applied well beyond glowering Wagnerian masses.

As with Gilbert Scott, the buildings that brick expressionists were hired for were often either industrial or ecclesiastical. The most thrilling examples to be documented in the book fall within a typology to which this architecture was ideally suited – that is, Berlin's first skyscrapers, all of them well out of the city centre. The main tower of the Siemens factory, designed by Hans Hertlein, the Ullsteinhaus in Tempelhof, for a publisher, and the Borsigturm in Reinickendorf (both by the architect Eugen Schmohl), and the especially gruff main tower of Hans Heinrich Müller's Kraftwerk Klingenberg, a power station in the city's far east, are all administrative blocks at the head of enormous factory complexes. They borrow from the skyscrapers of the Chicago School grids of upward-surging brick pilasters, and in the case of Schmohl's two buildings, the application of spiky neo-gothic adornment to the structure. The churches, meanwhile, are closer to Müller's power stations, with often near-windowless facades of clinker brick, stacked into stubby, blunt forms or assembled into aggressive towers, usually leading to subtly lit interiors (none of which are photographed here). Some of the architects behind this,

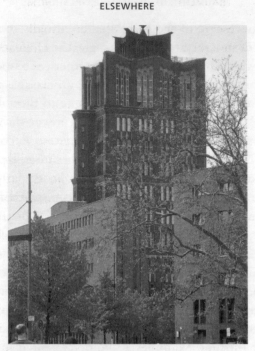

Berlin's First Skyscraper

such as Martin Kremmer and Fritz Schupp, specialised in industrial architecture; these two would go on to design the factory and power station of the Kraft durch Freude Wagen in Wolfsburg, in 1938. The best known of the many churches in this book is Fritz Höger's Church on Hohenzollernplatz, which was nicknamed the Kraftwerk Gottes – God's Power Station.

Looking at page after page of these photographs, with their bare dates and addresses, certain characteristics of this architecture start to become apparent. It is often a prestige architecture, with richly modelled surfaces and ornament. It almost never breaks with nineteenth-century urban continuity, unlike the arrangements of buildings in green space favoured by the Neues Bauen. Its organic rhetoric is reflected in the materials, with all that baked brick – you can often imagine how the buildings smell from looking at them. You'll also notice what is missing – housing, most of all. In the Weimar Republic, this was a preserve of the Neues Bauen, usually working for the Social Democratic trade unions, and the Heimatschutzstil, usually in the service of white-collar employee associations – their estates sometimes directly facing each other, as spatial polemic. There are two housing schemes in this book, one for Berlin tram workers, in an especially Fritz Lang style, and a basically Heimatschutzstil block with some mildly expressionist embellishments, at Ceciliengärten. Similarly, the cinemas and department stores of the era are almost wholly absent. This is no picture of the metropolis Weimar Berlin actually was or was bringing into being – but it is a picture of the usable past that its contemporary revivalists want to bring into being. For all Kollhoff's talk of eternal architecture, it evokes a series of cinematic clichés about 1920s Germany, the cityscape of *Metropolis* concocted using a collage of suburban factories. Like the reconstructed 1920s traffic light in Potsdamer Platz and the neo-expressionist Kollhoff Tower above it, it is a historical burlesque, the city Berlin would like to have been and never was.

The expunging both of commercial architecture and of the social planning of the left from the cityscape is not nearly so apolitical as the likes of Kollhoff and Rauhut would have us believe. They studiously avoid biography in the texts of the *Fragments* books, and there's a reason for that. Richard Brademann, for instance, joined the NSDAP in 1931, and delivered to Hitler a list of Jewish architects who were working on the Reichsbahn. Fritz Höger, who had been contributing to *Völkischer Beobachter* since 1927, joined the Nazis in 1932, and at the start of 1933 sacked, for explicitly racist reasons, his Jewish partner Ossip Klarwein, who had been the job architect on the Church on Hohenzollernplatz. Unable to work in Germany, Klarwein emigrated to Palestine the year after, although Höger wrote him a good reference. Neither Brademann nor Höger would manage to convince Hitler – a literal-minded neoclassicist – that brick expressionism was the appropriate style for the Third Reich, but both worked uninterrupted through it and supported it until the end.

The *Fragments* books are crowdfunded, and the success of the first volume led to a second, which curiously covered neither of the cities that are most associated with expressionist architecture, Amsterdam and Hamburg. Call it eternal if you insist, but the advantage of all this relentless glazed clinker brick is that it wears and weathers, unlike the white and coloured render of the Neues Bauen or the plaster ornament of the Wilhelmine era, both of which need constant care. It looks impressive even if you do nothing to clean it, and this comes across particularly well in *Fragments of Metropolis – Rhein and Ruhr*; whereas the Berlin industrial buildings have often been turned into business centres and suchlike, many of the expressionist monuments in the industrial sprawl of West Germany are now derelict. The Rhine–Ruhr region is here presented as another shadow metropolis, with another photomontage cover of its brick expressionist edifices, which, scattered in reality across an area with a population equivalent to Scotland's, again bear little resemblance to any actual metropolis. The region covered stretches way beyond the expected centres of the Ruhrgebiet (Dortmund–Essen–Bochum–Duisburg) and the two large cities adjacent to it, Cologne and Düsseldorf. Here, the research is formidable, with dozens of small towns showcased for their pugnacious brick monuments – although many are just neo-gothic buildings with a rather tenuous connection to expressionism. Again, the politics are quickly glossed over, although they were especially dramatic, from communist insurrections by the Red Army of the Ruhr to the occupations of the region by France and Belgium.

The foreword is by Paul Kahlfeldt, a neoclassical architect who, in a firm with his wife Petra Kahlfeldt, works alternately on extremely conservative private villas and on the restoration of several expressionist buildings in Berlin, including some of the BEWAG edifices. As with Kollhoff, the tone is polemical: 'Architecture as Paragon and Admonition' is the instructive title. 'Looking at some of the buildings presented here, the viewer cannot help being overcome by a certain sentimentality', caused by the buildings' 'consistent desire towards form', a vague expression which he then glosses with the explanation that 'the building masses are subdivided, the volumes structured' in what is grandly called a 'collective rebellion against the looming trivialisation of the metier'. By this, like Kollhoff, he means modernism and its attendant implication in mass housing and corporate homogeneity; today, he claims, this has devolved into a lamentable situation where 'bad behaviour in architecture is at best simply tolerated but sometimes even promoted and regarded as being contemporary'. Whither 'expression' in an architecture that is now openly admitted to be about good manners and context?

Christoph Rauhut's introduction stresses the importance of the coal and steel industries, of multicentric development rather than a coherently planned single city, and the complicated railway and river infrastructure that flows through the area – but again, he wants particularly to stress that 'what links all this architecture is the proud desire for progress through continuity'. Most of the buildings here are by local architects, and they're an interesting group: Heinrich Schmiedeknecht, an industrial architect in Bochum; Ludwig Freitag, the city architect of Oberhausen; Alfred Fischer, who practised widely in Essen and Gelsenkirchen; Kurt Haake, who was similarly prolific in Cologne and Düsseldorf; the Cologne-based church architect Dominikus Böhm; and the most notorious of the group, Wilhelm Kreis.

Again, they all worked in the middle style between Heimat and modernity, and again, all of them worked throughout the Third Reich, though the book coyly omits their work in the Nazi era. Some got in minor trouble during the period: Fischer, for instance, was more closely identified than most with the

Neues Bauen, and hence was pushed into early retirement, though he continued to practise in Bavaria; Böhm joined the NSDAP late, during the war. Kreis, meanwhile, was an enthusiastic Nazi and a leading member of the Third Reich's cultural elite. Biographical details of the prominent Neues Bauen architects show that a majority emigrated during the Third Reich. It has long been controversial that Mies van der Rohe kept trying to work in Nazi Germany until 1938, before eventually giving up and moving to Chicago. This dilemma was not a factor for the brick expressionists, unless, as with Ossip Klarwein, they happened to be Jewish – they kept doing the same jobs right up to the end.

The similarity of the architecture shown in *Berlin* and *Rhein and Ruhr* is interesting, given the notion that this is a regional or contextual architecture; culturally, geographically and architecturally, Cologne and Berlin have always been very different places. The brick expressionists did much the same stuff in East and West. *Rhein and Ruhr* includes more early high-rise office blocks, though unlike in Berlin, these are city-centre buildings: Kreis's Wilhelm-Marx-Haus, with its peculiar mixture of metropolitan scale and Hansel and Gretel chequerboard detail, or Paul Bonatz's Stumm Group office block, with its stepped rhythm of Gothic pilasters, both in Düsseldorf; the rather more clunky Hansahochhaus in Cologne, designed by Jacob Koerfer; the purple clinker and asymmetrical tower of Fischer's Hans-Sachs-Haus in Gelesenkirchen; and the awesome, articulated scale of Freitag's Rathaus in Oberhausen.

The churches by Böhm, such as St Engelbert in Cologne and St Kamillus in Mönchengladbach, are much more serious than the neo-gothic norm, with an interest in space and plasticity that served him well after the war, when he was one of the few of this group not discredited in modernist opinion – though the fact we're almost never shown any interiors means we can only guess at his spatial imagination. This is part of the architectural philosophy of 'good manners' that Hans Kollhoff and

Wilhelm-Marx-Haus

Paul Kahlfeldt insist upon – the important point is whether the work slots into the pre-existing urban ensemble without violence or discordance, with the street as a form of scenery. This is, of course, exactly what the Neues Bauen had least interest in: their project, particularly in terms of interiors but also in the arrangements for housing schemes, was to define new kinds of space, created both by new technologies and the proposed abolition of landlordism. That can be seen in the way that Bruno Taut's Berlin housing schemes dispersed their polychrome cubic buildings amid preserved forest trees, or Mies van der Rohe's floating interior spaces created out of 'almost nothing' in his Barcelona Pavilion or the Tugendhat House in Brno.

The architecture in these books, though, is literally facile, and all the discussion of clay and loam from the earth thrown towards the sky doesn't change the fact that most of these buildings consist of brick cladding applied to concrete or steel

Bruno Taut's Faceless International Modernism

frames. In the introduction to *Fragments of Metropolis – Rhein and Ruhr*, Rauhut draws attention to one of the more interesting examples of this process. In the centre of Düsseldorf is a remarkably coherent ensemble of brick expressionist buildings – or rather, given their regularity and order, something more like brick classicism – by Wilhelm Kreis, which now serve as a concert hall and a set of museums. These were created for GeSoLei, a temporary exhibition on health and social welfare, in 1926; yet Kreis treated them as if they were going to stand forever, at enormous expense, with travertine halls replete with mosaics and stained glass (not in this book, of course). This is something for which modernist critics criticised him harshly, which was 'part of a polemic debate being held at the time', as Rauhut curtly notes. As a result, they are still there, and in the book's illustrations they look as though they could stand forever. Kreis's last major buildings, though, were never built – a series of 'castles for the dead' to be placed on the scenes of major victories of the Third Reich in the East – great burial mounds to have been erected in Warsaw, in Greece and on the Dnieper.

If making a compilation of artworks from 1920s Germany and attempting to shield them from politics and polemics is difficult enough, the third and (so far) last volume of *Fragments of Metropolis* is simply subtitled *East*, and covers what is now Poland, Czechia and Slovakia. Naturally, in compiling a volume on what had up to this point been a distinctly Germanic architecture, in places that had all been at one point or another part of the Prussian or Hapsburg empires, a certain tact was necessary. The book is organised into several distinct categories, following the several state formations of the period covered. There's ex-Hapsburg and then independent Czechoslovakia, and several categories of Poland – those parts that were in Prussia/Germany before 1918–21, those that were in Germany until 1945 and the Free City of Danzig. These distinctions matter, because each of these had a distinct school of architecture – someone moderately literate in architectural history could at a glance organise many of these buildings into specific political formations. This is, not to put too fine a point on it, architecture from an era of nationalist mobilisation, in which architecture participated just as much as any other artform.

In her introduction to *Fragments of Metropolis – East*, Gesine Schwan, an SPD politician, sometime presidential candidate and political scientist specialising in East–Central Europe, makes considerable effort to sidestep any implication that a German architecture outside of Germany's borders might have uncomfortable implications. In fact, she tells us, the situation is quite the opposite. 'In a time when a cry for "homeland" rings out against the diversity and multiculturalism that globalisation brings, a book such as this is a welcome appearance', because it 'demonstrates that homeland does not always necessarily lie in opposition to the diversity and openness of a world city'; it presents an 'attractive alternative to a closed society', and 'in a time of newly awakened narrow-minded nationalism', the book and the architecture it catalogues can 'help to strengthen a shared vision of a peaceful, open and beautiful Europe'. This is standard bureaucratic Eurospeak, and the architecture presented here is staggeringly ill-suited to the task being set up for it.

Schwan's preface is followed by a more historical introduction by Beate Störtkuhl, an art historian with specialist knowledge of Wrocław in Poland, German Breslau in the period of this book. She takes some care to differentiate the at least five or six different political and national formations during this period, and their influence, and does her best to make sense of a rather capricious and incoherent selection of buildings. These come mainly in three distinct categories. Around half of the book is made up of German brick expressionist architecture, whether the modernised gothic of the Yachting Club by Gustav Gauss or the almost brutalist Gas Plant by Adolf Thesmacher, both in Szczecin (Stettin), Pomerania, or Paul Oehlmann's Catholic School in Legnica (Leignitz), Lower Silesia, or the tall, pre–First World War brick water towers in the Poznań (Posen) region. Wrocław/Breslau, one of the major centres of both expressionism and the Neues Bauen in the 1910s and 1920s, boasts a rich collection of buildings whose quality easily surpasses the Rhine–Ruhr in the same period; in particular, pre-war its works, such as the concrete-vaulted Jahrhunderthalle by Max Berg and the Junkerstrasse office block by Hans Poelzig, are foundational for all twentieth-century architecture, of any style. To see this work so lavishly showcased is very welcome, given that it is much less visited and publicised than buildings of the same period in what is now Germany.

The other half of the book is mostly made up of the cubist architecture of the Czech and Slovak lands, both before and after their union as an independent state in 1918; there is also a handful of buildings constructed in independent Poland proper, with an Art Deco church in Białystok, and the fabulous Warsaw School of Economics by Jan Witkiewicz-Koszczyc. This suggests that there was an initial plan to collect

Junkerstrasse Department Store, by Hans Poelzig

the expressionist architecture of the parts of the Weimar
Republic that became post-war Poland (there's also a fair bit
of it in what was the Königsberg region and is now Russia's
Kaliningrad exclave, but it seems the travel budget didn't
stretch that far). The air of revanchism and irredentism that
this showcase of the 'lost territories' of Germany could elicit
then required a change of tack, to encompass a totally different school of architecture that had almost nothing to do
with expressionism at all. This is not quite as progressive as
the compilers of the book seem to think. To rename the long-
established Czechoslovak cubist movement as expressionist
and yoke it to diverse unconnected phenomena is an erasure
of local specificity, rather than some marvellous union of the
local and the metropolitan. Similarly, of the buildings in Upper
Silesia, which was divided between Germany and Poland in
the aftermath of the Second World War by plebiscites and
Polish nationalist uprisings, all those included are from the
German side, with churches by Dominikus Böhm and several

clinker-clad offices and factories. That's because the Polish side of the divide, particularly its largest city, Katowice, opted for a version of the Neues Bauen, a confident and purely modernist architecture. Nothing was built there in the brick expressionist style there during the 1920s and 1930s, most likely because that architecture was strongly associated with Germany and Germanness, just as architects such as Fritz Höger and Wilhelm Kreis always said it was.

The cubist architects were liberals and rationalists, rather than angst-driven expressionist radicals, so the showcase of cubist architecture is presumably here because, like expressionism, it emerged out of a movement in painting. Some proponents took this relationship rather literally: conventional facades of houses and apartments were moulded with convex and concave rendered surfaces, as if a three-dimensional version of a cubist painting – though as Czech modernists pointed out in the 1920s, the flowing and intersecting spaces of modern architecture were actually a much closer analogue to the constantly moving, shifting sightlines implied by cubist painting. But this is what makes cubist architecture vaguely akin to the brick expressionist architecture showcased in the other two volumes. It's conventionally planned street architecture, especially in works like the House of the Black Madonna by Josef Gočár, now an integral part of Prague's tourist ensemble, whose puzzling facade and lush interiors practically proclaim, 'visit the city of Kafka!' The cubist works are most frequently villa architecture, comfortable and bourgeois nineteenth-century fare, only with a new fashionable kind of facade draped across the parlour rooms. There is also an evident dialogue with historical precedents, here the baroque more than the Gothic – most clearly in the cubist aedicule for the statue of St John Nepomuk in central Prague. A wave of rondocubism in the first few years after the war, as at the Adria Palace by Pavel Janák and Josef Zasche, or the Legio Bank by Josef Gočár and Otto Gutfreund (both in Prague), was a sort

A Czech Cubist Apartment Block

of combination of cubism and the rococo, with incredibly busy facades full of alternately curved and cuboid abstract decoration, a new invented language which aimed briefly to become a national style for the new country. It was quickly rejected, as Prague, Brno and Bratislava became showcases for modernism.

Again, though, Rauhut and Lehmann have distinguished themselves by the scope, if not the depth, of their research. Little-known works such as the Třeština Water Power Station by Josef Štěpanék show how easily cubism, like brick expressionism, could be applied to decorating industrial structures (and also, how its rendered and painted facades age much less well than those in brick). The book also includes little-known ceremonial buildings such as the Pardubice Crematorium by Pavel Janák, or the New Synagogue at Žilina, a highly uncharacteristic building by the master of the Deutscher Werkbund, Peter Behrens. This is the only synagogue in three volumes of books that are full of (mostly Catholic) churches. The curious politics of this can also be seen in the absence of one of the most dramatic buildings in Wrocław, Erich Mendelsohn's Petersdorff Department Store. Charging round a street corner, the building incarnates the ethos of motion and drama that animated the Glass Chain or the Workers Council for Art. But its materials – glass and steel; no brick, no stone – evidently disqualify it from the book. This is an absence that comes not from the trends of the time, but the prejudices of the present.

As usable pasts go, expressionism is ambiguous. Of course, modernist architects, as revisionist accounts on the Bauhaus anniversary have been keen to point out, were not quite as innocent of association with Nazism as was believed immediately after 1945. Forms derived from the Neues Bauen were still used for industrial architecture and in the design of wartime bunkers, and Bauhaus-trained architects such as Hans Dustmann and the hugely influential Ernst Neufert, author of the still-canonical *Architects' Data*, worked in Albert Speer's office – though always at the level of planning and engineering rather than high architecture. After the war, Nazis such as the Organisation Todt's architect Friedrich Tamms remained influential in German architecture and adapted to modernism in the 1960s when it became expedient to do so. The fact remains that Hitler's ceremonial buildings were stripped classical rather than brick expressionist or modernist, though some of the various NS-Ordensburgen (Castles of the National Socialist Order), the most fantastical of the Third Reich's buildings, would have fit well in *Fragments of Metropolis*. None of this changes the fact that the attempt to reimagine a twentieth-century architecture in which modernists lost the battle lends itself to the political right.

The furious inventing of tradition going on in these books may string together various unconnected phenomena for the simple reason that they're not modernism and hence an alternative to the terrible fall from grace that movement allegedly represented in architecture and planning – but the reticence about the actual politics of this architecture covers a guilty conscience. In her introduction to *Fragments of Metropolis – East*, Störtkuhl notes as an aside that 'looking back today, the architectural infighting of the 1920s is only an interesting historical phenomenon', of no relevance to the assessment of these buildings in the present day. I find this insistence deeply puzzling. When a successful, much-lauded architect literally inscribes an antisemitic poem in stone on a square dedicated to Walter Benjamin, then outlines an architectural philosophy based on an architecture rooted in the earth, equally opposed to Marxism and commercialism – and finds his historical justification for it in an architecture developed by committed Nazis – then we're dealing with a duck, that looks like a duck, quacking like a duck.

My Kind of Town: Warszawa

If I consider where I've thought, occasionally aloud, 'I love this city!' (Glasgow, Sheffield, Liverpool, Newcastle upon Tyne, Halifax, Bradford, Brussels, Hamburg, Moscow, Naples), there are usually certain common things getting me excited. Dramatic topography, unashamed modernity, space and scope, a history of struggle that avoids the stultifying museumification that afflicts conventionally attractive cities, an anti-classical urban montage of things that shouldn't really fit being thrown and meshed together. All these are part of what makes a city fascinating (to me).

The Polish capital fits all of the above conditions, except for the topography – its site, at least, is almost unremittingly flat. Another aspect that almost guarantees that a city will be interesting and rewarding (for me) is the disdain of received opinion. Cab drivers still assume that any foreigner in Warsaw is only en route to Krakow. The capital is pejoratively regarded as grim, grey and monotonous. This is largely because, after the suppression of the Warsaw Uprising in 1944, the Wehrmacht torched and evacuated what was left, with the destruction estimated at 85 per cent. Warsaw appears as a city entirely of the second half of the twentieth century.

There are few environments that embraced all the different approaches of twentieth-century architecture and planning so comprehensively and promiscuously as Warsaw, with each successive style/ideology rejecting the last, while occupying the same space. When I first went to Warsaw, I was taken round Żoliborz, a suburb built after the end of tsarist occupation in 1918. You emerge from Plac Wilsona metro station – a bizarre 2005 retrofuturist confection – and find yourself in the WSM Kolonie, a 1920s social housing estate to rank with the work of Bruno Taut and Ernst May; its architects, Barbara and Stanisław Brukalski, are not nearly so heralded. Turn out of these estates, built by a workers' co-operative, and you might

Co-operative Warszawa

find yourself in an area of conservative, neoclassical houses for officers, built for those who administered the colonels' dictatorship that ruled inter-war Poland; or in a post-war project, with neat CIAM-approved towers between tall trees; or in the mutant beaux-arts of a socialist realist estate.

Żoliborz is hardly all that remains of the pre-war city. The Old Town was famously reconstructed under Stalinism according to the paintings of Bernardo Bellotto; and in Praga, on the right bank of the Vistula, a nineteenth-century city still exists. Each of these says more about the twentieth century than any 'authentic' past: the Old Town is a dreamlike simulacrum, a surrealist animation given life, its mocked-up facades covering straightforward workers' housing. In the middle of it, a socialist realist escalator by the designers of the Moscow Metro takes the pedestrian to a motorway. Praga, meanwhile, is both a living exhibit of why modernism was necessary, with its overcrowded, jerry-built tenements unleavened by their peeling beaux-arts stucco decoration, and a showcase of the differing responses to it. Praga II, built in the fifties, veers between the modernist terraces by Szymon and Helena Syrkus and the proto-postmodernist axial monoliths of Plac Leńskiego (now Plac Józefa Hallera). Neither place is static, neither really feels stuck in the past.

Warsaw's immense tower-block periphery, its greyness now largely covered by layers of coloured insulation, is no less complex. Expressionist churches of the seventies make clear the extent of Catholic hegemony under Polish 'socialism'; shiny new towers are crammed into the interstices between blocks, with manor houses and villages subsisting just behind them. The city is linked – not as completely as it could be – by a typically spacious and reliable communist-era metro (finished in the mid-nineties) and an overground network constructed between the fifties and the seventies, whose concrete-shell stations by Arseniusz Romanowicz and Piotr Szymaniak are finally being appreciated and restored. The central public buildings, whether Stalino-Manhattanist (Lev Rudnev's Palace of Culture and Science) or surrealist-modernist (Stanisław Fijałkowski's National Library) are labyrinthine, practically cities in themselves.

Like many twentieth-century cities, Warsaw is visibly a little ashamed of itself, and a conformist, homogenising instinct is sadly dominant in its new architecture and its relentlessly neoliberal planning – its last really fine building, Marek Budzyński's University Library, a James Stirling–style exercise in contrast and montage, is over a decade old. Warsaw's incredible legacy of social housing and social planning is still mostly anathema. When the last estate is privatised and the last *bar mleczny* is closed, then Europe will have lost something very special.

— September 2012

4

Spaces

These four articles, three for the *London Review of Books* and one for the (briefly Arts Council–funded) Marxist arts journal *Mute*, are about the connections between ideology, buildings and space, experienced in the present day rather than retrospectively. They document and comment on what now seem clearly to have been major architectural and urbanist trends of the last fifteen years. These include the rise, and then the sharp decline, of the over-the-top, digitally engineered, ultra-futuristic architecture that accompanied both post-industrial 'regeneration' in the global north (particularly Britain in the 2000s) and the rise of petroleum monarchies in the gulf. Running parallel to it was an enormous rise of interest in post-war architecture, particularly its formerly most maligned strand, brutalism, very much in reaction to the bling and intangibility of digital regeneration architecture; and throughout the period, a middle-class return to the cities was taking place, with 'gentrification' replacing 'white flight' to the suburbs as the main means of property speculation. Also during this time, a lot of basic public amenities, from toilets to suburban libraries to youth clubs, were being cut back and erased, a loss that progressed from a gradual attrition to a flash fire after the financial crisis of 2008.

The section begins with a piece on the late Zaha Hadid, about whom, before her death in 2016, I wrote more frequently than any other living architect, partly because she seemed to be the one most explicitly trying to continue a version of the modernist project. The first of these was a 2007 article in *Socialist Worker*, of all places – the SWP's weekly paper was, let it be known, the first place to publish most of the mid-2000s bloggers, though with the exception of Richard 'Lenin's Tomb' Seymour, none of us were members or even fellow travellers. Rather, we owe our exposure to the commissioning talents of one of its former editors, Anindya Bhattacharrya (he later left the SWP during the 'Comrade Delta' affair, as did everyone with any integrity). The reason for my fixation with Hadid was the gulf between my unabashed enthusiasm for her designs – especially, but not exclusively, those on paper – and the depression I tended to feel about her built work as an expression of neoliberal urban policies. It led to a brief and interesting email exchange with her architectural partner and theoretician (and, allegedly, ex-SWP member) Patrik Schumacher, who instructed me to 'debate like a comrade, not like a prick'. Schumacher has recently attracted attention for arguing in favour of the abolishment of social housing and of building on Hyde Park, and for justifying the dominance of 'ultra-high net-worth individuals', so I stand by my style of debate.

The essay on brutalism also starts with the architectural effects of the October Revolution, and was also sparked by a combination of enthusiasm and irritation – and in this case, a feeling of having being culpable for at least a portion of the rash of books where intense young men write their *Bildungsroman* about climbing over crumbling concrete structures in the 1980s or 1990s.

A High-Performance Contemporary Life Process

Zaha Hadid Architects and the Neoliberal Avant-Garde

THE NEW AVANT-GARDE ACKNOWLEDGES ITS PRECURSORS
This summer, there was an exhibition at the Galerie Gmurzynska in Zurich entitled 'Zaha Hadid and Suprematism'. It was a 'dialogue' between the Anglo-Iraqi architect, winner of the 2010 Stirling Prize – and her apparent forbears, the architects and artists of the 1920s Soviet avant-garde. Her flowing, bristling forms whipped through rooms containing works by Kasimir Malevich, Alexander Rodchenko, Nikolai Suetin, El Lissitzky. Accompanying the exhibition was 'A Glimpse Back into the Future', a text by Hadid's right-hand man, the theorist and architect Patrik Schumacher. While some would disassociate constructivism and communism, or argue that Bolshevik 'totalitarianism' was the enemy of art, Schumacher had no such qualms. His text is impressively unambiguous in placing the political revolution as the very foundation of artistic innovation.

> Ninety years ago the October Revolution ignited the most exuberant surge of creative energy that has ever erupted on planet earth. While some of the artistic seeds were present beforehand, they blossomed and proliferated thousand-fold in the first ten years of the revolution. This amazing firework of creative exuberance took off under the most severe material circumstances – fuelled by the idealistic enthusiasm for the project of a new society.

We're very far from opulent Swiss galleries, although Schumacher does not make the unflattering comparison.

In fact, he argues, the next century of art and architecture was so indebted to this convulsive decade that literally nothing was developed later that wasn't already anticipated by the Soviet avant-garde. 'The pace, quantity and quality of the creative work in art, science and design was truly astounding, anticipating in one intense flash what then took another fifty years to unfold elsewhere in the world.' He gives particular attention to the way in which abstraction, carried to an extreme in the completely non-referential 'Non-Objective World' of Kasimir Malevich and the suprematist painters and architects that followed him, created a space where earthly rules did not apply.

> Malevich stands here for the enormously momentous discovery of abstraction as a heuristic principle that can propel creative work to hitherto unheard of levels of invention. Mimesis was finally abandoned and unfettered creativity could pour out across the infinitely receptive blank canvas. Space, or even better the world itself, soon became the site of pure, unprejudiced invention.

Schumacher does, however, take the Soviet painter a little to task.

> Malevich has been a pioneer of abstraction and a pioneer in directly linking abstract art with architecture via his seminal 'tectonics'. It is interesting however, to observe that these tectonic sculptures, which were conceived as a kind of proto-architecture, were geometrically far more constrained than his compositions on canvas. The tectonics are dynamic equilibrium compositions that strictly adhere to the principle of orthogonality and they are composed by cubic volumes with adjoining surfaces, thus excluding interpenetration. These 'cubist' restrictions characterized most of the modern architectural work in Russia and elsewhere.

There is a successor here, who will not be bound to the right-angle in the same manner: 'It is a well-established fact that the work of Zaha Hadid took its first inspiration from the early Russian avant-garde, in particular she directly engaged with the work of Kasimir Malevich'; that is, in her first major project, the 1980s work *Malevich's Tektonik*, a proposal for a suprematist replacement for London's Hungerford Bridge. So Hadid will go where the Russian avant-garde could not – into a completely non-objective world, freed from the last vestiges of spatial reality which Malevich still insisted upon. Yet in a very different context. 'These projects', writes Schumacher, 'in all their experimental radicality – had a real social meaning and political substance. But their originality and artistic ingenuity transcends the context of the grand Russian social experiment.' So it would be worthwhile to investigate the connection between Malevich's successor and the social and political world she inhabits.

Patrik Schumacher Declares Style War

Before we do, it's worth dwelling a little while longer on Schumacher himself. Hadid herself is no theorist, nor has she ever pretended to be. In the generation of deconstructivists which emerged out of architecture schools in the 1980s – Peter Eisenman, Bernard Tschumi, Steven Holl, Wolf Prix, Daniel Libeskind – she was always conspicuous in her refusal to justify her forms by quoting Derrida or Benjamin, although she has always cited the (similarly Marxian) Soviet avant-garde. So it's curious that Schumacher, her architectural partner for the last sixteen years, has increasingly become her abstract ventriloquist, writing intensely theoretical texts to go alongside every museum and opera house.

Schumacher is a little more ambitious than the average Deleuze-citing architect, however. Not for him the postmodernist fear of the grand gesture, categorisation and periodisation, the Hegelian historical sweep. Most of all, there is no hint of discomfort on the question of whether an avant-garde can still exist. In 2008 he declared quite unambiguously that there *was* a new avant-garde, and Zaha Hadid Architects, and a handful of others, were it. In a series of articles and one book over the last two years, he has attempted to prove the point.

He called the new style 'parametricism', a term derived from the computer scripting software that most large architectural firms use in designing buildings. Architects, especially in the UK, are an inconsistent bunch when it comes to theorising what they do. Most of them opt for one of a series of competing pragmatisms – the utilitarianism of high-tech, the dour 'social' concerns of 'vernacular' or most commonly a less conscious disdain for the idea of thinking too much about what they're doing. A minority in the more elite architecture schools immerse themselves in continental theory: Heidegger if you like natural materials and 'nature'; Deleuze if you like aggressive modernity. Schumacher is nearer to the latter trend, but his unabashed confidence in his own assertions marks him out.

In the 2008 paper 'Parametricism as Style – a Parametric Manifesto', Schumacher defines this new entity in terms fairly familiar from Deleuze and Guattari's *Capitalism and Schizophrenia*. On his list of 'don't's, or his 'negative heuristics', are a mish-mash of ideas from twentieth-century modernism and late twentieth-century traditionalism: 'avoid familiar typologies, avoid platonic/hermetic objects, avoid clear-cut zones/territories, avoid repetition, avoid straight lines, avoid right angles, avoid corners ... and most importantly: do not add or subtract without elaborate interarticulations'. Partly this is a list of bad things the earlier 'cubic' avant-garde does – all the unfriendly linearity and formal rigour that makes it boring to the architecture student. As for the 'positive heuristics', we're stuck in the *Thousand Plateaus*: we must 'interarticulate, hyberdize [sic], morph, deterritorialize, deform, iterate, use splines, nurbs, generative components, script rather than model'. There's yet more Deleuzery when Schumacher continues his definitions. We're immersed in multiplicities, and

> the assumption is that the urban massing describes a swarm-formation of many buildings. These buildings form a continuously changing field, whereby lawful continuities cohere

this manifold of buildings. Parametric urbanism implies that the systematic modulation of the buildings' morphologies produces powerful urban effects and facilitates field orientation. Parametric Urbanism might involve parametric accentuation, parametric figuration, and parametric responsives [sic].

The extreme syntactical inelegance is evidently part of the point, the tumbling onrush of pseudoscientific terms and the staccato sentence structure making the prose sound like an operative thing rather than mere description.

Moreover, Schumacher stresses how different this is from the modernisms that went before him and Hadid:

> Modernism was founded on the concept of space. Parametricism differentiates fields. *Fields* are full, as if filled with a fluid medium. We might think of liquids in motion, structured by radiating waves, laminal [sic] flows, and spiraling eddies. Swarms have also served as paradigmatic analogues for the field-concept. We would like to think of swarms of buildings that drift across the landscape. Or we might think of large continuous interiors like open office landscapes or big exhibition halls of the kind used for trade fairs. Such interiors are visually infinitely deep and contain various swarms of furniture coalescing with the dynamic swarms of human bodies. There are no platonic, discrete figures with sharp outlines.

It's an organic flow, but not a friendly one – rather an unstoppable, advancing force, dissolving anything solid in its path – yet the prosaic examples Schumacher gives (trade fairs!) add a note of bathos, which only intensifies the closer you get to the parametric edifice.

Initial responses in the architectural press have largely stayed at the level of ridicule, but Schumacher set out to challenge this with an extraordinary article in the *Architects' Journal*, easily the most aggressive, theoretical and indigestible piece of prose ever published in this trade magazine. 'Let the Style

Wars Begin' condensed and intensified his various more rarefied rhetorical interventions for public consumption, though with no concession given to the readership. It begins with a valedictory tone:

> in my Parametricist Manifesto of 2008, I first communicated that a new, profound style has been maturing within the avant-garde segment of architecture during the last 10 years. The term 'parametricism' has since been gathering momentum within architectural discourse and its critical questioning has strengthened it. So far, knowledge of the new style has remained largely confined within architecture

– but, he confidently asserts –

> I suspect news will spread quickly once it is picked up by the mass media. Outside architectural circles, 'style' is virtually the only category through which architecture is observed and recognised. A named style needs to be put forward in order to stake its claim to act in the name of architecture.

The insistence on *style* is interesting. The modernists of the 1920s attempted wherever possible to avoid the term, preferring the neutral and technocratic Neues Bauen or constructivism; when these were dubbed the international style by critic Henry-Russell Hitchcock and fascist activist Philip Johnson, it was as a deliberate attempt to celebrate the finer things, to hold up villas and 'an architecture style' against the 'fanatical functionalists' who wanted to build for 'some proletarian superman of the future'. The high-tech generation who are essentially today's architectural elders, Norman Foster, Richard Rogers, et al., always disdained the notion of style, claiming ever less convincingly to be above such fripperies, their work emerging from solely technological imperatives. Schumacher claims he will use style as a means of communicating with the public – which is lucky, as he was never likely to do so with his prose.

The term apparently has been unveiled *now* because years of laboratory work have made it possible:

> from the inside, within architecture, the identification of parametricism demarcates and further galvanises a maturing avant-garde movement, and thus might serve to accelerate its progress and potential hegemony as a collective research and development effort. As a piece of retrospective description and interpretation, the announcement of parametricism seems justified after ten years of consistent, cumulative design research. Prospectively, the announcement of the style should further consolidate the attained achievements and prepare the transition from avant-garde to mainstream hegemony. Parametricism finally offers a credible, sustainable answer to the drawn-out crisis of modernism that resulted in twenty-five years of stylistic searching.

The aim of achieving *hegemony* is again something that the technocrats, liberals and neoclassicists would never admit to. Schumacher clearly wants to destroy his woolly-minded opponents, and in that there's no doubt he's an avant-gardist.

It should be noted Schumacher isn't just suggesting that parametricism is the successor to the mini-movements of postmodernism or deconstructivism, but rather it's something more fundamental – 'the great new style after modernism', the final and long-awaited creation of something that owes nothing to the Soviet avant-garde. His contempt for all that came between is total.

> Post-modernism and deconstructivism were mere transitional episodes, similar to art nouveau and expressionism as transitions from historicism to modernism. The distinction of epochal styles from transitional styles is important. In a period of transition there might emerge a rapid succession of styles, or even a plurality of simultaneous, competing styles. The crisis and demise of modernism lead [*sic*] to a deep and protracted

transitional period, but there is no reason to believe that this pluralism cannot be overcome by the hegemony of a new unified style. The potential for such a unification is indeed what we are witnessing.

He goes on to frame this in *almost* political terms as a repudiation of Francis Fukuyama and his ilk, to insist that now something new *can* be created.

Modernism's crisis and its architectural aftermath has led [*sic*] many critics to believe we can no longer be expected to forge a unified style. Did the profound developmental role of styles in the history of architecture, as evidenced in the gothic-renaissance baroque-historicism-modernism sequence, come to an end? Did history come to an end? Or did it fragment into criss-crossing and contradictory trajectories? Are we to celebrate this fragmentation of efforts under the slogan of pluralism?

No, is his answer, and he has contempt for the idea that

any style today can only be one among many other simultaneously operating styles, thus adding one more voice to the prevailing cacophony of voices. The idea of a pluralism of styles is just one symptom of the more general trivialisation and denigration of the concept of style. I repudiate the complacent acceptance (and even celebration) of the apparent pluralism of styles as a supposed sign of our times. A unified style has many advantages over a condition of stylistic fragmentation. Parametricism aims for hegemony and combats all other styles.

This is for reasons *intrinsic* to parametricism itself, the way the designs apparently aggressively flood a space: 'Parametricism's crucial ability to set up continuities and correspondences across diverse and distant elements relies on its principles holding uninterrupted sway. The admixture of a post-modernist, deconstructivist or minimalist design can only disrupt the penetrating and far-reaching parametricist continuity.' Yet he also claims the design is more powerful because of the way it can join together or interestingly differentiate anything else in its path.

> The reverse does not hold, because there is no equivalent degree of continuity in post-modernist, deconstructivist or minimalist urbanism. In fact, parametricism can take up vernacular, classical, modernist, post-modernist, deconstructivist and minimalist urban conditions, and forge a new network of affiliations and continuities between and beyond any number of urban fragments and conditions.

To see what this actually looks like in practice, try Zaha Hadid Architects' Port Authority project in Antwerp, where a gigantic phallic insect mounts and violates a neoclassical building on the city's harbour.

Most of all, though, Schumacher insists that parametricism is not merely a style for the elite. 'It cannot be dismissed as eccentric signature work that only fits high-brow cultural icons. Parametricism is able to deliver all the components for a high-performance contemporary life process. All moments

Let's Declare Style War – ZHA in Antwerp

SPACES

of contemporary life become uniquely individuated within a continuous, ordered texture.' To leap from Vladimir Tatlin's or Malevich's three-dimensional hymns to the Communist International to the enticing prospect of a 'high-performance contemporary life process' is to appreciate the gulf between the old avant-garde and the new. Nowhere in Schumacher's now voluminous proclamations on the new style can you find much acknowledgement of politics, but you can find various little hints of the world outside his studio.

> Parametricism aims to organise and articulate the increasing diversity and complexity of social institutions and life processes within the most advanced centre of post-Fordist network society. It aims to establish a complex variegated spatial order, using scripting to differentiate and correlate all elements and subsystems of a design. The goal is to intensify the internal interdependencies within an architectural design, as well as the external affiliations and continuities within complex, urban contexts.

So this starts with acknowledging that there is a network society, and it's a 'post-Fordist' one (although anyone who has worked in a call centre could attest to the fact that networks and strict Taylorist disciplining of labour are in no way mutually exclusive). Schumacher has no particular interest in doing anything other than displaying this society, embodying it. In his manner, he fully acknowledges this: 'The avoidance of parametricist taboos and adherence to the dogmas delivers complex order for complex social institutions.' It mirrors the processes that go on within it; it is a mute avant-garde, an avant-garde without criticism. In a sense, this is a relief – none of the embarrassing claims by the likes of Rem Koolhaas and his Office for Metropolitan Architecture that designing offices for Rothschilds or Chinese state TV is in some way 'critical'.

It is easy simply to dismiss Schumacher, to shrink from his torrent of tortuous verbiage, to write it all off as forbidding and

Teutonic – to take the various positions adopted by the *AJ*'s readership, visible in the online comments under his article: 'what is it about Germans always trying to start the war?' or 'take a chill pill mate.' But to see what makes parametricism symptomatic of our unpleasant cultural and political circumstances, it needs to be taken seriously, and we need to suppress our aesthetic and syntactic revulsion. So, if we suspend disbelief for a little while, we can see that after all those morbid symptoms in the 1980s, 1990s and 2000s – the cowardice of pomo, the glorification of powerlessness and fragmentation indulged in by deconstructivism – the new is finally emerging.

Who is it that actually practises parametricism? Schumacher acknowledges only one precursor – the engineer Frei Otto, and only a handful of contemporaries – digital architect Greg Lynn, and two architectural schools – SCI-Arc in Southern California and the London Architectural Association under Brett Steele. Yet, perhaps appropriately given Schumacher's stated intent of total hegemony, the style has reached its greatest extent at the hands of its apparent enemies. It would be hard for the untrained eye – and after all, it's that eye Schumacher wants to catch, with his talk of 'mainstream acceptance' – to differentiate the bulging, organic, flowing, advancing forms of, say, the Sage in Gateshead by high-tech figurehead Norman Foster, or the Golden Terraces shopping mall in Warsaw, designed by American postmodernist Jon Jerde, from recent Zaha Hadid Architects projects such as the Guangzhou Opera House. The idea that an avant-garde only exists when hacks start stealing its ideas is a new one in architectural historiography. Nonetheless, there are at least a few signs that it really is an avant-garde, most notably the fact that many digital designers want absolutely nothing to do with so-called parametricism, considering Schumacher a mere *arriviste* who has co-opted the digital underground. The architect Daniel Davis wrote on his blog that, rather than truly entering into a design with the machines and programmes, Hadid and Schumacher created a design in a top-down, artistic manner, much as any other architect would.

> Whether ZHA uses a parametric model to generate the construction drawings of their signature is meaningless because the design was generated through a different medium. So Parametricism in this weird double-talk is Schumacher's attempt to associate ZHA (and even claim the ZHA created) a movement with which they have nothing to do. Stick at what you are good at Schumacher, making money, and let the third generation show you what this 'revolution' is really about.

In its political sniping and sectarianism, while simultaneously claiming the term for an unacknowledged underground, this statement is perhaps the nearest proof that there really is an avant-garde called parametricism, although perhaps Patrik Schumacher has little to do with it.

The Architect as CEO – Parametricism as the Architectural Logic of Late Neoliberalism

But what does Hadid herself think about all this? Her work has only recently started to fit the parameters of parametricism. Throughout the 1980s and 1990s, the firm's work built on the most disruptive and dissonant elements of modernist architecture – principally the Soviet suprematism and constructivism of the 1920s, and the architectural brutalism that flourished in Britain and Japan in the middle of the century – and did so without any particular theoretical baggage. The Deleuzian organic metaphors that Schumacher indulges in seem antithetical to these spiky, harsh projects. Her most famous early work, 1983's unbuilt The Peak club in Hong Kong, was a collision of rectilinear, repetitive forms that any Deleuzian would baulk at, a ferocious and sharp formalism. Perhaps the main link between this and what would come after, aside from the luxury clientele, is a certain geological bent to her structures, the sense

178

Council Housing for Berlin's IBA '87,
Zaha Hadid Architects

that they explode or erupt (rather than emerging or growing organically) out of the landscape.

As soon as this got translated into actual building, the results were more prosaic. A block of flats in West Berlin as part of the International Bauausstellung (IBA) in 1988 was a slightly wonkier than usual postmodernist tower, with only a mild lean to indicate Hadid's input. In the UK, where the Baghdad-born architect has been working since the late 1970s, she is best known for the rejection of her 1994 Cardiff Bay Opera House by both Tories (Virginia Bottomley didn't like it) and old Labour (neither did Rhodri Morgan). Until her work started suddenly to get built *en masse* in the middle of the 2000s, it seemed she would be best remembered for the paintings that preceded and accompanied each failed competition entry. These divide opinion greatly. For some they're prog-rock kitsch; for others – myself included – they're aston-ishing, genuinely worthy of comparison with El Lissitzky, a 'station between painting and architecture' of shuddering, overwhelming dynamism and power. Yet there was often a tragicomic gulf between these visualisations and the structures that resulted from them, as in the IBA block in Berlin, or when her harsh concrete structures for furniture designers Vitra in Weil-am-Rhein began to look as leaky and tired as any other ageing brutalist structure (and whether that is a bad thing or not is likewise a matter of opinion).

When Hadid's work finally began to get built, it was at the hands of two principal groups of clients: EU countries and Middle Eastern oligarchies. She has completed very little work in the United States or China (one completed building in each) and, notoriously, a tiny amount in the country where she has been based for over thirty years: her only buildings in the UK are a small cancer care centre in Fife, an unfinished and deeply forgettable transport museum in Glasgow and two structures in London – the Aquatics Centre for the Stratford Olympics, and the recently completed Evelyn Grace Academy in Brixton, to which we will come later. As it is, ZHA's work has tended to be limited to the most exclusive clients and programmes – museums, Alpine ski jumps, corporate showcase buildings (such as the BMW Central Building in Leipzig, or the various structures for Vitra). Hadid has occasionally expressed her dis-satisfaction with this, and her discomfort at being hired to design wilfully spectacular signature buildings, to be seen in isolation. 'What I would really love to build', she once told Jonathan Glancey, 'are schools, hospitals, social housing. Of course I believe imaginative architecture can make a difference to people's lives, but I wish it was possible to divert some of the effort we put into ambitious museums and galleries into the basic architectural building blocks of society.' She has regu-larly praised the grand public building projects of the 1960s, from Berlin's Alexanderplatz to London's South Bank, and their architects, from James Stirling to Rodney Gordon, with an admirable lack of retrospective hand-wringing. In a statement like the above, it seems she may even be slightly nostalgic for this era, when architects had a brief moment of national prominence, until the wave of popular anti-modernism in the seventies and eighties.

She has had some minor recent input in these 'basic architectural building blocks', inoffensively in Fife and more complicatedly in Brixton, as we will see. Yet the point remains, that these 'ambitious museums and galleries', like the Stirling Prize-winning MAXXI in Rome, are precisely what architects, particularly of the wilfully spectacular, dissonant variety – the avant-garde, if you will – are called upon to provide in the current climate. These are icons, gigantic three-dimensional advertisements, usually designed to 'anchor' a post-industrial area with a regular clientele of tourists, while the functional buildings that follow will be designed by corporate journeymen. It's unclear where all this fits in the conceptual paradigm erected by Hadid's partner. In a 2008 interview, Jonathan Meades attempted to take her to task on the firm's use of theoretical language, which he called 'the cant of pseudo-science – self-referential, inelegant, obfuscatingly exclusive: it attempts to elevate architecture yet makes a mockery of it.'

Hadid's defence is interesting:

> She claims to be not much of a reader of anything other than magazines, so the coarseness of the prose doesn't offend her. The point she makes is that this is the lingua franca of intercontinental architecture. A sort of Esperantist pidgin propagated by the world's architectural schools – the majority of which happen to be notionally anglophone, yet whose pupils and teachers come from a host of countries – and the world's major architectural practices which are international and polyglot ... the gulf between (her) clumsy, approximate jargon and precise, virtuoso design is chasmic.

So, in essence, this syntax is a true embodiment of the very post-Fordist globalisation whose ornamenter Schumacher wishes to be. Meades goes on to argue that the obfuscation might be the point. 'I suspect that Zaha has an ancient fear: that to discover how her processes work would be to jeopardise them' – (but) 'when Zaha talks about anything other than architecture, she employs an urbane vocabulary, a flourishing grammar and even the definite and indefinite articles.'

This doesn't go quite far enough in explaining why both ZHA's forms and Schumacher's verbiage have such appeal for the oligarchs who commission them. In a talk to the Architecture Foundation in London, one of the many sites in the capital that were supposed to host eventually unbuilt Hadid projects, the architect Patrick Lynch suggested another possible explanation. CEOs like Zaha because they think she's like them, and that the vaulting ambition of her buildings is a perfect fit. The swaggering 'fuck you' attitude, the rhetoric of transformation and aspiration, the sense of something ruthlessly and relentlessly crushing all competitors. The architect Sam Jacob went a step further in an article published in the midst of the 2008 crash, making a precise link between financialisation and parametricism.

Jacob notes that 'the ideology of the global market has been the context for architecture', which is a less romantic way of describing Schumacher's 'Post-Fordist network society'. 'These projects attempted to turn the flush of cash and credit delivered by fluctuations of abstract systems into something real: a thing or a place.' Hence, ZHA have produced a concrete monument to the demented extravagance of the derivatives-led boom of 1997–2008.

> It's created an architecture of spectacular, hollow unreality: based on unreal money, housing unreal programmes. This unreality has infused architectural production, often finding resolution in hysterical, liquid, fluid form at audacious scale – the kind of

thing recently dubbed 'Parametricism' by Patrik Schumacher. (Note: just as the height of building might be a warning sign of impending turmoil, the articulation of a stylistic manifesto is a sure sign of hubristic overconfidence).

The ideas of 'differentiation', the opposition to the 'fixed', has its own economic correspondent.

Displays of beyond-human formal complexity drop out of the computational design systems employed in the search for exoticism and difference – a difference that was demanded by the market pluralism of ultra capitalism. Appropriately, these projects seemed to use the very same kind of tools that have maximised, magnified, and deepened our current financial crisis. If the Modern movement had the abstraction of industry as its reference, millennial architecture had the systematised abstraction of late capitalism.

Jacob, writing after the visible collapse of financialisation, wrote of how 'this union of ideology and form has decoupled in dramatic fashion. The swift disjunction leaves a generation of architecture rendered instantly out of time – as un-possible as Gothic architecture in the Renaissance.' The piece ends on an ironic neo-romantic note.

Tomorrow's visitors to today's (or yesterday's) buildings will feel the swoosh of volumes, the cranked-out impossibility of structure, the lightheadedness of refraction and translucencies. They will marvel at buildings that hardly touch the ground, which swoop into the air as though drawn up by the jet stream. They will feel stretched by elongated angles that suck into vanishing points and confound perspective, and be seduced by curves of such overblown sensuality. And in this litany of effects, they will find the most permanent record of the heady, liquid state of mind of millennial abstract-boom economics. We might rechristen these freakish sites as museums of late capitalist experience, monuments to our quaint faith in the global markets.

It is appropriate, then, that ZHA's first completed building in London owes its existence to a hedge fund manager.

The Avant-Garde Builds Schools for the Future

The school in question, the Evelyn Grace Academy, is a city academy – that is, a non-selective school that is mostly state-funded but which receives a small percentage of its funding from a business or philanthropic non-state organisation of some description, for which it receives wide control over the curriculum. This should not surprise us. This is where architecture happens in schools now: there is a minority of spectacular and 'aspirational' academies, and a majority of what Alastair Campbell called 'bog-standard comprehensives'. The few schools that have achieved some architectural prominence over the last decade have been academies. Perhaps the most famous is Allford Hall Monaghan Morris's 2008 Westminster Academy in Paddington, a day-glo yellow and green box in the shadow of 1960s tower blocks and the Westway. Its most famous image, its 'iconic' capture, was of an atrium – that ubiquitous corporate feature – with a slogan defining each floor: '1 Communication'; '2 Global Citizenship'; '3 Enterprise'. In a perhaps inadvertently chilling article, Stephen Bayley made clear that this hectoring business ontology was extended to the teaching programme.

> Academies must respect key stage testing, but do not have to follow the national curriculum. This ventilates both the style of teaching and the plan of the building. The way it was explained to me was: we don't do French language and history, we do 'Napoleon'. This way, pupils learn about motivational leadership and acquire French language and history at the same time.

Indeed.

Another city academy prominent both for architecture and for an utterly craven managerialism was Norman Foster's 2003

Bexley Business Academy [now the Harris Garrard Academy], on the edges of the Greater London Council's (GLC's) failed 'town for tomorrow', Thamesmead. It has a 'simulated trading floor', although it is unknown whether it staged a simulated credit crunch. Recently, the architecture paper *Building Design* reported that it

> has been hit by a catalogue of maintenance problems, and the school's chief executive Sam Elms said that if she had her way she would move the school into a building more suitable for teaching … the problems include broken boilers, sewage defects, peeling paint, and a leaking roof which has continued to baffle experts.

Much as it's tempting to blame the helicoptering tax exile Baron Foster for the technical failings, he is perfectly capable of designing watertight buildings for prestigious clients. Rather, the defects were the consequence of New Labour's insistence on using the private finance initiative to build new schools – a procurement method that makes enormous amounts of money for lawyers, outsourcing firms and consultants, but has been less efficient for delivering sound buildings. Among other things, PFI contracts insist that architecture must be 'value engineered', a euphemism for the legal requirement that any component that can be made cheaper, must be made cheaper.

The cheapness of the architecture can only contrast with the opulence of those commissioning them. Evelyn Grace Academy was given its small proportion of private funding by a charitable organisation called ARK, which hence has overwhelming control of the school. It had been set up by a group of hedge fund managers, who deal in the same flowing, uncontrollable, weightless, non-referential and non-objective derivatives that Sam Jacob compares with parametricism. ARK's founders include Paul Marshall and Ian Wace, of Marshall Wace, and, most prominently, Arpad 'Arki' Busson, head of EIM Group, a fund of funds company. This prominence is due partly to the similarity between the charity's name and Busson's nickname, and partly to his status as the ex-boyfriend of Farrah Fawcett, Elle Macpherson and Uma Thurman, and as *Tatler*'s 'seventh most wanted person at a party'. As with Westminster, there is an assumption that the experience of trading in derivatives can be applied to education, which now, post-2008, should raise many more eyebrows than it used to. 'If we can apply the entrepreneurial principles we have brought to business to charity', he said to the *Guardian*, 'we have a shot at having a really strong impact, to be able to transform the lives of children.' He calls this 'venture philanthropy', and the fact that ARK's initials stand for 'Absolute Return for Kids' underlines the enthusiastic embrace of business ontology. Unsurprisingly, given that ARK have are particularly keen to apply their derivatives-derived wealth in impoverished inner cities, the grossness of the condescension has often been noted. In Islington, a local campaign 'forced ARK, a charity run by a group of bankers and hedge fund speculators, to pull out of a scheme to create an independent but state-funded academy on the sites of Islington Green and Moreland schools'. But in Brixton, in an area which had lacked a secondary school for some time, it got through.

It is worth reminding ourselves of what the academies are and were, given that they have been defended by some after their funding was the first major victim of cuts from the Tory–Whig government. A programme called Building Schools for the Future was the main conduit for the academies, responsible for both the destruction of the older schools and the construction of the new, but near the end of the Labour government's third term, it was also one of the main instruments for a brief burst of 'Keynesianism', with its funding guaranteed despite the recession. Michael Gove destroyed the programme almost immediately, but his counter-proposal for free schools essentially offered city academies without the architecture – according to Gove the only rationale for the programme had been to keep architects in business (the far more lucrative roles for the contractors and lawyers stayed unmentioned, of course). Businesses and charities, and perhaps the 'big society', would run the free schools at an even further remove from local authority control, but they could be housed in sheds for all Gove and his supporters cared. Journalist and free school enthusiast Toby Young has carved out a lucrative sideline in the architectural press, telling architects how useless their jobs are. It's in this context that the Evelyn Grace Academy limps to completion.

The Evelyn Grace website implies that the school may be inoffensive as city academies go. Pupils are reminded in assemblies that they are part of 'a special family, the ARK family', but mercifully, there are no trading floors or classes in creationism (both of which have been features of other City academies). The only major innovation appears to be the extension of school hours into a regular working day (8.30–5.00), and perhaps less obnoxiously the splitting up of the school into four smaller houses, each using a different entrance, which is fairly common practice. The rhetoric is certainly neoliberal, but in a similar vein to any comprehensive school today. Blairite buzz-words pervade the prospectus – we find unsurprisingly that 'developing an *aspirational ethos and mindset* is at the heart of our work', and that 'there will be a *zero tolerance* approach to behaviour that disrupts learning'. Meanwhile all students follow an intensive induction programme which teaches them to understand, follow and *buy into* all aspects of Evelyn Grace Academy's 'behaviour for learning policy'; and pupils 'will become *the leaders of tomorrow* in every walk of life' (my italics). This aspirational rhetoric is equally bureaucratic as, though rather less spectacular than, Patrik Schumacher's parametric syntax. Likewise, the theory opposes rectitude, reticence and no doubt also the rectilinear. In a talk on 'SEAL' (that's the social and economic aspects of learning), headteacher Peter Walker laments this as a kind of British reticence – it's tied up with liberalism, it's tied up with non-conformism, it's tied up with the history of the twentieth century, it's tied up with a natural reservation about the way the Americans treat the flag and so on; this whole area which is about dealing with how young people behave in an organisation. And I don't mean just bad behaviour and good behaviour, I mean learning behaviour; in order to learn effectively. We have a national resistance to that. We have a real hegemony still of subject learning in secondary schools.

So how does all this exclusivity – this aspiration, leadership and zero tolerance – fit into the local area? The description of the school itself, quite clearly written by Schumacher, talks of

an open, transparent and welcoming addition to the community's local urban regeneration process. The strategic location of the site within two main residential arteries naturally lends the built form to be coherent in formation and assume a strong urban character and identity, legible to both the local and neighbouring zones. The Academy offers a learning environment that is spatially reassuring and able to engage the students actively, creating an atmosphere for progressive teaching. To maintain the educational principle of 'schools-within-schools', the design generates natural patterns of division within highly functional spaces which give each of the four smaller schools a distinct identity, both internally and externally. These spaces present generous environments with maximum levels of natural light, ventilation and understated but durable textures. The communal spaces – shared by all the schools – are planned to encourage social communication with aggregation nodes that weave together the extensive accommodation schedule.

And so forth. The jargon remains, but note the change in velocity and intensity from the earlier manifestos and declarations of style war.

The building was not quite finished by the time the pupils arrived in September 2010, with the entrance from Shakespeare

Road still a mess of portaloos and waste; but the architecture is impressive. The school is on the same scale as the terraces, estates and villas around it, but without the slightest aesthetic concession to the London stock brick all around. It's a series of interlocking volumes, jagged and aggressive, with a certain flow, but without the monstrous organic formalism of the firm's more recent work. It's taut, compact, fierce, and its dynamism is undeniably seductive. City academies tend to have a deeply conservative architectural form, even when they're of the signature variety – with plenty of friendly slatted wood, atria and brightly coloured condescension. Evelyn Grace Academy has none of this – in its small way it's a deeply uncompromising and nonconformist structure, as much as it is wholly conformist, politically speaking. ZHA, a deeply publicity-conscious firm, has been a little quiet about this building, and although it was begun in 2006 and already under construction when the book went to print, it doesn't feature in the comprehensive 2009 *Complete Zaha Hadid*, which otherwise compiles the firm's every cancelled, unbuilt and speculative project. The project managers for the school were *Private Eye*'s 'world's worst outsourcing company' Capita, and to an extent it shows – the combination of precast concrete and grey cladding is admirable in its lack of ingratiating jollity, but the detailing is PFI cheap. The most spectacular part of the building, however, the bit that will be in all the photographs, is a bright red racetrack running under the school, while it hauls itself up on glass walkways. It's a combination worthy of the GLC architects Hadid cites.

Architecturally, there is little to criticise in this building. It might not be the embodiment of a new avant-garde, and Schumacher's new vocabulary is not all that apparent here; yet it does have some palpable connection with a historical avant-garde that aimed to revolutionise everyday life, that intended to take these standard Victorian streets by storm, to suggest that new ways of experiencing space need not be limited to an elite – that 'nothing is too good for ordinary people', as Anglo-Soviet

We Do Napoleon

constructivist Berthold Lubetkin put it. Yet it does this in order to inculcate in these people an utterly toxic ideology of patronising philanthropy and vacuous 'enterprise', which holds up the vain promise that they can enrich themselves through individual 'excellence' elevating them above their peers; in short, that *they can make it*, but damn everyone else. It is exactly the sort of building New Labour always said it was going to create, which gives it a definite bathos, given that it was completed under the millionaires' austerity government. It has hints, just hints, of the sort of structures we might want to build after neoliberalism; but in all other respects, it's impossible not to see it as what might be left of the avant-garde once all hints of critical or resistant politics have been evacuated. The avant-garde has moved from structures dedicated to the proletarian revolution to structures decreed by the super-rich, practically yelling at the proles below. '*Aspire*! Aim *high*, damn you!'

October 2010

Strange, Angry Objects

The Brutalist Decades

Speaking of his generation of modernist architects in the Weimar Republic, Steffen Ahrends told his son Peter, born in Berlin in 1933, that 'for us, the history of architecture started with the Soviet 1917 revolution'. It wasn't entirely a joke. For many modernist hardliners of his generation, and those that followed, 1917 had made possible a reconstruction of life on collective, egalitarian and, most of all, planned lines, which would mean a central position for architects, who would have the unprecedented opportunity of designing the buildings for an entirely new form of society. Peter Ahrends's self-published book, *A3 Threads and Connections*, is an oblique telling of this tale, through three generations of architects. The most historically important of these are the son, Peter – founder of the influential firm Ahrends, Burton and Koralek (now ABK)

Bruno Ahrends's White City

191

in 1960s London – and the grandfather, Bruno, who was one of the principal designers of the White City estate in northern Berlin, one of a cluster of Weimar-era social housing projects to have been given UNESCO World Heritage listing. It is a commonplace that modern architecture in Britain, as an ideology rather than as one of many possible styles, was an import from inter-war Central Europe – a gift dropped off en route to the US by Mendelsohn or Gropius, and continued by permanent émigrés – Goldfinger, Lubetkin, et al. – and this book is a document of how the architects involved saw this process.

Bruno Ahrends, like so many German-Jewish émigrés, was interned at the start of the Second World War as an 'enemy alien' – specifically, he was stuck for the duration in Douglas, Isle of Man. There, he created dream images straight out of the unbuilt projects of Weimar Berlin, monumental glass and concrete skyscrapers of the kind that would only be realised after the war. There is an undeniable undercurrent in these drawings, reproduced in *A3 – Threads and Connections*, of organising the shabby, stunted small towns of Britain, whose lack of planning wasted their natural assets, and composing them into something with futuristic vigour and ruthless optimism. Bruno's son Steffen had a more geographically exotic trajectory, taking him from the German-planned Soviet new town of Magnitogorsk to South Africa, and grandson Peter made his mark in the sixties and seventies with ABK, who designed a series of municipal libraries and university buildings in what was then called – though not by the architects themselves – the New Brutalism. Chichester Theological College was one of the earliest, a gruff, elemental series of brick and concrete pavilions, formed into sculptural towers with almost medieval slit-like windows; the most famous is the Berkeley Library at Trinity College, Dublin, where, similarly, hints of older architecture (this time, classicism and the baroque) can be found in an aggressive yet otherworldly design of breezeblock and granite. These are a long way from the elegant, neat

Ahrends, Burton and Koralek's Dublin Masterpiece, in Brutalist Weather

White City Bruno Ahrends had designed for the workers of Berlin forty years previously. In the process of its movement from Berlin and Magnitogorsk to Chichester and Dublin, modernism had transformed from a clean, clipped, stuccoed functionalism into a monumental, uncompromising and rather photogenic architecture.

In the book, this era ends with Peter's shocked reaction to the rejection of Ahrends, Burton and Koralek's winning competition entry for the National Gallery extension. Somewhat unimpressed with the brief, which entailed what they considered unwelcome concessions to 'market forces', such as office space to fund the galleries, ABK nonetheless composed a grand circus, culminating in a spiky, asymmetrical tower; it had no references to the style of the original gallery (a rather wan classicism), but tried to continue its use of civic, ceremonial approaches. In presenting the project to the Prince of Wales, Ahrends found that he didn't actually notice, and wasn't interested in, 'the plans, routes and squares we created', and wondered instead with some impatience why the building 'looked' as it did. In a speech to the Royal Institute of British Architects in 1984, Charles described the projected building as a 'monstrous carbuncle on the face of a much-loved friend', and followed this intervention with a book and TV series, *A Vision of Britain*, in which he expounded on his views. These were expressed in what Ahrends calls 'a mindless catchphrase language of "carbuncles", "glass stumps" and "fire-station towers"' – but what else could you expect of an architecture that was actually called *brutalism*? The upshot was that Ahrends, Burton and Koralek were thrown off the project, with the extension eventually being built to a design by Robert Venturi and Denise Scott Brown, which, whatever its programmatic 'complexity and contradiction', looked to the casual eye like just another part of Trafalgar Square, all Corinthian columns and Portland stone. ABK's career never recovered, and nor did the sort of modern architecture – committed to social change and uncompromising design – that the Ahrendses devoted their lives to.

It is telling that this intriguing, rather unprofessional account is told in a small, self-published book, with nineties graphics and unpretentious colour photographs. It will be easily lost among the rash of enthusiastic commemorations of the brutalist moment that was cancelled so finally by the intervention of the heir to the throne. There are coffee-table books full of archive photos, personal accounts by art historians, comprehensive historical monographs, National Trust tours, cut-out models, tea towels, prints and mugs; there are even flats for sale. There hasn't been such a wave of public enthusiasm for an architectural style since, in the 1970s and 1980s, the Victorian era was rehabilitated from the jerry-built eclectic slumland of Dickens and Doré into a much-loved part of the national heritage. This comparison is occasionally made by its advocates, who note that the discordance and aggression of brutalism, and its link with northern climates, connects it to the forthright, tasteless gothic of the high Victorians. This is certainly the impression given by an ambitious recent example of brutalist advocacy, Barnabas Calder's *Raw Concrete – the Beauty of Brutalism*, which makes the grand and meaningless claim that the period of brutalism was, in fact, the greatest architectural moment in Western history.

Almost every brutalism book not by an architect has an element of the *Bildungsroman* about it, the account of the moment when the author in his (almost always his) youth first encounters the style (I know, as I did this in my first book, *Militant Modernism*). Calder's story is of a young man who grew up in an

> Edwardian suburb of London (where) concrete architecture represented everything which was frightening and other: urban motorways, stinking, rowdy and flanked by decaying buildings; underpasses which reeked of urine, and seemed to have been expressly kinked to maximise the number of corners round which imaginary psychopaths could cluster; vast impersonal office buildings giving no indication of what was done within them; and above all council estates on whose raised walkways and deserts of patchy grass nameless but horrible crimes probably took place constantly.

It is admirably honest of him to make clear that he didn't have any sympathetic connection to these buildings until he came to engage with them as a student of architectural history; most other accounts begin much earlier, as we'll see, with some hard-to-recapture Proustian encounter between boy and *béton brut*. Conversely, Calder is always willing to tell us of his real fear upon his first tentative encounters with the likes of Trellick Tower. This isn't 'his' architecture, it has nothing whatsoever to do with where he is from.

Calder's selection of brutalist buildings, to make his argument about its eternal greatness as an architectural style, are eclectic and personal, and avowedly unpolitical. There is the

Hermit's Castle, Achmelvich, a totally private, bunker-like home, since disused (Calder, on a camping trip, places his sleeping bag with some relish on the built-in concrete bed). There are famous, listed masterpieces, such as Denys Lasdun's work in Cambridge or on London's National Theatre, and there is the 'good ordinary brutalism' of the University of Glasgow's demolished Newbery Tower. Calder has little to say about how the term brutalism came into being, making a glancing reference to its coinage in the London hipster circles of the ICA and the Architectural Association, but making much more of the brutalist generation's interest in historical architecture, 'a classically trained sense of the axis, the vista and the architectural set piece', so obvious in the work of Ahrends, Burton and Koralek – not for them, Steffen Ahrends's year zero in 1917. The current revival could be explained by 'a sense that the Welfare State was a worthwhile project, but more acutely by visual excitement at the excessive power, ruggedness and exoticism of buildings like this'. The book's strengths are twofold: one is a good architectural historian's flair at precise accounts of the formation of buildings, and the other is an argument about how much brutalist architects were used to give a 'radical' face to the constants of British ruling-class life – Oxbridge, the Royal College of Physicians, RIBA, Whitehall and of course property development. I'm not wholly convinced by this argument, which is based on a preoccupation with the most architecturally picturesque and unique examples of the style, rather than the enormous mass of work churned out by municipal architecture departments from the 1950s to the 1970s, meaning that by far the majority of brutalist buildings have been council housing, comprehensive schools and other public buildings – but it does reveal some important truths about a currently rather mythologised era.

This is a book of heroes and villains. The former include Ernő Goldfinger, and Calder's chapter on the Balfron and Trellick Towers stresses how important the personal conscientiousness of an architect could be in the 1960s. Both buildings were commissioned by the London County Council as part of slum clearance, in Poplar and Ladbroke Grove, respectively. The cult that both of these buildings have enjoyed, appearing now on innumerable trinkets, tea towels and T-shirts, is owed partly to their stark silhouettes, with their strongly emphasised service towers connected to the flats by skyways, and partly to the extremely high quality of workmanship. Goldfinger's personal arrogance, attested to by some of those who worked for him, meant in practice an obsession with quality – 'on budgets comparable to those of his contemporaries his buildings tend to be better detailed and better built than almost anyone's', with finely textured concrete kept in good condition by mouldings and details designed to stop staining and leaks. Some of these were nearly left unbuilt by the builders, and reinstated after the architect's thunderous intervention. Calder mentions his 'publicity stunt' in moving briefly from Hampstead to Poplar to discover what residents did and didn't like about the building,

Concrete Poured with Love: Lift Lobby, Trellick Tower

as well as his lesser-known but more consistent residency in Trellick Tower, where he kept an office from its completion in the early 1970s until his death in 1987. Calder also recognises the fact that Trellick Tower's rehabilitation (it was the first brutalist building to become popular with buyers) is owed not to yuppies moving in, but to the tenants' association who insisted on, and eventually got, a concierge and a pledge from the council that only people who wanted to live in the tower would be housed there.

Balfron Tower's uglier story is told in less depth. Poplar HARCA, the housing association the building was given to after a poll of tenants (who had been told that only a housing association could guarantee renovations) decided to sell the building in order to fund their renovation of other buildings elsewhere in Poplar. Ingeniously, before selling the flats on the open market, Poplar HARCA let them out to 'creatives', as a means of accelerating the long-established process whereby working-class people give way to artists who give way to bankers. Calder registers some discomfort at this, but this is not an angry book.

Rather, he is keen to remind readers that the Barbican, the one major brutalist estate to have been designed and managed for the wealthy (albeit by a local authority, of a unique sort), was a response to the possibility that the City of London's privileges could have been abolished by the reforming post-war governments – the Barbican was a 'bankers' commune' intended to keep the City's voting rights in place by building into it a resident population. Calder offers curt, unromantic analysis of the rim, short-term speculative capitalism that gave rise to the now celebrated but almost entirely demolished work of Owen Luder for the developer Alec Coleman, or to the semi-brutalist office and housing projects of Richard Seifert, such as the Anderston Centre in Glasgow, a half-finished and shoddily renovated sub-Barbican of monumental towers connected by walkways across a raised podium. Seifert, as Hugh Casson

Truncated Megastructure, the Anderston Centre

pointed out, had 'loyalty to his clients' where other architects felt a 'loyalty to society'; he was dropped from National Theatre design competition early on, for being 'too commercial – no principles', in the words of the judges. For his last major project, the wilfully sinister metal shaft of the NatWest Tower, for a few years Britain's tallest building, Seifert deliberately submitted an ugly low-rise and an elegant high-rise, in the hope that the latter would be selected (as it was). The anti-Seifert here is Denys Lasdun, the touchy, serious and wholly establishment architect who is Calder's real great love. Calder writes beautifully about the concrete work of the National Theatre, of how the Portland stone in the aggregate was calculated to harmonise with Somerset House, the Royal Festival Hall and Waterloo Bridge – which it does, since unlike so many owners of brutalist buildings the NT actually cleans it – and

The National Theatre, Outside, Where It Matters Most

most of all, about the complex process of creating that shut-tered finish. This was painstaking:

> air bubbles which naturally cling to the rough wood texture needed to be knocked loose by vibrating the wet concrete mechanically after it was poured but before it set, but not too vigorously: over-vibrating concrete would shake the gravel to the bottom.

He finds that even John Betjeman, the arch-Victorianist and founder of *Private Eye*'s 'Nooks and Corners' (originally called, in reference to the style, 'Nooks and Corners of the New Barbarism') admired the design, to the point where he wrote a letter of appreciation to Lasdun: 'I gasped with delight … it is a lovely work, and so good outside, which is what matters most.'

Like the original Victorian revivalists of the 1970s whom he so closely resembles, Calder likes to live the dream. He is over-come with enthusiasm in telling us about the months when he lived in a Lasdun-designed Halls of Residence in Cambridge, and in response to the problems brutalist buildings face with thermal insulation – which, naturally, effaces the rough, raw, tactile textures so important to lovers of the style – he tells us about a little experiment he made when living in a draughty Glasgow tenement, which he didn't heat one winter in order to prove his point that buildings didn't need UPVC and shoddy cladding. He recommends two duvets in the Glasgow winter and wearing jumpers indoors, but warns about an 'unwelcome dash to the shower' in the mornings. He is particularly anxious about the threat of unsympathetic alterations to his favourite brutalist monuments. He regards with pure horror the Blu-tacking of Students' Union posters to the red bricks of Stirling and Gowan's Leicester Engineering Building:

> of course I have sympathy with people's desire to make a place their own, and to customise everything from their choice of clothes to their wall decoration and their telephone ringtones. However, if you happen to find yourself in one of the two dozen best buildings of the twentieth century, you send round an email rather than putting up a poster.

One can be fairly sure that in the early 1960s when designing the building, grappling with a tiny budget, using whatever off-the-peg materials they could find, intoxicated with the bluff, articulated forms of industrial architecture, James Stirling and James Gowan could never have imagined that it would be treated by young enthusiasts in the twenty-first century as if it were St Paul's.

Calder is on his shakiest ground when he argues,

> the emphasis on visual excitement in the revival of interest in 1960s architecture is not a perversion of the real intentions of the style. Brutalism started out as a swing towards a politically neutral, self-propelling aestheticism cultivated by young architects afire with the thrill of Le Corbusier's post-war concrete primitivism.

This is not at all the impression that one gets when reading the earliest accounts of what the New Brutalism was. The title of the essay and book by Reyner Banham that first created and then summed up the style, was called, not by accident, *The New Brutalism – Ethic or Aesthetic?* The question mark was deliberate. Banham's book was on one level an exemplary piece of Cold War demonology. For the first decade after 1945, the pure white style of Bruno Ahrends's Berlin had been Anglicised – not in the direction of the monumental dissonance of brutalism, but into a friendly, rather cutesy amalgam of Scandinavian design and the English picturesque tradition; think here of the first new towns, the interiors of the Royal Festival Hall, the precincts of Coventry. Many of the architects behind this work, such as Frederick Gibberd (designer of Harlow new town) and Arthur Ling (architect of much of post-war Coventry), and a good chunk of the London County Council Architects' Department, were or had been card-carrying communists. In *The New Brutalism*, Banham argued – wholly spuriously – that Nikita Khrushchev's public denunciation of 'socialist realist' architecture in 1954 left these architects looking bankrupt and without an ideology to uphold (actually, politics notwithstanding, their architectural utopia was Stockholm, not Moscow). These CPGB Scandinavians called what they did the 'new empiricism', to which 'new brutalism' was a riposte.

On that Red-baiting level, the new brutalism was an amoral avant-garde response to the ingratiating nature of socially concerned, compromised modernists, but there were other things at work here too. Reading Banham's book, the essays by Alison and Peter Smithson later collected as *Ordinariness and Light*, with its telling epigraphs from Aneurin Bevan, or the various texts of Team 10, the international corresponding group that included most early brutalists, it is clear that there was a strong *ethic* in the work to which the *aesthetic* was often secondary. That mainly hinged on rejecting not just the picturesqueness of the Anglo-Scandos, but also the puritanism of the Berlin estates of the 1920s, clean-lined garden cities with depopulated public spaces. Instead, the New Brutalists were interested in the community life of the East End of London (more through Nigel Henderson's photographs than Willmott and Young's sociology), in the messy, chaotic nature of art brut and Eduardo Paolozzi ('Fuck Henry Moore' was one slogan), in vernacular architecture, in industrial buildings, and in Hollywood films and advertising. Their buildings were meant to be noisy and messy; for Banham, exemplars include Lasdun's cluster block at Keeling House, Bethnal Green, and Park Hill, in Sheffield, both attempts to recreate the bustle of a working-class street in the air. Aesthetics was secondary to this project; programme was all – in fact, the designers of Park Hill, Jack Lynn and Ivor Smith, boasted of the fact that they didn't draw a single elevation while designing one of the largest buildings in Europe. For Banham, this promised an *'architecture autre'*, where most accepted canons of form and order could be discarded, in favour of strange, angry objects whose appearance to the eye was wholly dictated by what they did inside and what the structure was made of.

Work like this was an amalgam of futurism and nostalgia which had more than a little to do with the fact that many of the brutalist architects were, like Banham himself (from a working-class background very rare in architectural circles, then as now) 'of redbrick extraction': provincials, northerners and some of them – like Peter Smithson, nicknamed 'Brutus' at the AA – classic post-war climbers, in his case from a respectable working-class family in Stockton-on-Tees. Keen to take this the whole way – and going one step further than Lasdun, who at Keeling House had embraced the once-horrifying thought that people might hang washing on balconies – Banham even praised one Japanese brutalist apartment block for the fact that fights happen in the walkways. Proof of authenticity. The relation of the New Brutalism to the working-class council tenants that would become its main inhabitants was ambiguous, though: brutalism was intended, according to Banham, as 'a brick-bat thrown in the public's face', which can't have endeared it to the public. By the time brutalist architects such as the Smithsons (in their Economist Building in St James's, a well-crafted, contextual work for an establishment client) had begun to embrace, in their spiky and personal way, an engagement with the classical tradition, it was all over for Reyner Banham – a 'betrayal', that sent him off to look elsewhere for his *architecture autre*.

None of this is discussed in any of the new New Brutalism books. The nearest that any of the shelf of brutalist revival volumes published in the last year come to acknowledging any of this strange, anachronistic and, one would think, interesting history is a few sentences in Elain Harwood's enormous *Space, Hope and Brutalism – English Architecture 1945–75*. It is some measure of the popularity of brutalism that Harwood has put it into the name of a book that is for the most part about other things, encompassing every aspect of post-war architecture, from streets in the sky to neo-Georgian country houses. Harwood is the ideal person to undertake the task. Every enthusiast, dabbler or fan of post-war architecture in Britain owes her a debt. As a case worker at English Heritage, Harwood was responsible for listing dozens of post-war buildings, right down to registering Sheffield's Park Hill as Grade II* in the face of a council that would clearly rather have knocked it down. Through this conservation work, and through several short books and guides, it's arguable that nobody since Pevsner has done so much both to preserve and to popularise modern architecture in this country, so it's gratifying that *Space, Hope and Brutalism*, a mammoth attempt to sum up the entire period, is published at a time when this architecture has never been so respected, or so fashionable.

Space, Hope and Brutalism aims to be the definitive reference work on the subject – its sheer weight means that it's most likely to be read specifically in reference libraries, most often, one suspects, by researchers. A chronological narrative is subdivided into several parts on particular aspects of the era: new towns; housing; private houses; schools; universities; transport; energy; industry and commerce; health; and leisure. Harwood's judgements are well considered, the historical detail is abundant and the photographs by James O. Davies are remarkable in their often-eerie glamour. However, this is very much the official story, coming from someone who, since her business has been the listing of buildings of exceptional quality, notices mainly the finest buildings of the era. One of the valuable things about this gigantic book is that it makes clear there is as much good architecture in the post-war era as there is in any other period – in fact, probably more of it. But the decision to excise much of the mundane work of local councils and, most of all, the dubious deals they cut with builders, particularly in the mid-sixties, in order to construct large quantities of prefabricated flats with great speed, means that the story is necessarily incomplete, tilted towards the best. Some of the most complete modernist environments in the country, from Broadwater Farm to Chelmsley Wood, do not feature, simply because they're of little architectural worth.

The narrative will be familiar to anyone who knows much about the period – the first ten years of 'New Empiricism', the wild experiments of brutalism, and then, in the 1970s, a sudden and sharp reaction, forcing architects into contrasting shifts towards a traditionalist 'vernacular' or towards the more technocratic 'high-tech' of Norman Foster and Richard Rogers. Because of this familiarity, much of the interest comes from unexpected details. On 'Energy', for instance, the account of Sylvia Crowe's landscaping of the grounds of nuclear power stations is an insight into the way that even the most unnerving of technocratic structures could be designed as integrated wholes with the landscape. Harwood's opening chapters are excellent in charting the shifts in planning in the post-war period, as plans for reconstruction of blitzed cities shift from beaux-arts Plymouth to New Empiricist Coventry to New Brutalist Sheffield.

The geography of post-war architecture as described here is also surprising, given how much of the enthusiasm for brutalism has come from cities other than London, such as Glasgow, Birmingham, Sheffield, Newcastle and Manchester (which even has its own retro-brutalist magazine, the very enjoyable *Modernist*). Rather than describing a more multicentric time, Harwood argues that London dominated the post-war decades in architecture almost as much as it does today. No local authority even remotely rivalled the London County Council in the scope of its architectural activity, and the cities and towns which were influential or impressive in their efforts were not those you'd expect: Sheffield, Coventry, Southampton and Loddon, Norfolk (a major holdout of the New Empiricism), feature here much more than Manchester, Birmingham, Bristol or Leeds. That's partly because of the bias for quality rather than quantity, so cities which embarked on huge programmes of rebuilding (like, say, Sunderland, or Portsmouth) get less of a mention if they opted for systems rather than architects. Birmingham, which had, as Ian Nairn approvingly pointed out in the mid-sixties, become unrecognisable in less than a decade, features little, beyond the mention of the exceptional local firm John Madin Architects.

Harwood often ends chapters with terse accounts of what was successful and what wasn't, and even more so, what survives and what doesn't (and why). Housing, for all the depredations of Right to Buy, survives far better than the buildings of the NHS and the comprehensive schools, both of which were decimated by New Labour and PFI, a development she notes with the aside that Blair 'assumed that old buildings could not deliver a decent education – never an argument made in the private sector', an attitude bound to make an English Heritage caseworker shake with fury. The few NHS hospitals of architectural interest, such as Powell and Moya's general hospital in Swindon, disappeared after less than forty years, to be replaced with the sub-architectural expression of accounting boondoggles. The best surviving typology of all, it seems from Harwood's account, is that of the private houses that architects built for the wealthy or for themselves, which appear in Davies's photographs as luminous, secluded time machines.

The coffee tables of these houses must be very well stocked at the moment. There are at least a dozen recent books which present the architecture of the post-war era in magnificently depopulated images, and in these, brutalist buildings are particularly well represented. This was anticipated by Banham, who considered the 'memorable image' one of the central tenets that made the New Brutalism so unlike the informal layouts and sleepy details of the New Empiricism. Brutalism was always meant to be photogenic – in their first public building, a secondary modern in Hunstanton, Norfolk, the Smithsons insisted upon its first coverage in the architectural press that it be photographed twice – once as a school, being used and beaten about by children, and once as a pure work of architectural space (designing buildings that were successfully both was not the Smithsons' strong point). Brutalism books, like the many brutalism Tumblrs that they draw upon, favour either stark black and white images taken when the buildings were new so that the marks of time aren't visible on the concrete, or, when

Memorability as an Image: Hunstanton School

the buildings are in better nick, new colour photographs where every pebble of the concrete aggregate is visible. The brutalism revival is a product of the internet – from Blogspot to Tumblr to Instagram, seemingly with less and less text and analysis as the craze continues. One building, for instance – the Ministry of Highways in Tbilisi, built in 1974 – features in at least five recent books of this kind. With its interconnected towers clinging to and then vertiginously dangling from a steep hill, it is a perfect internet image, so eye-catching that you'll stop checking Facebook or Twitter for all of thirty seconds while you look at it. Actually visiting the thing is another matter, and at least two of the books that use the image are written (or rather, compiled) by people that haven't.

A pretty typical, cheap and cheerful cash-in job here is Christopher Beanland's *Concrete Concept – Brutalist Buildings Around the World*, encased in a cardboard cover that 'wittily' evokes a nice grey slab of concrete. Here, the decisive encounter takes place in the West Midlands. 'Why do you like these ugly buildings?' he asks rhetorically. Because of

> dreams of brutalism. Dreams of blonde-haired girls lolling on roundabouts, outside towerblocks, beneath flyovers. An itch you can't scratch. And I know the culprit – Birmingham … from 2002 to 2007 I carved out some kind of life in 1970s-built concrete canyons and freezing offices and bars that stank of cigarettes, optimism and repressed lust.

This heavy-breathing stuff is derived from one of the central texts of brutalist revivalism, Pulp's 1992 fantasy 'Sheffield: Sex City', where the mundane concrete precincts of provincial British cities are eroticised by Jarvis Cocker's roving eye. In terms of the actual buildings, he's talking partly about the totally ordinary, but exceptionally monumental highway engineering that encases and courses through Birmingham, courtesy of its chief engineer Herbert Manzoni, and the architecture of John Madin, much of which is now being, or has just been, demolished. Like the work of Denys Lasdun or Ahrends, Burton and Koralek, this classically proportioned, obsessively considered architecture – Madin's Birmingham Central Library was designed using the golden section – was nevertheless connected by Prince Charles to bad things, in this case a place that 'looks like somewhere that books are burned, not read'.

Perhaps the only notable thing about *Concrete Concept* is its stress, correctly, on the International nature of brutalism. It may well have been cooked up by a clique of chippy hipsters in the ICA and the AA, but within a couple of years the term was being used to define anything heavy, rough and concrete; in the US, where it was largely used for university buildings, it never acquired any of the social connotations it acquired in, say, the UK or Japan. There, the building that kicked off brutalism was the Yale Art and Architecture Building by Paul Rudolph, a sculptural, self-conscious monument lined in 'corduroy concrete'. The ethic, here, was wholly architectural: a 'truth to materials' (here, concrete), an 'expression of structure' and, especially, an expression of the building's technical services, something which can make brutalist buildings exceptionally difficult to renovate, as these change as technology changes. Beanland won't let himself get bogged down in this, though. 'Brutalism emerged at the beginning of the jet age, as architects freely flew around the world pinching ideas from each other, carousing with fast women and driving fast cars, like in *Mad Men*.' Which presumably makes major brutalist architects such as Kate Macintosh, Alison Smithson and Lina Bo Bardi into the Peggy Olsons of the story. After this, and an A–Z of brutalism by Jonathan Meades, in which he gives more attention to the Atlantic Wall and Sir John Vanbrugh than the 'manifesto folk' who coined the term in the first place, we have a coffee table listicle, with breezy profiles of Habitat 67 in Montreal, Torres Blancas in Madrid, Preston Bus Station, the Washington Metro, Orange County Government Center or Basil Spence's New Zealand Parliament in Wellington ('shapes like this remind a chap of his egg cup or tea mug'). These are combined with what appear to be Google-sourced photos, and a potted bibliography.

A little more ambitious is graphic designer Peter Chadwick's *This Brutal World*. It is based on a Tumblr Chadwick has run for a few years called *This Brutal House*; the pop culture reference, to Nitro Deluxe's 1986 electro classic of the same name, connects electronic music, architecture and nostalgia, as does the introduction to his book. Chadwick's *Bildungsroman* is set in Teesside, and tellingly, the building that sparks the love affair is not strictly brutalist – the Dorman Long Coke Oven Tower, at the factory where his grandfather worked, near Redcar. Although this monumental, cast-from-one-mould object is not a million miles from some of the forms that James Stirling or Ahrends, Burton and Koralek arrived at by more circuitous routes, it is anonymous, not 'high' architecture, arrived at through functional necessity rather than direct expression. In a typical nostalgic detail, he tells us he first saw this building in the late seventies as a child, 'through the rear window of my father's white Ford Anglia ... uncompromising and faceless, this structure fuelled my imagination'. Then, rather serendipitously, he managed to see some of the other great modernist works of the north-east before puberty. He got to climb on Victor Pasmore's Apollo Pavilion in Peterlee ('from that moment on', getting his knees scuffed on the pavilion's rough surfaces, 'I fell in love with raw concrete'), and he got to gaze longingly at the Trinity Square Car Park and the Dunston Rocket, both in Gateshead, both designed by Rodney Gordon for Owen Luder Architects. On first hearing Joy Division, he realises that this is the landscape they were describing: 'up the tenth floor, down the back-stairs, into no-man's land'. This is interesting, if familiar stuff, but for most of the book, the elective affinity between brutalism and pop culture comes in the form of adding lyrical excerpts (among other improving quotations) to more Google Images–sourced photographs of monumental buildings.

While *Concrete Concept* sticks to buildings that would fit both Reyner Banham's and Paul Rudolph's definitions of brutalism, *This Brutal World* promises to be

> both an homage to Brutalism and a visual manifesto that celebrates this awe-inspiring style of architecture. I wanted to take the opportunity to reinvent and reappraise the term 'Brutal'. To celebrate the very best in the traditional canon of Brutalism ... and also to propose that Brutalism lives on in so much contemporary architecture.

The result is a Tumblr blown up unflatteringly into a lushly produced hardback, the format casting an unforgiving light on what might seem like an evocative juxtaposition when glimpsed on tablet or iPhone. There has been an effort at scattering the buildings so that the images complement each other, but it's a little trite: the Ryugyong Hotel in Pyongyang goes next to Skidmore, Owings and Merrill's Air Force Academy Chapel in Colorado Springs because, well, both have big sharp points. Only the chapel would fit even slightly into any previously conceived definition of brutalism. One thing the catholic selection of projects does is make clear how little being big and aggressive has to do with brutalism, either as theorised by Banham and the Smithsons or as practised by Denys Lasdun and Paul Rudolph. Brutal as the work of the late Zaha Hadid could be (lavishly showcased here), there was absolutely nothing she was concerned with less than 'truth to materials', expression of structure or the display of a building's services. That's not what the book is for, anyway – the pop quotations make that pretty obvious. Leonard Cohen tells us that 'there is a crack, a crack, in everything, that's how the light gets in', next to the clustered roof lights of the Zalman Aranne Library in Israel; Suede sing of 'two hearts under a skyscraper' next to some new glass towers by OMA in Rotterdam; and underneath an image of the bluntly expressionist Luckenwalde Hat Factory by Erich Mendelsohn, Nick Cave sings of how

Out of sorrow entire worlds have been built
Out of longing great wonders have been willed.

Aside from the question of what this could possibly have to do with the particular manner in which Mendelsohn chose to design a hat factory, it's hard not to giggle. Harder still, when an image of another functional structure, RMJM's Falkirk Wheel, a canal boat lift opened in 2002, is accompanied by Ayn Rand asking 'the question is not who is going to let me, it's who is going to stop me'. Maybe someone should have.

Among the 'influences' listed at the start of *This Brutal World* are Bernd and Hilla Becher, whose typological catalogues of deliberately decontextualised industrial structures, with people and surrounding objects pointedly cropped out to give prominence to a pure, abstracted form, have had some effect on the brutalist revival's approach to the subject. That's especially noticeable in what is, as a book of architectural photography at any rate, by far the best of these coffee table tomes, the Polish-French photographer Nicolas Grospierre's *Modern Forms – A Subjective Atlas of twentieth-Century Architecture*. There is talk at the start of the book alluding to the more poetic, theoretical end of brutalist revivalism: Grospierre insists that 'for me, modernism, and architectural modernism in particular, is the embodiment of one of the greatest ideas in the history of mankind – progress ... I can identify with the ideas of progress, I believe in them and I long for them.' That is, the photographs of buildings in this 'subjective Atlas' are intended as a commentary on the loss of faith in progress resulting from the demise of both state socialism and social democracy. The arrangement of photographs therein – a typological twinning, with two similar or complementary 'forms' facing each other, one page each – doesn't really manage to do this. Partly that's because of a certain falseness about the project, as with the work of the Bechers themselves. I know a fair few of the buildings Grospierre photographs, and I know that some of them are often humming with people, activity and often unaesthetic informal commerce. Presenting the buildings as ruined and empty – as a tiny handful are – makes the point about the failure of progress, modernity and suchlike, rather better than a somewhat battered but well-used public building might.

But what *Modern Forms* does well is, in part, create a selection of forms which are genuinely piquant, compiled from places that aren't easily found on Google Images, a pleasingly eccentric geographical itinerary of Poland, Lithuania, Latvia, Estonia, Israel, Lebanon and the United States. Most of the examples are brutalist, but many are in the concrete shell-roofed style particularly popular in roadside buildings in mid-century America and nicknamed 'Googie': a style where buildings became logos, designed to be seen at speed; appropriately, in terms of the simple architectural thrill of 'oh! What on earth is that?' the images deliver amply. Sometimes the book twins buildings which genuinely do look alike – a bandstand in Atlanta and a railway station cafe in Warsaw, with similar cylindrical glass shapes. Elsewhere, Grospierre cheats a little: the National Palace of Culture in Sofia only rhymes with the Interfaith Medical Center in Brooklyn because he's photographed it from the back, rather than from its formal, symmetrical entrance. More often, the similarity in form is combined with radical differences in typology – a kolkhoz in Estonia next to a multistorey car park in Texas. Shape is akin, function is alien, as with the House of the Soviets in Kaliningrad alongside another Dallas car park, or the Donbass Sanatorium in Crimea with the Jimmy Carter Presidential Library in Atlanta.

The real question here, given how these apparently similar approaches to monumentality or the enclosure of space look despite their totally different uses and histories, is: did modern architecture successfully create a formal repertoire appropriate to how people approach and experience a building? It is this, the superficial obsession of what the building merely *looks* like, which caused the mutual incomprehension between Peter Ahrends and Charles Windsor, leading the latter to complain of 'nuclear power stations' (the National Theatre) or '1930s wirelesses' (James Stirling's Number One Poultry) in respect of buildings whose function is made opaque or irrelevant to him by their unpleasant exterior form. This has long been one of the central criticisms of architectural traditionalists such as Charles's court architect, the Albert Speer apologist Léon Krier. For him, established architectural languages such as classicism, baroque and gothic tell you what a building is before you even have to read the sign. Now, that's not entirely historically accurate – in the eighteenth century, a roughly similar language could be used for a church, a country house, a terrace or the entrance to a factory – but it does explain some of the puzzlement with which the New Brutalism was met when it was actually new. So Grospierre juxtaposes the Vilnius House of Ritual Services (a Soviet type sometimes known as a 'sorrow palace', where funerals were held) and another jauntily angled

Poundbury Fire Station

thin concrete shell roof in Amboy, California: Roy's Motel and Cafe. Isn't this building – whose Lithuanian architects must have hoped to cast a sombreness and comfort appropriate to coping with bereavement – a failure, if it used the same formal language as a Californian diner? Look more closely, however, and you can see that the elements they share – such as a tension between jagged, cantilevered concrete volumes – coexist with many that they don't. The House of Ritual Services features a formal approach up a series of steps, to a niche-like entrance where the building's wings appear to shelter and welcome the visitor. Roy's Motel and Cafe offers none of these elements. Here, even the most intelligent purely formal, purely photographic account of brutalist architecture cannot but miss the way that buildings are actually experienced through use.

That, according to a certain, well-rehearsed criticism of brutalism, was the problem all along. Architects might have created images, sculptures, that they may have admired and expressed themselves through – but they didn't have to live in them, did they? In fact, they probably all lived in Georgian terraces. As indeed did Alison and Peter Smithson and James Stirling. It's all abstract for them, right? Wrong, according to Stefi Orazi's *Modernist Estates – the Buildings and the People Who Live in Them Today*. This is a clever move. The recent controversy over a petition signed by practically every major living architect, from Richard Rogers to Peter Eisenman, to save Alison and Peter Smithson's Poplar council estate Robin Hood Gardens from demolition, played out on exactly these terms. These architects, Tower Hamlets Council spokespeople pointed out, might well enjoy briefly looking at the 'daring' and 'fearless' design of these two long, dilapidated, careworn mid-rise concrete streets-in-the-sky; but if you like it so much, why don't you go and live there? Well, each of the people profiled in *Modernist Estates* has done exactly that, although none of them in Robin Hood Gardens specifically, which is currently being 'decanted', for a bland replacement in which, typically, it is unlikely many original residents will be able to afford to live. However, you don't need to demolish any buildings to price residents out of an area, and with the Right to Buy, and even more with the recent Housing Bill, that applies equally to council tenants as it does to private renters.

Most of the people in *Modernist Estates* have bought their flats. The book grew out of another Tumblr, where Orazi put up as they came on the market photographs and prices of modernist flats, most of them 'ex-council'; it was often hard to be sure whether the blog was making a satirical point about the decreasing status of social housing or not. That's not impossible, as Orazi, a graphic designer, tells us at the start of the book that 'I grew up in an architecturally unremarkable council estate in Sussex', and had always lacked the allegedly ingrained belief that houses are always better than flats, and private always better than public. In fact, in a claim that has a great deal more plausibility than Barnabas Calder's proclamation of brutalism as the architectural GOAT (Greatest Of All Time), Orazi calls the modernist estates of the 1950s to 1970s – or those showcased here, at any rate – 'Britain's best housing of the twentieth century'. Who are the 'people who live in them?' Well, you'll be surprised to learn that the people who live in modernist estates are not unemployed, are not working at warehouses or in supermarkets, but are in fact actors, graphic designers, lecturers, a 'digital project manager with a passion for analogue cameras', a Turner Prize-winning architect-artist, several architects, the head of the British Council's architecture section and 'a dealer specialising in mid-century Scandinavian furniture'. Not a single person is interviewed here who is not, in the parlance, a 'creative'. These are much the kind of people who made the architecture of the nineteenth century acceptable in the 1970s, turning former slums such as Notting Hill, Camden and Islington into desirable areas where within a couple of decades government ministers wouldn't be able to afford to live. In *Modernist Estates*, each of these enthusiasts is profiled in their home, and asked: what are the best and worst things, how are the neighbours and how has the building been treated?

The book is chronological, beginning with Wells Coates's full-blast, Berlin-style Isokon building, perhaps the first serious modernist building in Britain, and ends with the Anglo-Swedish architect Ralph Erskine's first phase of Greenwich Millennium Village, a late flowering of the New Empiricism. Neither of these are council estates as such (though both have social housing), and the book also features a private Span estate, one flat in Frederick Gibberd's private Pullman Court and a flat in the Barbican. These aside, each of the flats photographed and described is 'ex-council'. Sometimes, the proportion of council tenants has decreased shockingly with Right to Buy – in the Golden Lane estate, for instance, it's a mere 50 per cent – and elsewhere, as in Myatt's Fields, Lambeth, the subject is still a very normal council estate. And when asked to describe the best thing about their flats and houses, most residents answer in a similar way: they love the air, the openness, the freshness and the sense of living in something historic and idealistic. It's also fun to furnish them with carefully picked period furniture, as it was when you were moving into Islington in the seventies. The interiors are quite shockingly homogeneous, however much the buildings themselves are a disparate bunch, from fire-breathing, sturm und drang brutalism to friendly New Empiricism. Inside, you'll almost always find stripped floorboards, white walls, Swedish furniture with (depending on income) a bit of Bauhaus or fifties vintage, cushions with prints of brutalist buildings and tastefully framed exhibition posters. The contrast with most council estate interiors (a useful document here is the work of Stephen Willats, such as the recent *Vision and Reality*) couldn't be more glaring. Famously, council tenants, who will always point out of the most forbidding blocks that 'they're lovely inside', like to customise their flats as much as possible. Each flat is usually strikingly different; in 2008, a photography project on Robin Hood Gardens found

Park Hill: 'Let's Move to ...
a Utopian Socialist Experiment'

a dizzying range of interiors – kitsch, delicate, old-fashioned, modern. But here, everyone has the same good taste, as if this is the only possible appropriate response to modern architecture.

That's not to say that the queasiness of moving into and buying up something that was until recently a public good has escaped all the interviewees. Neave Brown, for instance, who was a designer at Camden Council in the 1970s, when it was designing what is almost certainly in terms of space, intelligence and construction quality the finest mass housing ever built in the UK. He moved a few years ago from one block of flats he designed to another, Fleet Road, in Gospel Oak. When asked, 'What is the best thing about living here?' he replies, 'Who am I to say, but it's beautiful.' When asked what the worst thing is, he speaks angrily of the fact that the ideals of his generation of architects were betrayed, and that working-class people can no longer get housing this good. Maria Lisorgskaya, a member of the arts and design collective Assemble, is interviewed in her short-stay flat as part of the gentrification of Balfron Tower; she is understandably prickly about this, annoyed both at the privatisation of the block (when asked what is the worst thing about the building, she mentions that 'people have had to leave due to the "glamorisation" of brutalism') and that she's considered, as a participant in the programme, as part of it. But who in their right mind would refuse a cheap flat in one of the most impressive structures ever built in London, even if it's only for a year until the owners strip it down and start moving the bankers in? No such qualms, however, seem to concern the lecturers living in Park Hill, used as a second home during the working week. Park Hill was given to the developers Urban Splash, on the proviso that a mere quarter of the estate stayed 'social'; flats in the part of the building that has been drastically renovated and redesigned are specifically marketed to 'creatives'. Thousands have been displaced from their homes in the process, never to return. The undertone behind the enthusiasm of many of the new New Brutalists is not hard to detect. Perhaps the problem wasn't buildings, but the people?

For Ivor Smith, one of the two designers of Park Hill, there is little to be upset about in the redesign and clearance of his building; in his new book *Architecture an Inspiration*, he tells us that in the work undertaken by Urban Splash, stripping out each flat in the part they have renovated, replacing bricks with brightly coloured anodised aluminium and adding a steel spiral staircase, 'I sense the same enthusiasm and excitement that Jack Lynn and I enjoyed half a century ago.' Smith 'qualified at a privileged time', though, when there was a 'sense of optimism and deep social concern', the latter of which surely has not entered into the equations of Urban Splash. In most other respects, *Architecture an Inspiration* shows how far Smith has travelled from the days when he and Jack Lynn boasted about the fact that they didn't draw elevations. 'In the middle of the 20th century', he delicately puts it, 'it was proposed that the elevation should automatically express on the outside what goes on within, and should honestly express its structure. This was simplistic rationalisation which, as we have seen, history contradicts.' His book illustrates the way in which, after being contradicted by history, architects who had once constructed outrageously confident concrete monuments shifted into something a great deal more modest.

Like Peter Ahrends's *A3 Threads and Connections*, this is a self-published book by an old man, and it has nothing to prove. The titles of both books, earnest and slightly ungrammatical, are remarkably unlike the percussive stomp of *Raw Concrete*, *Concrete Concept*, *Modernist Estates* or *Modern Forms*. It is intended as an introduction to 'architecture' itself for the casually interested or for beginning students, authored by a conscientious designer who has travelled a lot; many of the photographs are his, and it feels as though decades of thought have gone into the selection of these particular projects, out of all those he has encountered. A few years after Park Hill, Ivor Smith fell in with the Cambridge School of modern architects, such as the British Library's designer Colin St John Wilson, believers in uniting modernism and historical continuity, via an engagement with the city as it is, rather than as they would like it to be. The heroes here are Alberti, Palladio, Asplund, Lutyens, Aalto, Kahn, Moneo, architects concerned with order, precision and allegedly eternal values. The architects who would appear to be brutalism's heirs leave Smith rather puzzled: on appraising Richard Rogers's Lloyd's Building, which shares the brutalist joy in making visible its ducts and pipes on the exterior, he reflects that 'with such a strong celebration of the services, it's hard to know what the icon represents'. Architects of the early 1960s, when Park Hill was designed, would be surprised by the notion that they had to 'represent' anything but the building itself and what it does. They built civic structures, but the idea that there was a

The Cambridge School

particular code or language that civic buildings should use in order to communicate with the public would have left them entirely nonplussed. It would make complete sense to the younger architects who are currently taking on some of the larger commissions in London, though, such as Maccreanor Lavington, Patrick Lynch or David Chipperfield, all of whom owe something to the Cambridge School's concern for urban order, classical tripartite structures, colonnades, brickwork and stone. For them, brutalism's rupture with the existing city is a mistake to be rectified. Their buildings, office complexes for large developers and luxury flats instantly sold for astonishing sums, use a civic language which brutalists never thought was necessary for libraries, hospitals or council housing.

November 2016

Jane Jacobs Says No

In Enrica Colusso's film *Home Sweet Home*, on the subject of the recently 'decanted' Heygate Estate in the Elephant and

Castle, south-east London, a town planner explains to camera why nearly all the buildings around him – a large council estate, and a covered shopping centre – have to be demolished. They're not real streets, he says. They're a monoculture of one type of thing – housing here, shopping there – and worse than that, they're mono-tenure, one gigantic 'project' of poor people put in one place. Places like this are socially unhealthy – the people in them are *socially excluded* by being placed in great single-class ghettos. They are lifeless, homogeneous, boring, the result of 'top-down' rather than 'bottom-up' planning. Around him, however, swirl enormous amounts of street life. The covered shopping centre has a dense street market around it, and within its floors – at least at the time of filming – the sort of multicultural businesses that are usually praised by contemporary planners – a Polish restaurant, a Chinese super-market, several Latin American restaurants and grocers and, at the top, a bowling alley. The housing estates next door are – were – among the most multicultural places on earth, and as much as council tenants, you could find students enjoying the relatively low rents of 'ex-council' properties. But one thing the film shows is that while the shopping centre – and the traffic disaster in front of it, with its two roundabouts – are noisy and 'vibrant', to use the familiar cliché, inside the Heygate Estate was a green oasis, dense with trees, quiet. There were no 'streets', only walkways segregated from traffic, with far, far fewer people than there are in the shopping centre. The reason this place had to go, even before the interests of real estate and cash-poor councils are considered, could be summed up as: 'Jane Jacobs says no'.

This is interesting, as it is something like the reverse of the epiphany the freelance journalist Jane Jacobs experienced in Philadelphia in the mid-1950s, upon visiting new housing estates and old 'slums' with their planner Edward Bacon. Writing for a variety of publications, but mainly *Architectural Forum*, Jacobs had contrasted 'Olympian' town planners

such as New York's quango despot Robert Moses, addicted
to models and graphics, seldom ever getting out of their cars,
with 'pavement-pounders' such as Edward Bacon and the
shopping mall designer Victor Gruen, who truly knew and
explored their city on foot. Yet even they, it seemed, had failed
to create a 'real' city with the blunt instruments of state-driven
town planning. In Philadelphia Jacobs was taken to a 'bad
street' that she later remembered as being 'just crammed with
people, mostly black people, walking on the sidewalks and
sitting on the stoops and leaning out of the windows'. The
'good one', meanwhile, just had one boy kicking a tyre into a
gutter. Her biographer Robert Kanigel quotes her asking the
planner, 'Ed, nobody's here. Now why is that? Where are all
the people? Why is no-one here?' 'To her fury,' Kanigel says, 'he
just wasn't interested in her question.' Even a planner with the
best of intentions had failed to understand what made a city
interesting, exciting and economically successful, and create
new spaces that would follow suit. From this insight came the
impulse that led her to write what is probably the single most
widely read book on cities published in the twentieth century.

The Death and Life of Great American Cities couched itself
from the start as an attack on the orthodoxies of city planning,
as Jacobs saw them in the late 1950s and early 1960s. That
was, in Kanigel's words,

> a time when old city neighbourhoods were being erased, high-
> rise housing projects erected in their place; when slums were
> slums and everyone knew exactly what they were, or thought
> they did; when anyone who wanted to live in the city would
> have been seen as just a little weird.

The dominant urban ideas of the era were considered disparate
at the time, but were linked together by Jacobs into a scathing
portmanteau: *Radiant Garden City Beautiful*. The components came from France, Britain and the US, respectively: Le
Corbusier's mid-1930s Radiant City, a vision of a city of towers

in landscaped parkland, where housing was rigorously zoned away from industry, leisure and a central business district; Ebenezer Howard's Edwardian *Garden Cities of To-Morrow*, a proposal for the creation of verdant, self-contained new towns to accommodate what would later be called 'overspill' from the metropolis; and the City Beautiful Movement, which took hold of American planners in the 1900s, favouring the creation of grand, vaguely Parisian classical ensembles, usually for government, usually after clearing a non-'beautiful' part of city to create them, in the heart of American towns and cities. It's worth noting that the major building project in America at the time of Jacobs's writing – the creation of miles upon miles of low-density suburbs by private developers, subsidised richly by the Eisenhower-era state – doesn't feature in the portmanteau, as it didn't quite fit any of these three parts. That's because the argument was more about ideology than practice – the fact that Radiant Garden City Beautiful had seduced architects and urban planners to overlook what the city really was, the ways in which its built structure and economy worked on its own terms, in favour of a received idea of how cities 'should' be. The result, in her view, was 'the anti-city'. The anti-city destroyed the treeless pavements, which looked messy but functioned well, in favour of pointless greensward where 'Christopher Robin goes hippety-hoppety'. It destroyed human networks and replaced them with emptiness and formality. Her alternative to this was not a new proposal or a new image but something that, she claimed, already existed, and needed only to be strengthened and helped – 'the ballet of Hudson street', the vision of mutual aid and 'complex order' that she saw daily outside her window or as she sat on her doorstep in Greenwich Village.

Death and Life's reputation was bolstered as the sixties went on by the successful campaigns Jacobs herself was involved in, such as stopping the Lower Manhattan Expressway that would have destroyed her home in Greenwich Village, and which would have obliterated that ballet and replaced it with the linear forward motion of cars ploughing along concrete flyovers. Robert Kanigel takes his title from one of *Death and Life*'s most famous concepts, 'eyes on the street', which encapsulates well Jacobs's combination of humane optimism and anti-statist laissez-faire; crime, she argued, was actually lessened by the density and constant activity of the built-up nineteenth-century city, because so many people could see what was going on at all times, making policing almost unnecessary – if someone was robbed or attacked there would be dozens of eyewitnesses, an instant deterrent. The title of Samuel Zipp and Nathan Storring's Jacobs anthology, *Vital Little Plans*, quotes her alternative slogan to Chicago architect and City Beautiful ideologue Daniel Burnham's 'make no little plans – they have no power to stir men's hearts'. But the subtitle – *the Short Works of Jane Jacobs, author of the Death and Life of Great American Cities* – is revealing in a different way. An active writing career of seventy years, from 1936 to 2006, was dominated by that one book. Both Kanigel and Zipp/Storring are keen to make a case for what she did before and after *Death and Life*, but the space devoted to the various parts of her career tells its own story. Only a quarter of *Eyes on the Street* is devoted to the fifty years of Jacobs's life that succeeded the book's publication.

Jane Butzner was born in 1916 into a wealthy Protestant family in Scranton, a declining coalmining town in Pennsylvania; she did not go to university, but managed with impressive speed for the time to carve out a career as a copywriter and freelance journalist, largely for a metallurgy trade journal, *Iron Age*, and married Robert Jacobs, an architect specialising in hospitals. She published her first book in her twenties – *Constitutional Chaff*, a long-out-of-print annotated collection of discarded drafts and failed proposals for the Constitution of the United States (*Death and Life*, published twenty years later in 1961, is often described incorrectly as her first book). In both *Eyes on the Street* and *Vital Little Plans*, you find Jacobs discovering 1930s New York as a revelation; and some of that is already couched in the terms of *Death and Life*. Kanigel notes that one single block of Jones Street, location of her first Manhattan flat, had at the time she moved there, terraces of 1840s houses interspersed with 1920s apartments, a sweet factory, a French laundry, an ice dealer's cellar, a barber shop and three speakeasies, all unaffected by zoning regulations. Yet she was susceptible then to the alternative visions of imaginary cities that she would later do so much to discredit decisively. One highlight was the 1939 World's Fair, organised by Robert Moses as a vision of spaced-out towers, flyovers and abstract, futuristic architecture. Much later, she recalled to an interviewer, 'I thought it was so cute. It was like watching an electric train display somewhere.' Did you have an inkling that this was going to turn out to be Dallas in 1985?, asked her interlocutor. 'No, of course not.'

Vital Little Plans ignores her dabbling in constitutional archaeology, and instead begins with two New York microcosms Butzner had published in *Vogue* in the mid-1930s. Zooming in on the 'flower district' and the block or so of diamond sellers on the Bowery, these are amazingly similar to her later work. There is the interest in complex economies, urban activity and trust – 'there has never been a robbery in the centre', she claims of the diamond district – and there is her ability to sketch dramatic and somewhat sentimental urban panoramas, full of activity.

> Under the melodramatic roar of the 'El', encircled by hash-houses and Turkish baths, are the shops of the hard-boiled stalwart men, who shyly admit that they are dotties for love, sentiment and romance ... apprentices, dodging among the hand-carts that are forever rushing to or from the fur and garment districts, dream of the time when they will have their own commissions houses. Greeks and Koreans, confessing that they have the hearts of children, build little Japanese gardens.

It is not coincidental that this sort of thing sounds so close to contemporary urban marketing copy, whether offered by magazines like *Monocle* or by estate agents, when selling 'vibrant' inner-city neighbourhoods. Jacobs's densely populated, living vision won out comprehensively, in Europe and North America at any rate, against the long-obsolete dioramas of the world's fairs and architects' models; even the biggest developers, and the most enormous projects, now try to, in the words of Michael Bloomberg, 'build like Moses with Jane Jacobs in mind'. The editors of *Vital Little Plans* tell us that we live in a 'triumphant era of urban symphony', where the things that once marked Jacobs out as a subversive and eccentric – a love of street life, old and worn city-blocks, informality and small-scale capitalism – are total orthodoxy. Her pamphleteer language, vividly readable and unafraid of causing offence (or of caricaturing opponents) has been codified into town planning cliché: social exclusion, mixed use, mixed tenure, active frontages.

Reading between the lines of *Eyes on the Street*, however, the major reason for Jacobs's transformation from cranky freelancer to universally feted urban guru ('the Mother Teresa of urbanism', as Mike Davis, a rare dissenter from the church of St Jane, once put it) becomes her encounter with the slum, as concept and, decreasingly, as reality. It was the slum, for the planners of Radiant Garden City Beautiful, that made drastic urban transformation necessary. At first, Jacobs did not disagree with this. But gradually, between the 1930s and 1960s, she came to reject the notion that slums even existed. This can partly be blamed on the editors of the Soviet daily *Izvestia*. One of Jacobs's many freelance jobs was for *Amerika*, a magazine financed by the state department from the Second World War onwards as a showcase of American life for the Soviet market. Her work for this magazine – and her membership at that time of leftist institutions including the United Federal Workers and the American Labor Party – earned her surveillance from the FBI and a thick file during the McCarthy era. To her credit, she responded angrily to their enquiries, asserting (truthfully) that she had no sympathy with communism but condemning their surveillance in the strongest terms. While working for *Amerika*, Jacobs wrote a piece on contemporary American architecture. Published in the early fifties, at the height of the Cold War, the piece immediately elicited a hostile article in *Izvestia*, which pointed out her avoidance of the question of slums. In an era when, according to her subsequent collaborator Daniel Seligman, '17 million Americans live in dwellings that are beyond rehabilitation – decayed, dirty, rat infested, without decent heat or light or plumbing', this was a fair point, however much those slums might have looked rather desirable by comparison with the urban Soviet Union at the time. 'Let's see if we can't clear up what a slum is', challenged the *Izvestia* editors. Arguably, Jacobs would spend the rest of her career trying to do precisely this, by declaring the concept obsolete – that is, asserting that slums, as conventionally understood, didn't exist. The worst thing a place could be was not noisome, impoverished, dirty or crumbling, but boring; an insight she later expanded into the assertion that the worst thing an economy could be was stagnant. In the early 1950s, however, she still believed in replacement, rebuilding and the inevitable clearance that came with that, writing in *Amerika* of 'futuristic apartment complexes, slums erased, a new American cityscape replacing them'.

'A too-hasty glance', Kanigel writes of the famous house on Hudson Street from which Jacobs watched her ballet, 'might have suggested that (the Jacobs family) had moved into a slum.' It was rat-infested when they moved in, with a garbage dump in the yard, and they did a lot of work to make it nice – their own contribution to what Jacobs would later call 'unslumming'. The change in her perspective came when she started freelancing at *Architectural Forum* and began visiting the new projects that were replacing the slums. At first, she saw the work of Ed Bacon and the architect Louis Kahn in Philadelphia as a third way, between blanket clearance and laissez-faire. She even advocated the destruction of the city's old market – 'slum markets are like slum housing: there are big profits in them for some people, at the expense of all people' – but then, upon finding the small boy kicking his tyre around, she came to reject Bacon's Philadelphia, much as she did the work of Robert Moses in New York, which she had always disdained. The shift comes in a series of essays at the end of the 1950s, most importantly 'Downtown Is for People', published in the widely read paperback anthology *The Exploding Metropolis*, edited by William H Whyte under the auspices of *Fortune*, where the essays by Jacobs, Whyte, Seligman and English contributors Ian Nairn and Gordon Cullen were distinguished by the fact, unusual for the time, that they 'were written by people who like cities'.

Jacobs's argument in these essays – that cities can and should be understood on foot, by ordinary, non-expert people – gradually becomes an overwhelming fixation with the damage done to cities by *projects*. Here she uses an expanded definition which goes beyond just the conventional public housing project – the American analogue to the English council estate or the German *Siedlung* – to encompass any single-use development in the inner city, anything which has been zoned so that it is just housing, just industry, just culture, just business. The specific projects that offended Jacobs were the 'urban renewal' of much of East Harlem, moving the population into large, spacious high-rise flats such as the George Washington Houses, the 'middle-income' (a euphemism for what would now be called luxury flats) towers of Stuyvesant Town in Lower Manhattan, and the cultural 'ghetto' of the Lincoln Center, which itself faced a dense concentration of housing projects such as the Amsterdam Houses. These projects were, and are, heavily segregated in terms of class and race – indeed, only the ones that mainly housed working-class people of colour were

actually called 'projects' – but for Jacobs, they were all essentially the same thing, pieces of the deadly anti-city imposed on
the teeming life of America's greatest metropolis. The interiors,
facilities, living standards and maintenance all differed – as
did residents' perception of their new homes – but this was
all irrelevant. Each of them did the same thing: they killed
the street.

In the *Architectural Forum* essay 'The Missing Link in
City Redevelopment' – included in *Vital Little Plans* – Jacobs
rightly stressed the unthought-out consequences of destroying
the dense, multifunctional old streets and their replacement
with, at best, one or two 'community centers'. 'The stores
themselves', she pointed out, 'already work as "social centers",
especially the bars, candy stores and diners.' The ground-floor
units where the shops usually are were not solely used for
commerce, either. 'Most political clubs are in storefronts.
When an old area is levelled, it is often a great joke that ward-
heeler so-and-so has lost his organization. This is not really
hilarious.' And what were they replaced with? In the George
Washington Houses in East Harlem, she notes, there is a 'community center, but it is a children's center' … 'eradicating the
hand-to-mouth co-operative nursery schools, the ballet classes,
the do-it-yourself workshops, the little exotic stores which are
among the great charms of a city'. The replacements are utterly
inadequate, and because of this residents are forced to impro-
vise, creating social spaces out of what were intended as solely
functional entities: 'absolutely the only place that showed signs
of working as an adult social area was the laundry. And we
wonder if the planners of the project had any idea its heart
would be in the basement.' What *projects* do, Jacobs writes in
'Downtown Is for People', is, 'whatever the activity', to 'take
a part of the city's life, abstract it from the hustle and bustle
of downtown, and set it, like a magnificent island, in splendid
isolation'. Commerce here is big business: 'when a new building goes up' in these new, shiny, high-rent spaces, 'the kind of

ground-floor tenants it gets are usually the chain store and the chain restaurant'.

All of this was based on a fundamental lack of interest in what a city is, rather than what a city could be. 'No-one can find what will work for our cities by looking at the boulevards of Paris, as the City Beautiful people did; and they can't find it by looking at suburban garden cities, manipulating scale models, or inventing dream cities. You've got to get out and walk.' This sounds like excellent advice. It would certainly have been useful for the planners of the new Elephant and Castle to have got out and walked before they used Jacobs's lines to denounce the 'projects' of the Elephant and Castle, wilfully blinding themselves from the fact that they had all of the 'exotic stores', co-operative institutions and urban activity she claimed was impossible in an anti-street 'project'. The problem is that the primacy of walking eventually led Jacobs into a theory of urbanism based almost solely on what you'll see from wandering around. 'We are apt to think of big cities as equalling big enterprises, little towns equalling little enterprises. Nothing could be less true.' This is the sort of Jacobs slogan that sounds much smarter than it actually is – cities have long been as much a matter of big business as they are of 'mom and pop stores'. Her approach also tends to ignore the less pleasant aspects of small-time commerce. Her ethical, functional and economic preference for small business over big business, constantly reiterated in her work after *Death and Life*, would sound odd to many people who have ever rented from a small landlord, or worked for a small shopkeeper; when someone's livelihood depends on your rent or your work, discipline may well be more brutally enforced than it is by a distant, indifferent corporation or municipality.

What Herbert Gans, one of Jacobs's informants when writing *Death and Life*, called a 'blindness to race and class' comes out again and again from these essays, partly due to political changes Jacobs could not have anticipated. In 'A

Living Network of Relationships', a 1958 speech to the New
School, Jacobs describes an advertisement for the luxury Park
West development in Manhattan, a typical project in her terms.

> Three apartment houses set upon a vast meadow. The scene is
> more rural than anything within twenty miles of New York,
> let alone above 97th street and Amsterdam Avenue. 'Your own
> world in the heart of Manhattan', says the ad. This advertise-
> ment, objectively a lie, is unfortunately subjectively true. It is an
> honest picture of the fundamental rejection of the city which is
> part and parcel of New York's slum clearance and rebuilding
> program. None of us can have our own world in the heart of
> Manhattan.

If you weren't paying attention, this could sound like an attack
on the rich of Manhattan annexing space the city badly needs,
but that sort of rabble-rousing is quite far from Jacobs's intention. It wouldn't matter, qualitatively, for Jacobs, if it were
former slum residents given this 'vast meadow ... in the heart
of Manhattan'. It simply shouldn't be in Manhattan at all, for
it is the anti-city, a space that can only be wanly contemplated,
but which has no function, no use, no life, no point, a gratui-
tous, wasteful and dangerous void without eyes on the street.

'None of us can have our own world in the heart of London'
could be taken as a rallying cry by Southwark Council and
Lendlease in their densification and destruction of the projects of the Elephant and Castle. Within those slab blocks of
the Heygate Estate was a green, tree-filled environment – not
necessarily a vast meadow, but nonetheless a space with no
function other than to be pleasant and quiet for the residents
of one of the noisiest and most polluted places in Europe. The
architects of these projects would have congratulated themselves for the fact they made it possible for the London poor
to gaze out on a vista of trees and listen to birdsong right next
to two of the most congested roundabouts in Britain; such
spaces were intended to be a salve and a relaxation from lives

of hard factory and dock labour, and a relief from housework. None of this features for a second in the accounts of *Eyes on the Street*, or in the essays of *Vital Little Plans*. In Jacobs's city nobody suffers, except from the tedium-inducing consequences of urban renewal. Even aside from the old questions of slum housing – overcrowding, vermin, dilapidation, damp – nobody on Jacobs's street has a tiring and grim job, nobody is struggling to pay the rent, nobody has the anxiety of unemployment and nobody is much bothered about inequality, which barely exists. How could it, when the mainly black and Latino social tenants of George Washington Houses and the private owners at the whites-only Stuyvesant Town were actually in the same place without realising it?

Kanigel and Zipp/Storring are both refreshingly keen to point out how some of this was anticipated in criticism of *Death and Life* at the time of publication; for a book which has become such an unassailable classic, *Death and Life* received some very harsh reviews. A lot of this was a matter of attacks from vested interests, and offence was taken at Jacobs's lack of qualifications; there was pearl-clutching over her forthright language, often there was casual misogyny, and sometimes there were informed and serious critiques. The notorious attack by her former supporter Lewis Mumford, 'Mother Jacobs' Home Remedies', managed to combine all of the above. Some critics simply missed the point. One of *Death and Life*'s most poignant moments is an account of walking round Boston's North End with a planner, cheerfully discussing how well it works for the people who live there, only to be met with the response that, delightful as it is, it's a slum and it has to go. A Boston planner attacked the book because these Boston streets were 'no model', still flawed and impoverished; the fact that it wasn't a model but a normal flawed part of the city was exactly her point, she retorted.

But among the more penetrating critics were her former collaborators when she was working on the book, sociologists such as Gans, who accused her of recreating a 'physical fallacy' where buildings are given what another critic, the urbanist Kevin Lynch (whose *Image of the City* is otherwise close to Jacobs's preoccupations), calls 'a very singular power to change people's lives'. Ellen Lurie, who had shown Jacobs around the projects of East Harlem, was keen to point out that while many were bored and depressed by their new neighbourhoods, many more residents preferred their new flats, with their heating, running water, views and quiet. A conference in Chicago saw her refusal to discuss race to any substantive degree – in the American city of the fifties and sixties, of all places – met by residents pointing out that the packinghouse neighbourhood she praised was 'known to exclude black people'. *Death and Life* ends with a programme as rigid as any modernist plan, right down to fixing blocks to as short as possible a length so as to maximise street activity, and enforcing mandatory densities that would make everywhere as concentrated as Paris. Few of these latter recommendations have been followed. More criticisms would come later, when planners and developers and city governments would adopt some version of Jacobs's theories as a 'model'. Sharon Zukin argued recently that her obsession with planners meant that other actors in the modern city – developers, insurance – passed almost without comment. The planners and architects of public housing projects are certainly much easier to deal with, much less intrinsic to the workings of the capitalist city. Yet the insights into how planners refuse to consider the real life and typology of the existing city were so strong that the book couldn't be written off as charlatanry, as insights gained from walking expanded into an all-embracing urban theory. That came later.

Jacobs had a tendency to absolutism; in Gans's words, 'She imposes her tastes and values on the city more than any planner would dare to do.' That is richly evidenced by the insults she uses for those who don't share her liking for dense and loud inner cities. I happen to share most of her tastes and many of her values, and I agree strongly with Jacobs that the large city provides more visual pleasure and more excitement, is less wasteful of resources and less destructive of the environment than the suburban anti-city that she denounced – although I find it much harder to believe that the economies of these cities are necessarily stronger or more 'vital' than those of low-density sprawl, given that Newcastle and Pittsburgh are not notably more affluent and economically dynamic than Surrey and Silicon Valley. The problem is partly that her scorn for new towns and suburbs extended to those who moved into them. In fact, it seemed to baffle her that anyone could ever have chosen Levittown over the West Village, or Harlow over Stepney. In a now-famous passage, she wrote that Ebenezer Howard's garden cities – which would become official policy in Britain, with the post-war new towns – were 'really very nice towns if you were docile and had no plans of your own'. This is a weird way of looking at suburbia and new towns, and a dated one. In his *Lost World of British Communism*, Raphael Samuel recalls that Manchester's inter-war council suburb Wythenshawe, both a project and a Radiant Garden City Beautiful if ever there was one, was prime recruiting territory for radical politics, because it was inhabited by workers with the self-discipline and drive to move out of the slums, even if it meant paying more rent. The post-war new towns were most likely to attract people who had plans of their own, plans which involved getting themselves out of what they considered hopeless, dead-end places where they didn't want to bring up children, and embracing something new, fresh and modern; it was those who stayed in the inner city who were considered passive. Many early suburbs and new towns were places of joiners and activists, not of passive recipients, or 'children', yet this is exactly how Jacobs characterises them. Anyone who disagrees with her is an infant. New York 'is never going to get finished', she asserts against those planners who would have wanted it 'solved' by the provision of projects; and 'this should not really be discouraging to anybody over the age of eighteen'.

It was easy, as Mumford did, to argue that Jacobs's lack of interest in poverty and the real grimness of slum life came out of romanticism, and in being what would later be called a 'gentrifier', a middle-class incomer dazzled by the big city and making it her own. Jacobs did practise what she preached in this regard. Her commitment to inner-city industry, part of her disdain for any notion of zoning, was no joke. Kanigel recounts that

> the Fisher chemical warehouse was just down Hudson Street; [Jacobs's son] Jimmy, not much older than 12 at the time, would walk there for a litre of potassium chlorate, some sulfuric acid, potassium hydroxide pellets, and purple dye, pay for it with a little pocket money, and head home to concoct crazy 'experiments'.

He doesn't consider the less cutesy things that might happen when a child meets a large quantity of raw chemicals. Many parents may have been less laissez-faire about where their children played (one of the most startling facts in *Eyes on the Street* is that one of Jacobs's sons was illiterate at the age of nine, without her knowledge – she rectified the problem quickly).

Scornful as she was towards the escapees from the city, Jacobs was unusually sympathetic to the people who lived in the inner city and tried to make it work for themselves. Inner-city dwellers, used to being considered as a problem rather than as people, have accordingly often been grateful for her sympathy. Her explanation for why places like Greenwich Village had gone from being considered slums at the start of the twentieth century to the desirable places to live that they were already becoming when she wrote *Death and Life* was that their residents, rather than planners, governments or developers had 'unslummed' them. One of the most frustrating things in her work is her failure to explain exactly how unslumming happens, as it undoubtedly does. One explanation, which she certainly wouldn't have considered plausible, is that it was a knock-on effect of the garden city. Of her three adversaries, the garden city was the only one that didn't envisage clearance or erasure of the existing city – the point of it was to relieve pressure and overcrowding in the older cities by providing alternative new centres. Lecturing in Kraków in the 1910s, Ebenezer Howard was asked by his hosts what they should do with their city, which they held in low esteem. To their surprise, he answered that they didn't need to build a garden city, because they already had one – all they needed was to build a bit more workers' housing to alleviate overcrowding. The population of the big cities fell sharply in the post-war era, because of the new towns and the new suburbs, and it's very likely that this, along with full employment and increased education, gave slum residents the free time and breathing space to sort out their neighbourhoods themselves. The state and local government could do things for inner-city residents other than wield Robert Moses's self-described 'meat axe', but Jacobs wanted to limit authorities' field of activity as much as possible. After *Death and Life*, these urban strictures would be extended to cover the whole of economic activity.

The backhanded compliment of being Jane Jacobs's second-most-read book goes to the 1969 *Economy of Cities*. It is best known for its advocacy of import replacement, its folksy concept of 'new work', some penetrating comparisons and historical digressions, and some very ill-advised forays into speculative archaeology. The latter consists of her invention of New Obsidian, an imaginary metropolis which, she asserted, proved that cities actually preceded agriculture, an argument she based on her interpretation of the remains of Çatal Hüyük. She insisted that these theories would be widely accepted by archaeologists within a couple of decades, which has not proven to be the case. The rest of the book, much of which is reprised in essays featuring in *Vital Little Plans*, is less easily mocked, though is in many ways equally questionable. Her notion of 'the creation of new work' comes in a discussion of the problems of single-industry cities such as Manchester, and later Detroit, as compared with cities such as Birmingham and New York. The single-industry mass-production metropolis, which the likes of Marx and Engels expected to be the harbinger of the future, was actually a clumsy and lumbering thing which could achieve brief and rapid growth but would quickly collapse from its own inflexibility; when other cities learned how to mass produce textiles as Manchester did, Manchester became obsolete, whereas the metal trades of Birmingham, with their abundance of small producers and skilled workers, constantly produced splinters and side-effects, with each individual workplace able to create another workplace doing something different.

As far as it goes, this is accurate enough, but like so many of Jacobs's just-so oppositions, it isn't quite as clever as it looks. The future is Birmingham, she claims, and yet many of the megacities of the twenty-first century are industrial monoliths as inflexible and mass producing as Manchester – electronics assembly in Shenzhen, textiles in Dhaka, and so forth. That's because mass production was and is something that can create massive profits in the short term, but it is also because mass production is exceptionally useful if you want adequately to feed and clothe 7 billion people. *The Economy of Cities* attempts to create a theory of capitalism suited to the 1968 generation, a sort of Schumpeter for hippies, where the small tradesmen of Birmingham become the real drivers of technological and economic change; it is Schumpeter's emphasis on 'creative destruction' without the destruction, or any of the suffering that comes with it, with the Nietzschean entrepreneur replaced by the plucky, family-run small business.

The opposite of the dynamic economies that generate 'new work' are the stagnant monoliths of the projects. Yet these places have generated new things, and, in their way, new industries, usually in places where Jacobs wasn't looking, and particularly in music – the birth of the multi-billion-dollar industry that is hip hop from the projects of the Bronx in the late 1970s being an obvious example. For someone who appeared to love cities and modernity so much, Jacobs had an interesting lack of curiosity about twentieth-century culture, which is especially strange given how far her insights have been assimilated into the notion of a 'creative class'. 'Common sense' is her benchmark, and accordingly the often strange and discordant popular culture created in the projects as much as the streets of New York is beyond her remit. So too is much interest in art or architecture. A rare comment on aesthetics appears in her explanation of modern architecture's failure as the consequence of its excessive abstraction, caused by the loss of common sense. It's also possible that the new work generated by a city could be enormously destructive: organised crime is a trivial example, but much less so is the domination of New York after its 1970s crisis by finance, insurance and real estate, which are utterly unproductive and dubious in Jacobs's terms, despite being the main drivers of the 'triumphant era of urban symphony' that the editors of *Vital Little Plans* celebrate. As it is, *The Economy of Cities* was a philosophy of urban history that could only be found remotely convincing in the post-war boom, and as a critique of its fetish for Platonic, zoned, heavily planned megaprojects. To explain the twenty-first-century city with it would be a much more difficult proposition.

Jacobs's later books – *Cities and the Wealth of Nations*, or *Systems of Survival* and *The Nature of Economies*, the latter two written in a 'Platonic dialogue' form – inched her ideas closer to what is normally understood as neoliberalism. Her disdain for planning and state-driven development led her into some deeply odd claims, including that the Marshall Plan was a failure, based on the evidence of continuing poverty in Southern Italy. Her critiques of expressways – another of which she campaigned to block almost as soon as she moved, in the late 1960s, from New York to Toronto – now read as deeply prescient, despite being based on a silly distinction between 'foot people and car people' (if the two really were fixed categories, then the increased use of public transport, walking and cycling in many European and American cities would have been impossible). However, Jacobs had trouble with large-scale, inflexible publicly funded transport networks such as underground metros; she preferred something called the Carveyor, or StaRRcar, a sort of single-car, no-timetable, on-demand tram only ever built in Morgantown, West Virginia.

The lexicon changes in her later work, with the old dichotomies such as car people and foot people, pavement-pounders and Olympians, replaced by the more ambitious 'Guardians and Traders', who were the kind of people who worked in government and business, respectively. She liked to keep these apart, avoiding the 'monstrous moral hybrids' that were entailed by public–private partnerships. Certain things – policing, healthcare, prisons, schools – were guardian functions, and pretty much everything else – Jacobs was an early privatisation advocate, one of the founders of Canada's pro-privatisation Consumer Policy Institute – was to be left to the traders, including post and rail. As the bad place where the bad things happen, *project* was replaced by *plantation*, a stagnant mass-production typology which she apparently managed to separate from her alternative, the dynamic metropolises like London and Amsterdam which actually set up most of the world's plantations. In all this, the theory of new work developed in *The Economy of Cities* remains a constant. One example of her cutesy theory of technical change comes in the last essay in *Vital Little Plans*, where Jacobs describes how the frames of her glasses went from metal to plastic, due to technology transfer: 'plastics designed for toys, fishing rods and surfboards' ended up making her famous specs more comfortable. It's easy to list the major transfers from technologies developed in bad, stagnant projects such as the military and the space programme into similarly benign and domestic consumer goods, but that would upset the family-firm theory of capitalism. Kanigel ponders on what side of the political divides that emerged after the sixties Jacobs could be placed, and decides she was beyond conventional left–right dichotomies. This seems indulgent. Actually, with a few caveats, such as her liking for local democracy and opposition to private–public partnerships, Jacobs's ideas slot neatly into the 'third way' politics of New Labour and the New Democrats – a market economy, with the state's role limited to the maintenance of order.

Jacobs lived long enough to see her own ideas become an orthodoxy. Some of this she dealt with well, refusing to be flattered by her apparent disciples. As Zipp/Storring point out, Jacobs 'shared (with) modern architects and planners a whole-hearted belief in the primacy of function in design', and so she found the attempts of the New Urbanist movement to reconstruct the historic city (Celebration in Florida, Poundbury in Dorset, among others) to be largely facile – however much they looked like historic cities, these were projects, the Radiant Garden City Beautiful reincarnated, and their 'centres were not really centres'. Her responses to the new problems thrown up by the death of the planner-state and the life of the neoliberal market were barely adequate. She did anticipate the possibility of gentrification in *Death and Life*, as a possible consequence of too much success in unslumming, which would lead to increasing homogeneity as big business moved in. But she had little idea what could be done to stop it – many of the plausible instruments, such as rent controls or more public housing, weren't quite organic enough. She suggested the state help the new small businesses to buy their premises, which would have no effect whatsoever on the rise of rents in housing when a place becomes 'vibrant' enough to gentrify, but might well help cool places to stay cool. Asked about the problem that had made her Greenwich Village uninhabitable to all except the exceptionally rich (her Hudson Street slum house recently sold for $3 million) or the few lucky public housing tenants, she answered that 'it attested to how much people really *wanted* diverse and vibrant neighbourhoods'. The growth of the anticity in the 1960s meant that 'we stopped building places worth gentrifying' – so that 'demand outstrips supply', and that this is the reason for the rising rents. It's a breathtakingly flimsy response, and one which is easily falsified by the fact that many projects – such as the council estates of inner London – are already undergoing gentrification.

But it's not altogether clear whether it makes much sense to read Jacobs to understand London – or any other city outside the United States of America. The estates of, say, the London County Council are not particularly similar to the projects of Robert Moses, unless regarded superficially; and lack of maintenance, employment and public transport links, rather than spatial layout, have proven in most cases to be the conditions that turn an estate back into a slum, much more than whether an estate follows a conventional street plan. Moreover, American public housing projects were always intended as a stopgap, a means of getting people out of the slums, before they can get back on their feet and into private housing – building them to the standards of private housing would have been heavily criticised as tantamount to socialism. You can see this even in the one New York scheme in which Jacobs had a minor hand – the West Village Houses, an extensive project of infilling gap sites with new, low-rent, walk-up flats, successfully presented as an alternative to a mooted clearance and high-rise project. To an English eye, these look every bit as stark as the towers to which they were meant to be the polemical alternative; a blunt profile, tiny windows, dun brick, just like every other project in Manhattan. This parsimony of provision was seldom found in London or Vienna, where public housing was usually superior to private for much of the twentieth century; in Stockholm or Berlin, it was indistinguishable from private housing (one of the few European cities where such an obvious divide can be found is Paris, a city which, unlike New York, was essentially declared 'finished' in the 1960s, pushing new development into the *banlieues*). In none of these examples was the density of pre-clearance commerce replicated, but in exceptionally few of them were the only community spaces to be found in basement laundries.

When Jacobs refers, in her 1992 foreword to a reprint of *Death and Life*, to London's 'grandiose but bankrupt Canary Wharf project', which she believes destroyed the 'much-loved Isle of Dogs community', it is obvious she didn't know London very well. She remains an extremely American thinker. When, in a 1990s interview included in *Vital Little Plans,* she recounts how 'all my life I have had a couple of imaginary companions: Thomas Jefferson and Benjamin Franklin', she isn't joking, and is very much the writer who compiled a book of drafts of the US Constitution. Its values – a vigorous yeoman democracy, freedom of speech, freedom of capital and a wilful ignorance of the divides created by class and race – were her values. Accordingly, much of the power of her work – or at least, of *Death and Life* – comes from how accurately she described the homogenising effect of a public–private meat axe upon America's great cities. Transferred elsewhere, many of her ideas have the quality of a cargo cult.

However, London has followed her advice, as has every-where else. Sometimes, the results have been decent, in their own terms. On the subject of the dynamiting of St Louis's Pruitt–Igoe public housing scheme, she insists, 'I don't think things should be blown up ... we should learn to knit them back and make them part of the fabric of the city.' In one project, the South Bank Centre, our nearest analogue to the Lincoln Center, the monoculture of culture was soon supple-mented with skateboarders and second-hand bookstalls, and in the 1980s by the opening of the foyers to the public and new neighbours in the co-operative housing of Coin Street Community Builders; this was followed by more cultural megaprojects such as the Globe Theatre and Tate Modern, and, more recently, the public bodies who own the place have sold off little parcels of the site for chain restaurants and book-shops. The result is a hugely important and much-loved part of the city, albeit of a rather tamed sort.

Less than a mile away in the Elephant and Castle, the change came because the new shopping mall couldn't tempt the sort of chains dominant elsewhere – always a little point-less, with a largely poor population around it and the West End so nearby – and so the low rents of the units meant that shops serving the local community emerged there instead, encour-aged by the mall's owners who had let a messy street market fill part of the underpass below. The housing, offering as it did big, airy flats in the centre of London, went from being 'hard to let' to becoming a desirable commodity via the Right to Buy; a government office block by a famous architect opposite the Heygate Estate was turned into a block of luxury flats. Like much of London's more interesting spaces, it was suc-cessful because of a combination of capitalist investment not working quite as intended and social housing working exactly as intended. But it broke every single rule in the good book, in *The Death and Life of Great American Cities*. The new development, with its 'street food pop-ups', short street blocks, ground-floor shops, massively reduced open public space, densely packed flats and overwhelmingly private owners, is already ticking all of the boxes. I strongly suspect Jane Jacobs herself would have hated it.

July 2017

The Socialist Lavatory League

The Jubilee Line used to be one of the better London Under-ground lines to travel on if you have Crohn's disease. When it was extended in the late 1990s, some of the new stations – Green Park, Stratford, Canada Water, North Greenwich – were equipped with toilets, a great rarity on the Tube. They weren't very nice – if you were in the more than half of the population who sit down to use the toilet, you had to do so on a metal pan with no seat – but at least they were there. If you're liable to need urgently and frequently to use the toilet and yet you want to leave the house, it's nice to know that your means of transport has provided for you, albeit grudgingly. So, a couple of months ago, when my disease was in one of its active periods and I was on a journey from south-east to east London, I was urgently informed by my digestive system that I would need to get off early at Canada Water and use the facilities there; it was now or never, as I was about to change for the London Overground, a completely toilet-free line. As I got off the escalator, an unexpected sign read 'THERE ARE NO PUBLIC TOILETS AT THIS STATION'. *There bloody well are*, I thought, I know, I've used them, and so I walked towards them as quickly as I could, hoping at least that there was a disabled cubicle that I could open with my radar key. There was a toilet there, but it was locked and there was no hole for the radar key; instead there was a set of buttons to input a code – probably so that it could be used by staff at the adjacent bus station, as their legally mandated toilet facility. Luckily the library opposite was open late for some sort of youth theatre performance, otherwise my only option would have been a dirty protest.

This and similar experiences – not all of them such lucky near-misses – have been part of my life since my early twenties, when I first became ill with Crohn's; it has a variety of symptoms, with the results of chronic bowel inflammation being the most persistent and embarrassing. Much of the time the problem is relatively minor. Public toilets are a joke, barely existent in London. I sometimes amuse myself by imagining that there are people who actually take the municipal street signs seriously, and try to follow their arrows to a toilet, a mistake I learned early on not to make; but you can walk to the nearest pub and ask nicely, something helped by the official-looking Crohn's and Colitis UK 'Can't Wait Card' I carry with me. But when the drugs stop working – which they usually do around a week before each eight-weekly intravenous dose of Infliximab – more is needed. Recently, that drug atypically stopped working four weeks before the bimonthly dose, during a month when I had a large amount of travel planned. Living on soup and water, I used Google Maps to ascertain where cafes and service stations would be on my walks, looked up the facilities at every station on the Tyne and Wear Metro (toilets only at two interchanges with the bus network, if you're wondering) and ended up helpless on the way home from my sister's house in Catford at midnight, with the pubs closed and nowhere else to go.

I've written about this occasionally, but editors often find it to be *too much information* – I recall one description of the consequences of the lack of public facilities in Birmingham being removed from a work in progress by the editor at a left-wing publishing house because 'readers don't need to know this much about your bathroom needs'. Perhaps not. But as the Canadian journalist Lezlie Lowe points out in *No Place to Go*, those needs are not quite as unusual as they might appear. Near the end of the book, she quotes one expert estimate that at least a quarter of the population regularly needs to use public conveniences urgently. 'Seven percent have paruresis. Another 7 per cent are incontinent. You're already up to 14. You throw in menstruating women, parents with kids, people with ostomies … too many to count.' And yet it's a subject discussed in giggly terms, as if it's beneath us to talk about it, much less make policy around it ('go behind a hedge', toilet campaigner Clara Greed was told by the manager of Paddington Station, when she complained about the inaccessibility and inconvenience of their coin-operated 'conveniences'). Lowe contrasts this with disabled access, where a very similar issue – people being unable to use public spaces because they are designed as if their bodies do not exist – has led to firm legislation and widespread retrofitting, at least in the countries she focuses on (the US, UK and Canada). Rather than being an embarrassing and marginal problem, she finds that this failure of public provision brings together a wide range of issues – austerity, regeneration and re-urbanisation, gender, automation, the ageing of the population – all of which have direct bearing on whether or not you can find a public loo.

Her own account begins with the experience of trying to use a public space in an affluent, well-planned city – Halifax, in Canada – with young children. Halifax Common is, like so many others today, 'a place built for leisure. Unless, that is, you're the kind of person who uses the bathroom.' The facilities are rudimentary, frequently locked and badly designed, but 'every time I'm out with my infant and toddler, I need to change a diaper or respond to the urinary urgency of (my) children', and as a result she has to carry around a replacement pair of child's underwear in her handbag. Oddly, for a town that is so concerned with its place in Quality of Life rankings, it does not consider toilets to be a particularly important part of public infrastructure – recently, it published a Parks and Open Spaces Masterplan without mentioning them once. Lowe notes the usual explanations for this – the expense of upkeep, vandalism and, most of all, the fact that all sorts of people, such as drug users looking for places to inject, homeless people wanting a place to shelter and gay men meeting for sex, may want to use the park toilets as well as middle-class mothers. This is rooted in something fundamental in the attitude to the city: 'providing bathrooms means welcoming the world and being okay with it' – an acceptance that a wide and sometimes unsavoury cross-section of people will use the facilities. But 'keeping some out is more easily achieved by keeping everyone out'.

The book flits between historical accounts of the rise and fall of the public toilet and current attempts to try and make it workable in the present day. Naturally, this includes much material on the profound inequalities in the way toilets are designed – most of all, in the way that male and female toilets are designed to identical dimensions, despite the fact that women, as was statistically proven many decades ago, have quite different needs; even aside from such frivolities as make-up, it takes them longer to pee and longer to undress, and then of course there's menstruation. Lowe had an early and unpleasant realisation of this inequality as a child, pissing herself 'in the bathroom line at a community hall dance', as 'all the while, the boys' bathroom hung ajar, the light on, the room unoccupied. I could literally *see* the toilet. Not a single girl in that line made a move'. The world's first flushing public toilets were installed at the Great Exhibition in 1851, but the first permanent public toilets that also had provision for women were not installed until 1893 (on the Strand – it's a bar now). These inequalities have recently seen some attempted redress through the increased use of unisex toilets. Lowe gives the transphobic scare story about malevolent 'men' exploiting a newfound access to women-only spaces the short shrift it deserves, but notes that the de-segregated toilet brings about its own problems for those who adhere to orthodox religious rules about the non-mixing of the sexes. The solution – cubicles for everyone – would involve a large and expensive project of retrofitting, in a context where toilets are frequently barely provided at all.

The main focus of the book is the provision of public toilets per se, rather than their design. Here, Lowe finds the decline in Britain to be much more shocking than that of the relatively rudimentary networks of conveniences built in North America, where for the most part there was less of a legacy to destroy – with some exceptions, such as the New York Subway, where 1,500 toilets have been reduced to 75, due to 'security concerns'. In the UK, every town has often elaborately designed public toilets built from the late nineteenth century onwards, originally attended by permanent staff, as an inextricable part of the 'gas and water socialism' of the era, part of a general effort of urban democratisation, along with libraries, sewers and schools. It was uneven and discriminatory, but it was something rather than nothing. Lowe cites a 2016 Freedom of Information request that revealed a total of 1,728 public toilets had been closed in the previous decade. In London, half of all council-run public toilets have closed in the same period. One consequence is that 'some of London's ornate underground Victorian-era facilities are being sold off and transformed into kicky little cafes and hip restaurants' – and if you're polite and you look reasonably clean and together, they might even let you use their loos. Like other campaigns to preserve aspects of the British welfare state, the various efforts to save council toilets 'aren't for better provision, but to keep what's there now'. The incentives for councils under austerity to sell up their toilets and the land they sit on is enormous – as one council worker tells Lowe, you can sell a toilet for 4 or 5 million pounds, or you can spend half a million pounds maintaining it.

Ironically, given the conversely impressive efforts in expanding disabled access in Britain, one reason so many Victorian public toilets have been closed is the expense involved in providing for exactly that. Disabled access is now mandatory and statutory, which is not the case with respect to the provision of public toilets. So, given that it's expensive and fiddly to retrofit a Victorian loo reached by steep iron steps, it's much easier just to close it; the public loo is partly disappearing as the result of a conflict of different levels of rights, between the legally mandated and the merely advisory. Lowe refers to 'the British Standards Institution's Guide to Standardisation for public toilets', a precise and detailed fifty-four-page document rendered completely pointless by the fact that 'these universal best-practice standards aren't universally implemented, because they are voluntary'. One rare area where there is actual public toilet legislation, in the US, is in service stations.

'There's a master's thesis in this somewhere; bathrooms for pedestrians being replaced with bathrooms for drivers' – a useful indicator of what groups' needs the government thinks are worth legislating for.

Where public toilets have been erected in the last twenty years, they tend towards a particular model – the automated kiosk, with advertising bolted on to pay for it. This, like a lot of automation, sounds a lot more impressive than it is in practice. These are self-cleaning contraptions, obviating any need for the apparently grim and degrading profession of toilet attendant (or for anyone to need to pay their wages), which let you use the box for a certain amount of time, to deter rough sleepers, and when you're out they completely wash and dry themselves. The technology is fine, but it's the aspects that need human assistance that are the problem. There are seldom seats, in case they get ripped out, soap and paper are often absent, and then there are the UV lights, which are often used to make it hard for heroin users to find a vein – which, Lowe finds, have the unintended side-effect of encouraging more people to use them for sex, as many apparently find the lights erotic. 'Even the boon to operators – that automated bathroom fixtures lessen the need for human oversight – isn't an absolute given,' Lowe notices.

> When automated flushers and faucets and hand dryers stop working, no human is there to know except the users, who have, precisely as a result of automation, been alienated from the space and feel no need to go out of their way to report, for example, a non-flushing and rapidly filling clogged toilet.

There is some acknowledgement in a couple of American cities that these often vandalised and bleak coin-op kiosks aren't good enough. Lowe points to the Pit Stop programme, developed by advertisers JCDecaux in San Francisco. These provide various things that others don't – needle disposal units, and receptacles for compost, recycling, dog waste – but most importantly, 'they are staffed. That's it', albeit by 'former state prisoners paid sixteen dollars an hour'. The attendant does some crucial things – maintaining the queue, making sure only one person goes in at a time and making sure the toilet is clean and stocked with paper and soap. The scheme saw a massive rise in public toilet use in the city, with the Pit Stops used 'not only by homeless people, with limited access to indoor bathrooms, but also by tourists, families with young children, and other people with unconventional toilet needs', such as Uber drivers. This is the profit-making version of the idea; but the municipal Portland Loo scheme in the Oregon city provides a similarly high-quality, staffed service.

If automation is not the solution, and if it's hard to imagine local governments as they currently exist and are currently funded paying for upgrades, attendants and maintenance of existing loos, the usual response is to encourage people to use the facilities in malls, pubs and cafes. This is the approach taken by Manchester City Council, which has closed every single one of its public loos in the city centre. 'Go behind a hedge' has been replaced with 'go and use Starbucks'. This has multiple problems. As Rudy Giuliani's former deputy mayor Fran Reiter admits, 'You know as well as I do that if some homeless person, some bag lady, walks into Tiffany's, they are not going to let her use the toilet.' Lowe points out that this provision is almost entirely conditional on spending money in said place before staff will give you the code or the key. Shopping malls, meanwhile, tend to signpost their toilets in a deliberately oblique manner, intended to keep you endlessly circling around the mall – I remember walking, flushed and desperate, around a mall in East Kilbride for about ten minutes before I eventually found what I was looking for.

The problems with this 'solution' are probably encapsulated by something I watched in a Nottingham Starbucks, next to the railway station. For reasons best known to themselves, the staff lock the toilets at 6 p.m., some hours before the cafe closes. A local 'character' lingered around, telling the many people who walked in the direction of the loos that they were now closed; he could probably have been gainfully employed to attend some actual functioning public toilets. Lowe suggests that the free-to-all toilets of public libraries are a good alternative to the purchase-conditional facilities in the mall or the cafe. She evidently hasn't been told – as I was recently by the librarian at Chandler's Ford Library, Eastleigh – to use the toilets in Waitrose instead, as 'we don't have any'.

Of course, as Lowe points out, they do. Every single workplace that has a roof (and some that don't, like building sites) in Britain and North America does, because they have to, by law. That doesn't mean, 'Can't Wait Card' notwithstanding, that they're going to let members of the public use them. I briefly had a job compiling traffic surveys on a busy junction in London suburbia, for Colin Buchanan and Partners, in the morning rush hour. The inevitable happened, and I had to ask the places that were open – newsagents, the Post Office – if I could use their staff toilets, and was politely told that I could not in each one of them (I quit the job soon after). One of Lowe's interviewees, who has Crohn's, points out to her that whereas 'people with physical disabilities – the ones others can see – have fought hard to have their accessibility needs met, and they've mostly won', those who have diseases that can't be seen have so far had little of the same success. This is now starting to change, albeit slowly. 'Not all Disabilities are Visible' signs on disabled toilets are a minor but widely discussed example; Jeremy Corbyn wore a Crohn's and Colitis UK badge at Prime Minister's Questions for Crohn's and colitis awareness week in December 2018. Yet there is no new policy. The nearest thing to this has been in the Welsh Assembly, where the Public Health Bill drafted in 2014 by then health minister (and now Welsh Labour leader) Mark Drakeford included provisions for the first time to make it legally mandatory for all local authorities to have a 'public toilet strategy'. The bill was defeated, largely because it also included strict restrictions on the smoking of e-cigarettes in public places, which antagonised Plaid, the Tories and the Lib Dems. Typically, this wasn't an important enough policy to stand on its own, and was abandoned because of something completely irrelevant to it.

So it continues – whether it's a local authority in the Valleys or a powerful infrastructural behemoth like Transport for London, every public body in Britain is washing its hands of public toilets, to be partially replaced with cafes and malls that may or may not let you use their private toilets. This is obviously not going to work. Lowe's Crohn's interlocutor leads her on to an extremely radical solution, but one which is increasingly the only possibility, given the scale of the closures. The key issue, if you have Crohn's or colitis, isn't what sort of toilet there is, but that you can use it, and immediately, regardless of whether or not it has glory holes, needles or a 50p charge – the point is that it exists. 'Help for people with most diseases of the bowel comes not from design modifications, but by way of fast and easy access to bathrooms. Everywhere.' It 'boils down', she writes, to the following request: 'Please, stranger, let me use your bathroom right now, because I really, really need it'. Any legal provision for people with Crohn's or colitis on the scale of that which has been made for those who can't walk will have to factor this in. Accordingly, austerity makes something very dramatic suddenly quite thinkable – the legally mandated public use of private toilets. In 1973, Kenneth Tynan wrote the following in his *Diary*.

> During the night I have a dream in which I join a subversive organisation called the Socialist Lavatory League. Its purpose is to bring all private loos into public ownership. Everyone will have the right to use anyone else's loo – which will mean the end of private peeing. The dream wakes me up giggling, but on reflection I don't think it is all that bad an idea.

There is some considerable irony in the fact that it is as a result of the complete abandonment of any concession to one of the most basic human needs – unless it can be used to generate profit – that we can now imagine the utopian dream of the Socialist Lavatory League actually coming to pass.

May 2019

5

Screens

The screens in these four pieces are those of television, cinema and the internet, and with the exception of the essay on Peter Mettler's *Petropolis*, they bring us back to the place where we (or rather, I) began. That is, blogs, in the middle 2000s, and the group of depressive, overeducated and underemployed (mostly) men and (sometimes) women who self-published them. In much the same way that the blogs were an attempt to try and recreate some of the pop-modernist culture of a relentlessly dumbed-down music press, they were also a reaction to the way in which the likes of Channel 4 and BBC2 went from providing public access to the work of the avant-garde, into becoming the home of reality TV and 'let me take you on a journey' documentaries.

Because of these absences, we did have to 'make our own fun', so to speak. A rare attempt to take that particular scene out of a tightly bound south London clique and into a public space was a film club, Kino Fist, where we would screen double-bills of, say, *The Bed-Sitting Room* with *Threads*, at warehouse 'spaces' in the London Borough of Hackney. The 'Boredom' event entailed screening, back-to-back, Michael Haneke's horrendously bleak *The Seventh Continent* with Věra Chytilová's exuberant *Daisies*; my blog post on the latter, printed here, had nearly been worked into my first book, but was left out for reasons I can't remember. It is closely tied to the PhD thesis on Soviet Americanism I was working on part-time at Birkbeck College; part of this, on slapstick comedy, was eventually published by Pluto Press several years later as *The Chaplin Machine*. The *Daisies* post itself was written in response to a thread on the forum Dissensus, which was set up by Mark Fisher and Matthew 'Woebot' Ingram; conversations often devolved into scraps between musical and intellectual factions, and this was the result of one of these scraps.

The last essay here is in memory of Fisher, to whom I owe an enormous personal debt – I was practically adopted in 2005 by the group of bloggers for whom he was the obvious leader. To me, they were already celebrities of a sort; I would say to myself in amazement, 'I am sitting in a cafe, with K-Punk and Infinite Thought.' The resultant friendships did not last, but they were extremely intense while they did. Partly because of this I published this review of the anthology of Fisher's work initially in Russian in the journal *Emergency Rations*, edited by Kirill Kobrin, one of those Russian figures who resemble English pop culture critics in the breadth of their interest in culture both high and low. I was nervous about the piece, but a few years later I don't think publishing it in English will upset anybody; it is certainly not intended to. Meanwhile the article on Adam Curtis reverses this focusing on how the internet has gradually affected the work of the last Reithian at the BBC – the unexpected meeting point of the online self-publishing culture we were creating in the 2000s, and the 1950s–1980s public media culture we were so nostalgic for.

Decadent Action: Věra Chytilová's *Daisies*

*For all those who are soured by the sight of trampled-down
lettuce – only!*

In a recent Dissensus thread on film, the questions of anti-
naturalism, Bertolt Brecht, 'laying bare the apparatus' and
other *Measures Taken* hobbyhorses came up a few times. One
of the more common objections to this approach, which runs
through the epic theatre to late-sixties film and post-punk, is
that without naturalism, representation and identification one
is left only with intellectual aridity, political grandstanding,
'greyness' – an argument which has much in common with the
idea that, without capitalism, our society would be denuded
of its colour, its abundance of sensations, its chaotic cities, its
sexuality and the hyperactivity of its culture industry. This is
of course reinforced by the perception that the various forms
of 'actually existing socialism' from 1917 to 1989 were one
enormous bread queue, presumably in front of a grey concrete
building housing a state bureaucracy of some description.

At various points in this history though, there are sudden
outbreaks of violent colour, of an anti-naturalism which
entirely sidesteps the international style and its Platonic greys
and whites. Some particularly violent examples are the late-
1920s posters of the Stenberg brothers, sculptors turned movie
advertisers. Without ever falling into the mere picturesque of
art nouveau or its sixties revivals, their designs are dialectical
juxtapositions in green and red, depictions of cinematic conflict by angle and gesture. Most striking is their implicit link
between movement, futurist dynamism and colour – a synaes-
thesia that recurs here and there, such as in Sergei Eisenstein's
writings on contrapuntal colour, and in the ANS, an enormous
synthesiser residing in the terrifying totalitarian-gothic edifice
of the Moscow State University and most famously played by
Eduard Artemyev on the soundtracks to *Solaris* and *Stalker*,

that relies essentially on 'painting' a sound, creating discrete, shimmering chromatic stabs.

Or, from Czechoslovakia just prior to its brief experiment in 'socialism with a human face', there is the extraordinary formalism of Věra Chytilová's 1966 film *Daisies*: one of the most stunning profusions of effects, colours and jarring techniques in cinematic history, a film utterly in love with its own aimless exuberance. It has always been treated somewhat sniffily, both by the apparatchiks who banned it and by Western critics, for whom the film failed to conform to the sombre mode of East European film – no struggles against a Kafkaesque bureaucracy, no method-acting male heroes, no interminable Kunderan love affairs and an irritatingly ambiguous political import, as the film could be interpreted easily enough as Stalinist, consumerist, sexist, feminist or anarchist, depending on one's prejudice. More precisely, the director herself described it as being about 'destruction or the desire to destroy'.

The plot, such as it is, follows two young women, Marie 1 and Marie 2, who decide (to a montage of newsreel footage showing destroyed cities and collapsing buildings) that as the world is 'spoiled', so will they be. The acting channels the constructivist infatuation with Charlie Chaplin, who incarnated their principles by transforming himself into a marionette ('Chaplin is not human' – Gilbert Seldes). Similarly, Marie and Marie decide that they are 'dolls', and act accordingly: in the opening scenes the movement of their joints sounds like the creak of a door, walking round the room produces a metallic clatter. Their 'spoiling' takes the form, first of all, of going on innumerable dinners with older men, in order to eat and drink as luxuriously as possible. This escalates until, eventually, they receive an ambiguous comeuppance.

An example of how the film 'works' can be seen in the section where the two Maries go to a restaurant to see a dance act. As an Eastern Bloc ragtime plays, a man and a woman do twenties-style dances, dressed in flapper-era garb. The girls get progressively more and more drunk and begin breaking things, annoying the other guests. The dancers are suddenly unnerved, frown worriedly between their moves – the other customers make complaints, and Chytilová disrupts the action by constantly changing the colour filter, draping the restaurant either in an art film grey or in sudden, severe reds and greens, the beer flowing over the table becoming a kaleidoscope of coloured bubbles. The music is reminiscent of the dialectical film music advocated by Hanns Eisler and Theodor Adorno, which would be contrapuntal, working against whatever was on screen – the music playing is clearly from a live recording, and as the diners become more irked and the staff more disgruntled, there are ecstatic cheers and applause. The girls make themselves a spectacle, create from their everyday life something more than passivity – the dance of destruction is slightly reminiscent of the end of Jacques Tati's *Playtime*, though without Tati's humanism, without his sense of a public.

The film is a depiction of gross abundance and profligacy, and takes the same approach to its own construction. The effects that it uses are there purely for themselves – take for instance a scene in which a train departing from a station is abstracted into kinetic, opposing, multicoloured lines, for no purpose other than excitement. Appropriately for a film so brutally edited (it clocks in at around seventy minutes) the Maries are fixated with cutting, taking a pair of scissors to everything from food to magazines, creating in their room an array of magazine photographs, scribbles, depictions of abundance. In one ecstatic scene this escalates to them chopping off each other's limbs, heads, until in a scissor fight the entire frame is cut up into millions of tiny pieces, dancing around the screen. They secede from the human decisively here, their transformation making them no longer subject to the laws of physics.

Remember the one who kept asking 'what will happen to us!
What will happen to us!'?
The one who died?

As described, *Daisies* might sound like mere individualism, a joyous consumerist protest interrupted by a statist bureaucracy. The film was critiqued by its censors for similar reasons, for the amount of food squandered on screen. Chytilová maintained that in fact the film was a critique of consumerism taken to its limit – and however much the film might glory in these devourings, it would be difficult to find in it a simple celebration of consumption. The Maries seem to need constantly to prove their own existence. In one scene, finding a trail of their own half-eaten vegetables, they joyously march along chanting 'we are, we are, we are!' – they can only define themselves if there is something that definitively bears their mark. At another point they seem accidentally to walk into a socialist–realist film, as Czech men cycle down cobbled streets on their way to work through a romantically misty morning. Horrified, they realise that not one of them notices their presence.

The protagonists' action is essentially based on an aggressive infantilism, a total refusal of the adult world – though not the kind of infantilism that marks late capitalism, where one has to pretend to be fourteen in order to cope with colossal working hours, etc.; this is an utterly dogged and dangerous infantilism. For all their bikinis, short skirts and dating of various deluded men, Marie 1 and Marie 2 are asexual. In one scene one Marie attempts a mock-seduction of a butterfly collector, though when finally at risk, pleads 'do you have any food in the house? At least some jam perhaps?' Instead, the girls' behaviour marks a collusion in their own commodification. At the film's end, they stumble onto a military-industrial complex, and carry on their campaign of destruction therein. Straying accidentally into an imposing building, all bare ducts and pipes and warning signs on the wall, they walk into a food elevator, past a kitchen and a symphony orchestra, and then arrive at a table laid for a rather unsocialist-looking baroque banquet. Their gleeful destruction of this is what finally elicits censure and leads to their punishment.

You really mean something serious? That something is?

Bookending the film are images of terrifying destruction, newsreel filtered through the same demented chromatism as the rest of the film. A camera flies over a blitzed city. A missile connects with a ship, an atomic bomb explodes. Destruction takes various forms: the minor destructions perpetrated by the Maries, and the actual, life-destroying destruction carried out by power. There is no ostensible moral or conclusion in *Daisies*, presumably the reason for its unpopularity; if watched at all now, it's generally considered as an odd, psychedelic curio or as a piece of titillation. Rather, it is a film unique both in terms of its experimentalism – the film is *sui generis*, has had no noticeable trace in cinema since – and in its radical ambiguity. The shortages and grimness that supposedly characterise state socialism are totally absent; instead we have circumstances that could be easily transferred to our own society, in which war and famine appear to happen elsewhere while smoking and eating too much salt are legislated against, in which an ever-present sexualisation masks a virulent puritanism, and in which deferred resistances are made through hyperactive conspicuous consumption. The difference is that the protagonists of *Daisies* refuse to stop – they consume and consume until finally power has to force them to stop.

January 2006

The Petroleum Sublime

One of the most sad and beautiful sights in Britain is offered by a place called Fawley, on the edges of Southampton. This is the site of an enormous Esso oil refinery, the largest in the country, and at one time in Europe. It is best viewed from the other side of the estuary, from the serried tower blocks and blasted shingle beach of Weston Shore, or the park where the almost equally vast Netley military hospital used to be. What you see is a skyline of chimneys of elaborate, picturesque complexity, their tubular steel winding into mindbogglingly complex patterns and tentacular lattices. Container ships and oil tankers slowly make their way up and down the waterway, and at night, when the flames from the top of the pipes is combined with bright, multicoloured lighting, Fawley is a magnificent, glittering metropolis, an entire city of oil, a deeply unflattering contrast with the rather more prosaic city of people a couple of miles back up Southampton Water.

Fawley was the site of an oil spill in summer 2010, where a leak from one of the tankers led to the temporary closure of the beach on Weston Shore. This event did not receive as much press coverage as it might have done, for the entirely unsurprising reason that it paled in comparison with another, much more vast and terrifying spill in the Gulf of Mexico, the largest in history. The images of the spill caused by an explosion at the Deepwater Horizon drilling rig were not of gleaming manmade refineries, but of nature defiled, of animals choked by the viscous black fluid, which seemed unstoppable through nearly the whole year, an almost unsolvable problem. All the horrors of the dying oil economy – the social atomisation and spiralling death rate caused by the motor car, the neocolonial resource wars, the extraction of oil from ever more unlikely places, the apocalyptic effects of burning even the oil we know we have left, Sarah Palin – seemed to coalesce into this image of a leak that couldn't be plugged. Yet the iconography of petroleum has had a presence in film and photography over the last decade which, even when critical of its increasingly devastating effects, has also registered the sublime qualities of its structures, and the harrowing beauty of the landscapes it has transformed.

The latter is the subject of one Peter Mettler's elegiac 2010 documentary *Petropolis*. The film, funded by Greenpeace, consists of a series of aerial tracking shots of the Alberta tar sands, a huge extraction project in Canada. It takes a God's-eye view of a project of truly improbable scale, swooping over the bituminous sands and the industrial structures that pockmark them, an entirely alien moonscape. Despite its activist funding, it keeps a contemplative distance from the material, with the pin-sharp digital film making it sometimes resemble an apocalyptic *SimCity*. Clouds gradually fade into the plumes coming from the bitumen upgrader, while the camera spins around effortlessly. There is no sense of a 'human scale' in this man-made space, but the moment when a human being is the focus is one of the most vividly estranging – the camera pans out from a lone figure to a perfectly rectilinear, illegible structure resembling a Mesoamerican ziggurat. More often, we veer from the refineries – awesome in their complexity, both the mathematical and the dynamic sublime – and the landscapes, which look as though they've been scrawled over, vandalised. The overwhelming impression is of something uncontrollable – man-made as it is, the tar sands appear as a force of nature, of such massive scale that the process, once set in motion, can't possibly be reversed, and all we can do now is contemplate the enormity of what we have done. The impression is reinforced by the film's soundtrack, which veers between silence and an advancing drone that suddenly cuts out when the tracking shot ends, the noise of a (temporarily) postponed disaster.

Perhaps there's a bad faith in this. What Mettler films is, in its traumatic and horrifying way, deeply beautiful, and any inflammatory or agitational quality is quickly replaced by awe. The film's credits cite photographer Edward Burtynsky, whose compendious 2009 collection *Oil* is still the most astonishing presentation of the petroleum sublime; in its introduction, Burtynsky admits that the initial motivation was 'a sense of awe at what we as a species were up to', and that awe, mixed with horror, the picturesque and a certain amount of *Neue Sachlichkeit* pervades his photographs, the contemporary equivalents of Romantic painter John Martin's transfigurations of the industrial revolution into visions of Hell. They're thrilling when they show the cities oil built – the Cyclopean expressways of Shanghai, the skyline of Detroit – and have a malevolent grandeur when depicting the aftermath, the drained, deserted world of rusting derricks and collapsing platforms in Azerbaijan, formerly the Soviet Union's petroleum belt. No doubt aware of Brecht's admonition that a photograph of a factory tells us almost nothing about the relations inside, *Oil* is partly made up of analytical texts on the history of its subject, contextualising the awesome, awful images.

Another recent book takes a more specific, if less analytical approach, though shares with *Petropolis* and *Oil* a certain elegiac quality, the sense of something ending, albeit dying the most violent, unwilling death. Mitch Epstein's *American Power* depicts petroleum as an inescapable product of the American Century, and its desuetude as a symptom of its decline. Photographed mostly in the mid-2000s, while the Iraq war raged far enough away to be only an implicit reference ('Terror-Free Oil', claims one petrol station) it takes satiric glee in showing how the American dream of anti-urban dispersal and cute dream homes relies on the most massive, ultra-modern structures. Cooling towers overshadow weatherboarded bungalows, holiday-makers survey scarred landscapes. The most emblematic photograph shows the BP Carson Refinery in California decorated with a large, torn Stars and Stripes flag. The implication, here and elsewhere, is that the US will give up oil over its dead body, and the images of wind farms that are interspersed through the concrete and steel in *American Power* seem unlikely to induce the same sense of nationalistic identification and affection.

Mettler, Epstein and Burtynsky all try to hold on to a critique of some sort, to combine awe and ethics. This is markedly absent in the work of a less famous photographer, the Slovakian Branislav Kropilak. His series 'Factories' is entirely made up of refineries, all shot at night. It's pure formalism, a concentration on effects: the metallic sheen, the glaring lights and the tint of rust upon the intersecting pipes and uncanny domes of an entirely generic complex, rendered with a cold but adoring eye. It's a work of aestheticisation, and among other things Kropilak's work is a reminder of how much twentieth-century architecture – from constructivism to Archigram to Richard Rogers's Lloyd's Building – is essentially a more polite, more artistic version of these places. There is no terror, no sense of approaching collapse in these images, only a precise gaze at the improbable formal achievements necessitated by functional processes. They're decontextualised, depoliticised and utterly beautiful.

Most of all, Kropilak captures the seeming irrationalism, the uncanniness of the refineries, presenting images of a weirdly organic technology, the pipelines' endless connections and intersections displaying an industrial non-aesthetic seemingly more inspired by fevered dreams than calm *Sachlichkeit*. Although unfortunately the 1970s did not throw up a programmatic text on 'Learning from Fawley Refinery', this kind of structure is one of the main inadvertent parents of high-tech architecture. As supported by Reyner Banham's debunking of the international style's pretensions to up-to-the-minute technology in *Theory and Design in the First Machine Age*, such spectacles showed an industrial aesthetic that was neither calm nor ordered, that had little in common with the serene Platonic volumes Le Corbusier saw in grain silos. Instead they were busy, seemingly chaotic, overcoded and overdetailed, wildly impure. Banham himself, in the 'Non-Plan' he composed in 1969 with Cedric Price, Peter Hall and Paul Barker in a famous issue of *New Society*, imagined giving Fawley *son et lumière*, recreating it as a visitor attraction.

It would be strangely Ruskinian to suggest that the refineries are beautiful *because* of their fulfilment of function, especially given that their complex nature means the function can only be guessed at by someone looking at them for aesthetic reasons. But they raise an intriguing question – what is the appropriate form for an honestly technological architecture in (very) late capitalism? As everywhere, when you look for a genuinely contemporary industrial architecture, you find the buildings of today's production and distribution centres, as profiled with lugubrious relish in Chris Petit's *Content* – you find gigantic, blank, rectilinear distribution sheds, an architecture more bare, more white, more Platonic and more blandly pure than a Corbusier could possibly have wanted. The aesthetics of extraction and refining have a Faustian drama completely lacking from the seamless world of the Big Sheds.

The industrial romanticism of Kropilak's *Factories* is reminiscent of 'Stanlow', a song on Orchestral Manoeuvres in the Dark's 1980 album *Organisation*. The song refers to a large Shell oil refinery in Ellesmere Port, Merseyside, where singer Andy McCluskey's dad worked, and it is already a lament as much as a hymn to a dying faith in human technological achievement. 'We set you down to care for us, Stanlow ... a vision fading fast, Stanlow'. In almost all these various meditations on the dubious and thrilling aesthetics of petrol, there is a sense of imminent disappearance, but also an astonishment at the sheer scale and drama of construction and industry, an impulse which could so easily be put to less destructive use. Near the climax of *Petropolis*, a brief voiceover tells us how many million years the sun has left to live, and then states that petroleum has only been extracted in the current manner for eighty years. It then asks – over alternately poignant and alarming images – the question 'what will we do next?' It sounds open, promising.

January 2011

And Then the Strangest Thing Happened ...

When Adam Curtis's new documentary *HyperNormalisation* premiered on the BBC's online iPlayer service last autumn, the journalist Chris Applegate compiled an 'Adam Curtis Bingo' card that circulated widely on Twitter and Facebook. The card contained many of the tropes that have become extremely familiar in the documentary filmmaker's work over the last twenty years. With this simple game, you could have a drink whenever Curtis's distinctive, slightly harsh Received Pronunciation narration – what used to be called BBC English – began with 'this is the story of ...' or 'but one man ...'; when he asserted that so-and-so 'was convinced that ...' over 'electronic bleeps and bloops' and imagery that included 'grainy film of oil sheiks' or 'footage of old-timey computers and reel-to-reel tapes'. 'A disturbing vision of humanity' might be outlined while a 'Burial track plays', and a montage of ''80s Russian punk musicians' and 'people in the '50s or '60s dancing' could accompany a story about a group of men whose 'aim was to create a new world, one which ...' 'Aerial footage of a city at night' would suddenly switch to an 'ominous foreshadowing shot of the World Trade Centre'. It was all very accurate, though by now, the director's tropes are familiar enough to have spawned their own subgenre: the Adam Curtis parody video. There are several on YouTube, all of them trying – with varying degrees of success – to ape the voiceovers, the montages and the general ominousness.

The dramatic Curtisism 'but one man thought differently' occurs in each of the parodies, but in *HyperNormalisation*, the 'one man' is Curtis himself. 'What was meant to be a ...' – a declaration of counter-propaganda – here turns out to be something quite different and more modest: a mere reflection of the filmmaker's own very personal version of recent history. *HyperNormalisation* is the Curtis film that most resembles the parodies. There is nothing in it he has not done before, except that – as with 2015's *Bitter Lake* – his pace is increasingly relaxed, with lengthy, drifting, wordless sound/image juxtapositions that feel closer to contemporary 'artists' film' than anything on television. You could read this languor generously, as a conscious new direction in Curtis's work. Or it could simply be the sign of burgeoning self-indulgence, the kind of thing cult figures often become susceptible to. Or perhaps, at this late stage in his career, Curtis is deliberately producing self-parody in order to please a semi-ironic fan-base, in a contorted attempt to comment on the very medium – the internet – that has transformed his approach.

Curtis's highly distinctive style emerged fully formed in three multi-part documentary series he made for BBC2 between 1992 and 1999 – *Pandora's Box*, *The Living Dead* and *The Mayfair Set*. With the exception of the Burial soundtrack (they hadn't yet made any records) and footage of the World Trade Center (it hadn't yet been destroyed), all three would lead to severe intoxication after a game of Adam Curtis Bingo. You can see nascent Curtisisms in his earlier films – such as *The Great British Housing Disaster* (1984), on the failures of industrialised housing in the UK, or *The Road to Terror* (1989), on the way the Iranian revolution came to devour its children – but these 'current affairs' documentaries, which you could imagine airing on the History Channel, are much more conventional than the later work. The authoritative voice – here, not Curtis's own – is less mannered, the montage a little less delinquent.

The Great British Housing Disaster tracks, through archive and specially shot footage, as well as interviews with major protagonists (such as Newcastle City Council boss T. Dan Smith, then only just released from prison for corruption), the way the housing crisis created by the dual legacy of Victorian slum-building and war damage was supposed to be resolved by mass production – and how the shoddiness and built-in obsolescence of that production led to a wholly new set of problems. The narrative would become familiar – left-leaning technocrats in alliance with finance and industry creating something that was not at all what any of them expected – but at the time this was not a familiar angle of approach. The documentary's subject is the intersection of naive local governments, a particularly short-termist industry and a poorly understood and even more poorly deployed technology, rather than a then-commonplace – and ultimately less disturbing – narrative: that you could blame urban failure entirely on the pipe dreams of sinister architects and planners obsessed with concrete, 'cities in the sky' and Le Corbusier. Curtis bends the facts a tad, however: the tracking shots of concrete high-rises (now rather piquant in their starkness and graininess, perfect sample material for present-day Curtis) frequently scan towers that aren't system-built and that still stand today. The film's final assertion – that the policy by local authorities to reclad badly built prefabricated towers with layers of insulation would create its own set of technical disasters – appeared not to have been borne out – at least, not until the Grenfell Tower fire, which was far more lethal than the collapse at Ronan Point (ironically, Grenfell itself was not system-built and was only made unsafe *by* its cladding). Meanwhile in *The Road to Terror*, the authoritative voice disappears altogether, with a first-person narrative of bereavement running through the opening sequences. The film's lingering shots of atrocity would re-emerge in Curtis's more distinctive later work, as would the repeated obsession with revolution and its unintended consequences.

But leap just three years to *Pandora's Box*, in 1992 (billed, typically, as 'A Fable from the Age of Science' – Curtis always coyly and disingenuously claims to be a mere 'storyteller'), and you have practically everything you'll find in *HyperNormalisation* twenty-four years later. Part 1, 'The Engineers' Plot', deals with the defeat of Soviet central planning via the heroic Taylorist future envisaged by the Proletkult poet Alexei Gastev; Stalin's ambiguous relationship with engineers – who were essential for five-year plans, but also victims of the first show trials;

and the USSR's abortive experiments in the 1960s with decentralised planning via cybernetics and computerisation. 'To the Brink of Eternity' covers the RAND Corporation, game theory and mutually assured destruction; 'Black Power' is on Kwame Nkrumah's Ghana and the fate of his non-aligned pan-African socialism; 'A is for Atom' is about atomic power; 'Goodbye Mrs Ant' is on the unintended effects of the pesticide DDT; and 'The League of Gentlemen' tackles monetarism and the formation of neoliberalism in Britain. These themes will be familiar to anyone who has watched Curtis's recent documentaries: 2011's *All Watched Over by Machines of Loving Grace* is partly an expansion (or remix) of 'To the Brink of Eternity'; the replacement of direct colonialism with neocolonialism features heavily in *Bitter Lake*; and the failure of Soviet technocracy has a glancing role in *HyperNormalisation*. But it is worth pausing to note just how extraordinary this narrative was in the early 1990s. Curtis's real story – explored here for the first time, and central to his later work – is how the hopes of mid-twentieth-century political movements that human problems could be solved (common to decolonisation and Third-Worldism, the revitalised Soviet socialism of Khrushchev's Thaw, the America of the Great Society and the Europe of social democracy) were crushed, partly through their own actions and partly through a faith in technological solutions to political questions. The subjects here are always select groups of high-level political actors (the masses, rather questionably, are usually inert or mob-like, driven by vaguely understood desires, easily manipulated). Unlike others of his generation, Curtis does not gloat over the failure of these modernising elites, and does not see the 'end of history' as remotely positive. The cruelty and atrocity many of his films linger over – luxuriantly soundtracked by Brian Eno – are the main result of this failed project of egalitarian modernisation.

Curtis obviously lives in archives, and *Pandora's Box* is a showcase of suggestive imagery and historical montage that would be fascinating even with the sound off. But what is specially interesting, and specially lacking in the recent work, is the density of interview footage. Curtis is a terrific interviewer, and questioning leads to some of the best moments in his films. In *Pandora's Box*, the monetarist economist Alan Budd recounts his worry that, rather than being a neutral exercise in economic theory, the squeeze on interest rates may have been deliberately intended to crush trade union power and create a 'reserve army'; a cab driver, taking Curtis past the hulking offices of Gosplan next to Red Square, tells him that its edicts regulate how far he can take a passenger. There is much of this too in the three parts of the subsequent *Living Dead*, broadcast in 1995. Its account of the uses of nostalgia is shockingly contemporary, with only an analysis of the then nascent internet absent. The focus on the uses and abuses of the Second World War presages the weaponised historical discourse in Russia and Ukraine in the aftermath of the Maidan protests and the annexation of Crimea; the episode on Margaret Thatcher's obsession with Winston Churchill is particularly frightening viewing after the UK's vote to leave the European Union. For all the audacious historical melange (a BBC production of *The Turn of the Screw* is deployed with particular sly intelligence), the interviews are among the documentary's most shocking moments, as when the American literary historian and ex-GI Paul Fussell speaks of the incomprehensibility and horror he felt when fighting in the Second World War – and the need to suppress that specific memory of combat as quickly as possible.

Much work by British writers, historians, critics and artists since the financial crisis is contained in these films. It is not necessarily that people rip Curtis off, more that you might later realise that he got there first. Mark Fisher's work on *Capitalist Realism*, Andy Beckett's genealogy of British neo-liberalism, Douglas Murphy's studies of failed architectural futurism, Francis Spufford's novels about code-breakers and Soviet cyberneticians (and, to be honest, much of my own work on post-war architecture) – it's all in here already, but with pictures and music and many more interviews with people who were actually there. The sense that Curtis was writing history on the hop, at a time when most commentators were lost in the vacuous optimism of the Blair and Clinton boom, is especially strong in 1999's *Mayfair Set*, which sees the birth of the 'but one man ...' motif. The film consists of four picaresque stories about the ways that neoliberalism, deindustrialisation and neocolonialism were enforced in Britain and its empire, told through the actions of a handful of former habitués of the Clermont Club in the aristocratic London district of the title: SAS man David Stirling, and the financiers James Goldsmith, Tiny Rowland, Jim Slater and Mohamed Al-Fayed.

We watch these charismatically horrible people as they plot coups (executed in Yemen, mooted and then abandoned in Britain), asset-strip industries and plunder raw materials (in Britain and in Africa) and destroy industrial towns (on both sides of the Atlantic). A story that sees the reassertion of the stock market's dominance of the economy in the 1970s – or the destruction of British industry – as something hatched over poker in the Clermont Club is obviously incomplete, and this extreme level of personalisation is a central target for critics of Curtis's films. But as personifications of historical forces, you can't do much better than these insufferable, barely sane English grotesques. Right-wing historians such as Martin Wiener and Correlli Barnett argued in the 1980s that British industry's world dominance declined due to excessive regulation, powerful unions and the loss of an 'industrial spirit'; they expected unsentimental, Thatcherite capitalism to save and expand British industry, but in the event, it was decimated still further. *The Mayfair Set* provides an explanation: production was simply less profitable than speculation. Curtis's narrative of how this happened has the virtue of being funny and frightening, rather than hectoring or depressing.

The first Curtis series I saw was 2002's *The Century of the Self*. It is worth remembering that at this point British television was still dominated by five channels, so whatever was on could receive huge ratings and become a talking point in workplaces and playgrounds; you could also find yourself watching it by accident. Switching from the banal, 'let me take you on a journey' documentaries that dominated BBC2 or Channel 4 (the designated 'sophisticated' channels) to one of Curtis's dizzying montages was an experience that could reassert your faith in television as a medium. This cast Curtis himself (along with Jonathan Meades, a very different figure of a similar age) as the last, delinquent heir to the project of patrician populism – explaining unusual ideas to a mass audience, which was associated with its first director general John Reith (and generally known as Reithianism) – upon which the BBC once prided itself. (The conservative Reith would have found Curtis a puzzling successor, but he might have noticed a kinship in both the seriousness with which Curtis approached concepts and histories and the disbelief in the autonomy of any action taken by ordinary people.) *The Century of the Self* follows the Freud family – Sigmund, his nephew and propaganda pioneer Edward Bernays, his daughter the 'ego psychologist' Anna Freud and, more bathetically, his great-grandson and nineties PR man, Matthew Freud, whose significance is perhaps overstated but is used as a convenient means to tell the story of New Labour – as they enshrine psychoanalysis at the heart of consumer capitalism and its mass media. Here, Curtis's montages become increasingly formal, delighting in slogans and juxtapositions. In a randomly chosen ten-second sequence from *The Century of the Self*, you'll find fragments of Technicolor advertisements for consumer goods cutting into police beating protesters cutting into cheerful dogs in suburban front gardens cutting into images of office blocks, as the RP voice describes the formation of the first focus groups. You'll then shift to a face-to-face interview with one focus grouper, who tells us the story of how psychoanalysis managed to increase sales of Betty Crocker cake mix. Analysing the results of the focus groups, the resident Freudians decided that women felt guilty about the ease of making cakes from the mix, so the recipe was changed slightly, as the housewife was told to add an egg (symbolically, of course, granting her husband *her* eggs). Sales shot up.

The psychedelia and the hall-of-mirrors effects that creep into *The Century of the Self* become rampant in subsequent films like *The Power of Nightmares* (2004) and *The Trap: What Happened to Our Dream of Freedom* (2007). But these later documentaries still have strong theses, and they still aim, above all, to convince the viewer of a certain position, rather than losing themselves in anecdotal flux as do *Bitter Lake* and *HyperNormalisation*. *The Power of Nightmares* is an elegant expansion of the oft-made link between the families Bush and Bin Laden, following instead their intellectual heritage in the conservative reaction to mid-century America shared by Sayyid Qutb and Leo Strauss. The film was controversial when it was released for explicitly claiming that Al-Qaeda, as a coherent organisation rather than a vague brand, was to a significant degree a figment of the US State Department, although that argument no longer seems quite so shocking, given the degree to which ISIS made this a central part of their dispute with the longer-established group. *The Trap*, meanwhile, is another brief history of neoliberalism, this time via Isaiah Berlin's concept of 'negative freedom'. Here you start to find ideas thrown out with ADHD-level haste, such as an exceptionally dubious aperçu on the putative influence of Frantz Fanon and Jean-Paul Sartre on the Khmer Rouge. These two films, with their international, polemical bent, expanded Curtis's cult from shared DVDs and VHS tapes in the UK into US broadcasts, awards, film festivals and the art world; his next film, *It Felt Like a Kiss* (2009), was originally part of a gallery installation and dispensed with conventional narration in favour of rhythmic sloganeering on the subject of American colonialism and consumer seduction.

And then – to put it in Curtisese – the strangest thing

happened. If, in *The Mayfair Set* or *The Century of the Self*, Curtis was our last Reithian, the last documentary filmmaker in Britain to respect a mass audience's intelligence, his more recent work has been both about and usually distributed through the internet. The mission of educating and informing – and making coherent arguments that could be conveyed in a multi-part series – was gradually replaced by a diffuse, intentionally disorienting approach that replicates the bafflement which Curtis argues is deliberately created by those in power. The tics remained the same, but something had shifted.

Ironically, at this point, as the montages became more abstract and alienating, Curtis alienated much of his internet-left fanbase by attacking them, in *All Watched Over by Machines of Loving Grace* (2011), which traces the 'Californian ideology' from its birth in game theory, to the coterie around Ayn Rand, to Silicon Valley, and through to the unintended consequences of environmentalism in central Africa and the internet-enhanced 'revolutions' of the twenty-first century and their apparently abortive results. The argument that the new, internet-facilitated horizontal networks of the left (Occupy, *et al.*) merely mirrored those of neoliberalism was coupled with a more pointed claim that they simply had no idea what they wanted, only what they opposed. Here is where the parodies come in, most of them almost certainly made by people who had once been devoted fans. At the same time, the internet lends itself to Curtis's work, in its elective groups of people sharing an endless loop of in-group information. In her autobiography *Trans*, Juliet Jacques recounts binge-watching Adam Curtis films while recovering from her gender reassignment operations; I had a similar experience recovering from Crohn's disease–related surgery. The later films really are ideally watched one after the other, through a haze of prescription opiates, with the mind only half following the line of argument. They're a ride, a trip, not a 'story' or 'fable' anymore, let alone a thesis. They also possess a humour that works well if you're a little stoned. One sequence of *All Watched Over ...* implies that, with Alan Greenspan and his 'machines' running the country, Bill Clinton had nothing much to do in the White House – cue slow-motion footage of Clinton surrounded by adoring young women, Monica Lewinsky among them. This approach mimics the passivity both lamented and reinforced by the films – Curtis isn't exactly pleased with the notion that we cannot improve the world, but he drives it home through flowing montages of high-tech violence.

Though its increasingly vague and allusive approach to argumentation was new, *All Watched Over ...* still retained the interview material, and as with Curtis's earlier films much of this is hugely memorable. A member of the Ayn Rand collective tells him how she gave away her husband in order to make Ayn happy. 'Wasn't that *altruism*?' Curtis asks. 'Yes – and I'm not proud of it,' she responds. These moments are totally absent in *Bitter Lake* and *HyperNormalisation*. The result would seem to push Curtis ever closer to, say, the film-essay tradition of Harun Farocki, the Otolith Group, Thom Andersen, Chris Marker and Patrick Keiller. These have seldom featured on television – they belong, instead, to the arthouse, the *Kunsthalle* or YouTube. Both films were distributed only on iPlayer, and both are long – *HyperNormalisation* clocks in at nearly three hours. They will have been watched almost entirely on the internet, by an international rather than solely British audience. These films were also much cheaper to produce. Rather than having to jet off around the world to interview economists, think-tankers and Silicon Valley gurus about their achievements and present them with their failures, Curtis now works solely in the archive. The result is mutually satisfying: the BBC, which clearly regards him as a puzzle, and commissions nothing even remotely as sophisticated for their arts channel BBC4, have to outlay a pitifully small amount of money (*HyperNormalisation* cost £30,000 to make); and Curtis, in return, gets complete control, without an editor to keep an eye on his excesses and longueurs. So while Curtis is exceptionally good at pointing out the deleterious effects of the internet on economics and politics, he seems wholly satisfied with its effects on his own work.

The best thing Curtis has produced in the last few years is his BBC-hosted blog, The Medium is the Message. Here he presents works in progress and tells tall tales, but the tight format of the blog post keeps him on his toes; the posts, illustrated with archive footage, on Murray Bookchin's influence on Rojava or on the sheer extent of Soviet penetration into the British secret services, are better than anything in his recent films, precisely because they aren't corralled into a wafty thesis about how 'we' can no longer conceive of 'alternatives' and how 'our world has become' a baffling and illegible media landscape where 'nothing is true anymore', and so forth. *Bitter Lake* and *HyperNormalisation* are, however, absolutely full of material that would make for excellent blog posts and decent one-hour TV documentaries. *Bitter Lake*'s account of Saudi state formation and its cogent critique of the British occupation of Helmand, or *HyperNormalisation*'s juxtaposition of the mirror images presented to the West by Gaddafi and the elder (Hafez) Assad, are superb, and are good reminders of one of Curtis's greatest strengths: his genuinely global and historical vision of US/European/Middle Eastern relations, something lost both in the right and left versions of debates about why 'we' are in the Middle East. They are still often very funny in that giggly, stonerish way, though the humour seems to belong not just to a different movie, but to a different medium: sequences about Donald Trump and Jane Fonda, and a hysterical montage of pre-9/11 destructions of American cities, are better made for GIFs and Vines, rather than extended, three-hour argumentative film-essays. What grates most in the new, untrammelled, non-Reithian Adam Curtis – aside from the surely by now intentional, fan-pleasing self-parody – is the way he drifts over long images of destruction and horror, the victims (somehow more unnamed, more voiceless than ever before) exhumed, immolated or tortured as Eno's 'On Some Faraway Beach' plays yet again. If Curtis once appeared to want to explain late, neoliberal global capitalism and tell (always admittedly tendentious and picaresque) stories about 'how we got here', by now he seems to be content with adding to the helplessness. Worst of all, he seems to be enjoying it.

March 2017

From Boring Dystopia to Acid Communism

In autumn 2018, I spent a day in the town of Loughborough, in the East Midlands of England, the town where Mark Fisher grew up. I knew Mark well, at one point – from around 2005, to 2009, we were close friends, and we remained in sporadic contact after – but I had never been to Loughborough, and he certainly wouldn't have suggested it. I wasn't there for a sentimental journey, but for an assignment to look at the University of Loughborough, founded a century ago as Loughborough Engineering College, inextricably linked with the industries of the town. In the 1960s, that college was expanded with a strikingly ambitious plan by the architects Arup Associates, with, alongside it, a huge public art programme, which ran for several decades. Concrete towers and pedestrian walkways would connect the college buildings with integral new communities, rolling green hills. Between them were avant-garde sculptures, by artists such as Lynn Chadwick and Peter Peri; in the early 1980s, the largest of them were placed on prominent hills. Paul Wager's harsh metal constructivist sculptures, one of them called *Strike*, had been erected around the time of the great miners' strike of 1984–85, which was hugely important in this mining area – many East Midlands miners had refused to join the strike, as their pits were profitable. The campus

278

was impressive, but it was obvious that it wasn't cared for. Makeshift fences surrounded some of the sculptures; pedestrian paths would suddenly stop, and you'd walk through car parks. There were few maps, and you could get easily and frustratingly lost. New buildings were cheap and tacky, looking like they would be blown to pieces by the wind.

But that hadn't prepared me for the town centre. Like a lot of British town centres, it is on a small scale, but with none of the consolatory pleasures of quaintness or elegance. Shops are, with the exception of a handful of supermarkets and restaurants catering for Chinese engineering students, chains: Costa Coffee, Caffè Nero, Wetherspoons, the same everywhere. In the mildly ornate Victorian town hall, one of the forthcoming attractions was 'Strictly ... Ann Widdecombe', an evening with a Conservative politician who was once, as the minister responsible for prisons in the mid-1990s, best known for enforcing the shackling of pregnant women prisoners even while they gave birth, but who has since become a 'national treasure' after appearing on the TV show *Strictly Come Dancing*. Public transport was rudimentary, and after the chains, came half-derelict streets of warehouses and disused factories. The trains were all late. Mark used to call this landscape 'Boring Dystopia'.

I'm starting this article with this description of Loughborough because it exemplifies a lot of things about Mark's – I can't really not describe him with the familiar 'Mark' – work. It is ordinary, as he was ordinary, but it wanted to be more than that, once. 'Mark Fisher' is, to an English ear, an incredibly ordinary name. Search for authors called Mark Fisher and you'll find around five, usually appearing in the same search. He used to regret the fact that he'd chosen to publish under the name on his birth certificate when he made the shift from blogger and para-academic theorist to popular writer, in around 2008 – in his twenties, he'd published under his mother's maiden name, as Mark De Rozario. Yet within the ordinary, there are all kinds of unexpected avant-gardes lurking – 'The Weird', as he'd call it – just below the surface. So here, on the one hand, there is the development of a sort of popular modernist culture, funded by the state, which reaches way beyond London, Oxford and Cambridge into the life of provincial towns, symbolised by all those sad, lost abstract sculptures. And then there's the failure and replacement of that culture with a *boring dystopia* based around reality television, lowered public expectations, goofy populism and a depressive *capitalist realism*. It was all there, but of course he wasn't.

Mark became a cult figure with the publication in 2009 of *Capitalist Realism*, an account of depression and depoliticisation in a neoliberal yet culturally moribund system that he called 'market Stalinism'; it was published with Zero Books, the press he'd founded with an old friend from the University of Warwick, the novelist Tariq Goddard. *Capitalist Realism*'s focus on the affective consequences of new patterns in education, work and consumption meant it was an unusually emotional and convincing account of processes usually recounted in drab academic prose. Because of this, the book was a huge success, especially for such a tiny publisher – it has since been published in German, Spanish, Turkish, Czech and Russian, among other languages. I remember his plans for what to do next. His blog, K-Punk, which he ran at various domain names between 2003 and 2016, had become a formidable archive, and he was going to fillet it for three collections – one on the concept he'd borrowed from Jacques Derrida's *Spectres of Marx*, 'Hauntology', which he had reconceptualised as a descriptor for the 'lost futures' of both social-democratic public culture and pop culture. There would also be one on 'Glam', a persistent obsession which ran through many of his writings on music, film and fashion, and one on 'Love Songs', which was hard to imagine, because he'd only written about one or two of these, particularly through his love for Rihanna's 'Umbrella' – but then at the time he told me this, he had just got married. A lot with Mark depended on mood and chance. Then there was going to be the follow-up to *Capitalist Realism*, which would be on what he called 'Post-Capitalist Desire', which was rather enticing.

In terms of books that you can buy in shops, this is not quite what there is. *Ghosts of My Life*, with Zero, was the 'Hauntology' collection. It was published much later than expected, in 2014, and included a lot of his best work, and a lot of occasional pieces on musicians and filmmakers less interesting than he was. It was followed – on Repeater Books, the publisher he and Goddard had founded after Zero was run into the ground by its owners – with *The Weird and the Eerie*. This was a strange, deflated, troubling and rather pointless book full of truncated versions of K-Punk posts, essentially a more limited version of the earlier anthology. I remember picking up a copy in a bookshop on its release, and wondering what on earth he was doing publishing it – I hadn't spoken to him in over a year. It was published barely a week before his suicide in January 2017. *K-Punk*, taking its name from the blog, is yet another collection, this one absolutely vast – over 800 large-format pages. It includes the only completed segment – a long introduction – of that book on 'Post-Capitalist Desire', which he had decided to call *Acid Communism*. Baldly, that's what we have here, and I will try to give an account of what is in this book. Specifically, I'll try to test whether or not the claims that are increasingly being made for Mark's work – that he was the greatest English critic of his generation, in short – are tenable. But I won't be able to keep my memories out of it. I owe Mark a debt that I will never be able to repay. From 2005 on he took me under his wing as a writer, became my friend, and filled me with a confidence I would never otherwise have had. I'm very far from the only person to be able to say this, but even so, I am not an impartial observer. This is not only because of what I owe him, but also because I have often implicitly aimed work at him, as I tried to get out from under his shadow. I would do this rather than ask him what he thought, because I feared his rejection. How tediously *Oedipal*, I know he would think.

Then there is a second difficulty, which is explaining Mark's work to a Russian readership. *Capitalist Realism*, of course, has been translated, but it is by far his most accessible, least cranky and personal piece of writing, one which could, by and large, be understood by any reasonably literate person living under any 'free market' economy today; it was intended to be universal, and for all that it extrapolates from British experience, it is. That isn't the case with the rest of his work. There are two particular problems that I think have to be properly explained. One of these is political – the necessity of explaining why it is that he settled upon the name 'Communism' for his political ideal. But in some ways, this is easier to explain than the enormous emphasis he gave to two forms of media that have simply never had the same significance outside of Britain – television and pop music. The first was a result of the programming of the BBC, ITV and Channel 4, between the 1960s and the 1980s, when various of its 'plays for today', serials and one-offs could be highly experimental and political; and the second is unusual because of the intrinsic connection between music and its discourses. For Mark, the important thing was an interconnected network of music and theory, via the *NME* (in the 1970s and early 1980s) and *Melody Maker* (from the mid-1980s until the mid-1990s), a network which never existed to the same degree in the US, let alone elsewhere in the world. The blogs of which he was at the centre were an attempt to recharge this culture, when the mainstream had ceased to provide it.

In *K-Punk*, academic Darren Ambrose collects all of these into thematic rather than chronological sections, on books, film and TV, music, politics, interviews, and 'reflections', with the *Acid Communism* introduction at the end. He largely carries out this task very well. There are, obviously, things he has done that I wouldn't have done, and places where I think he has misunderstood certain interlocutors and certain ideas, but that's inevitable given that so much of this was about the instant back-and-forth of blogging, comment boxes and forums (Mark founded one, Dissensus, with the musician and writer Matthew Ingram, who blogged as Woebot). As I was part of this network, I might smile at being reminded in Ambrose's footnotes that Code Poetix was the poet and programmer Dominic Fox, Scanshifts was Justin Barton, with whom Mark collaborated on the radio collages *London under London* and *On Vanishing Land*, and that Infinite Thought was the philosopher Nina Power. Yet there are many other interlocutors quoted in here that Ambrose either doesn't know about or has deliberately sidelined. We don't learn that Heronbone was the poet Luke Davis; Savonarola was the philosopher and political scientist Alberto Toscano; Bat was the Trotskyist and occasional UK Garage DJ Anindya Bhattacharyya and *not* Giovanni Tiso, author of the blog 'Bat Bean Beam'; or that Voyou was the Marxist academic Tim Fisken; nor, even, that Glueboot was the writer Siobhan McKeown, Ambrose's partner. But then, many of the blogs being referred to have simply disappeared, taken offline by their authors, making their pseudonyms into illegible oddities, the hyperlinks that identified them absent.

The results are extremely uneven, but they have a continuity, one which Ambrose, in his well-judged introduction, calls 'Fidelity', a fidelity to the things that first set Mark off on his intellectual and political path – usually, given his background, these were pop and television. Ambrose argues that 'fidelity is key, because it provides the animating fibre that underpins the vast collage which he somehow synthesises into an effective and operative worldview'. Accordingly, certain fixations recur and recur, even when Mark's style and tone changed sharply over the years. It's to this which we'll now turn, proceeding in the episodic, thematic manner that the book is arranged – as each could easily have been a book on its own.

❧

The most puzzling of Ambrose's decisions is why he considered it worth including an entire section on literature (beautifully titled *Methods of Dreaming*), let alone why he decided to open the book with it; in fact, Mark wrote more often about football than about literature, and this book's non-inclusion of any mention of football leaves room for perhaps the only other possible book to be made out of Mark's oeuvre – otherwise, this book is so massive and comprehensive as to make some sort of Walter Benjamin or Tupac Shakur–style posthumous publishing afterlife impossible. He could write well on Kafka, Lewis Carroll, Dostoevsky, H. P. Lovecraft and M. R. James, but there was one literary exemplar for Mark, and he towered over everyone else – J. G. Ballard. Tellingly and typically, Mark had found him via music and the music press. So there are essays here on Ballard's 'Why I Want to Fuck Ronald Reagan' and its satirical yet successful circulation as a focus group paper at the Republican Party conference; there is much on his extraordinary, high-modernist, late-1960s series of 'condensed novels', *The Atrocity Exhibition*; and there is the following very K-Punk statement on prose, with reference to the cipher-like characters in Ballard's books: 'most of Ballard's characters (are) little more than spokespeople for the author's theories. Which is fine, of course: we need more "well-drawn characters" like we need more "well-wrought sentences".' But then there's something else, an essay on David Cronenberg's 1996 film of the 1973 book *Crash*, a sustained, completely thought-through text that was written, uploaded on the blog, read for free and then hotly debated, which is how most of this book was first produced.

I happen to know that this essay – entitled 'Let Me Be Your Fantasy', a sly little rave reference – comes from a 'Porn Symposium', embarked on by the interconnected network of blogs that had grown up around Mark and K-Punk. (Presumably, this was because the most Web 2.0 thing around, aside from blogs, was the sudden massive availability of pornography – and what else are you doing online when not working or blogging?) At her blog Infinite Thought, Nina Power contributed an essay on 'vintage porn', the silent stag-party fare that preceded the mass-market porn industry; on my blog Sit Down Man, You're a Bloody Tragedy, I wrote on Dušan Makavejev's film *WR: Mysteries of the Organism*. Nina and I both put these posts into our Zero books – her *One-Dimensional Woman*, my *Militant Modernism*, both published in 2009. Both are extremely light compared with Mark's contribution, which reflects a conception of sexuality that emerged equally out of glam and Jacques Lacan, one that he presented as more ideologically and theoretically correct than any other.

Cronenberg's *Crash*, cold and composed, is favourably contrasted with the orgiastic overspill of fluids in Ballard's book. 'Sex here is entirely colonised by culture and language. All the sex scenes are meticulously constructed tableaux, irreducibly fantasmatic, not because they are "unreal", but because their staging and their consistency depend on fantasy.' True enough. Yet it's what happens next that is unusual: 'far from being some nightmare of mutual domination, this is Cronenberg and Ballard's sexual utopia, a perverse counterpart to Kant's kingdom of ends.' It is a rather stark utopia: 'our deepest desire', we're told, 'is not to possess an other but to be objecti-fied by them, to be used by them in/as their fantasy'. The sexual ideal is 'to be objectified by someone you also want to objec-tify'. As a description of what is happening in these works, it's accurate enough, and as a sexual taste, I'm not interested in *kinkshaming* it. The problem is the barrage of insults for the vitalists and sentimentalists who might find the Lacanian injunction that 'there is no sexual relation' bleak, limiting and faintly misogynistic.

The same harsh sexual worldview emerges straight after, in another extremely tightly argued blog post, on the photog-rapher Steven Meisel, and his series for *Vogue Italia*, 'State of Emergency', which featured pornified images of military and security friskings, inspired by the 'War on Terror'. Mark

juxtaposed this with the obsession with 'realness' on the part
of the 'Young British Artists' who were still then dominant –
Damien Hirst, Tracey Emin, Sarah Lucas. 'The used tampons
and pickled animals of Reality Art offer, at best, tracings of
the empirical. Their quaint biographism reveals nothing of the
unconscious.' This is condensed and devastating, but it's in the
service of the following claim: 'Meisel's elegantly staged photographs, meanwhile, drip with an ambivalence worthy of the
best surrealist paintings. They are uncomfortable and arousing
in equal measure because they reflect back to us our conflicted
attitudes and unacknowledged libidinal complexities'. They
do? Perhaps. But perhaps we don't actually unconsciously
want to torture anorexic women. Women, in particular, may
not. And then he moves on to a point about systems of cultural value, where he's obviously completely right: 'reframed as
Art, the *Vogue* photographs would no doubt be described – in
the all-too-familiar terms of art-critical muzak – as "negoti-
ating with ideas of violence/terror/etc." As high fashion, they
meet instead with a type of liberal denunciation that is no
less familiar.' This is absolutely true, and it is a very K-Punk
point – the laws of the high (fine art) and low (fashion) are
held to be very different and a double standard pertains. But
as a defence of the work as such, it is as theoretically watertight as it is deeply grim. These essays, with their litany of
Ballard, Lacan and Sacher-Masoch, represent a side of what
Mark was up to which he kept out of the anthologies he compiled himself. Perhaps he was keeping them for a glam book;
it's equally plausible that he had simply outgrown this rhetoric.
But putting them in this book is a reminder of what drew a
lot of people to K-Punk in the first place – the very fact it was
so harsh, unreasonable, vehement and ideologically consistent
in an era, the 2000s, when criticism was at an extraordinarily
low ebb of PR speak and chirpy idiocy.

More familiar are the essays on David Peace and Margaret
Atwood. The latter might seem an unusual choice, given

Mark's sometimes uneasy relationship with feminism, but she was a crucial figure, both for *Surfacing*, a novel that he saw as an indictment of 1960s counterculture, and for her dystopias, *The Handmaid's Tale*, *Oryx and Crake* and *The Year of the Flood*. What is especially useful in his alternately fascinated and frustrated essays on these is that Mark was someone who, unlike most novelists, completely understood pop culture, and was utterly immersed within it – there was never a sense that he had to condescend to understand it. So he finds Atwood's later novels hard to accept largely because of her poor understanding of branding in the descriptions of futuristic corporations – this might seem like a minor point, but that would be deceptive.

> AnnoYoo, HelthWyzer, Happicuppa, ReJoovenEssens and – most ungainly of all – Sea(H)ear Candies: these practically caused me physical pain to read, and it is hard to conceive of any world in which these would be the leading brands. Atwood's mistake is always the same – the names are unsightly plays on the functions or services that the corporations offer, whereas capitalism's top brand names – Coca-Cola, Google, Starbucks – have attained an asignifying abstraction, in which any reference to what the corporation does is merely vestigial.

Mark wrote extensively on David Peace's semi-fictionalised novels of British crime, politics and football, and some of this is collected in *Ghosts of My Life*. Peace's 'political Gothic' is first traced here in an intense blog post on his *GB84*, an overwhelming novel about the miners' strike of 1984–85, which turns up again and again in this anthology. Peace was a K-Punk figure for the aggression and pulpiness of his prose, his understanding of the importance of pop and media, and for his unforgiving account of the political defeats of the 1980s, the crushing of the miners that made possible Thatcher's reshaping of British society in radically individualist form. The other pivotal moment for this was the 1989 Hillsborough Stadium disaster, when ninety-six Liverpool FC fans were crushed to death as a direct result of contemptuous and inept policing; it also led to the formation of an elite Premier League in British football, via sponsorship deals with Rupert Murdoch that were considered the only thing that could pay for the allegedly required stadium upgrades. Mark was at Hillsborough, on the other side, supporting his team, Nottingham Forest – now a minor club, but once, under the management of the charismatic socialist Brian Clough, a major international force. Clough was the subject of Peace's best novel, *The Damned United*. I wish there was more about this in *K-Punk*, as football was as intrinsic a part of Mark's worldview as music and TV; it feels odd to be gleaning the football insights as a side-effect of literature.

Mark's politics were as complicated as everything else about him, but reading back from this book, and from what I know myself, I think they developed as follows. You can see him in many of these essays as a teenage socialist, then facing disillusion with the consecutive electoral defeats for the Labour Party of 1983, 1987, 1992 – and more importantly, the defeat of organised labour in the 1984–85 strike. This, as we now know, and as Peace details at length, came via militarised policing and a series of black operations by MI5, which included an alleged secret service mole, Roger Windsor, acquiring the role of chief executive in the National Union of Mineworkers. A friend who knew Mark when he was a postgraduate at the University of Warwick in the late 1990s claims that he referred to himself then as a 'working-class Tory', and that doesn't sound at all implausible to me. His work with the Cybernetic Culture Research Unit (CCRU) at Warwick frequently displayed an awed admiration for the ruthless workings of neoliberal capitalism, derived from Deleuze and Guatarri's *Capitalism and Schizophrenia* and Jean-Francois Lyotard's *Libidinal Economy* – the CCRU's guru, Nick Land, would maintain that position to this day. In the early essays of *K-Punk*, Mark still holds on to these ideas to some degree, a body of thought that would later be called 'Accelerationism' – if you can't beat it, revel in it. But two things threatened this, and pushed him towards an increasingly recognisably humane communism: one was his experience of teaching at a further education college in the south-east London suburb of Orpington (so, teaching mostly working-class school-leavers of sixteen to eighteen), which was the main source for *Capitalist Realism*; the second was his disillusion with the cultural results of neoliberalism, especially by comparison with those of 'moribund' and 'sclerotic' social democracy.

One way of explaining this shift is through Mark's writing on the television writer Dennis Potter – another transplanted, alienated working-class boy – who created his best work between the mid-sixties and mid-eighties, and died of cancer in 1994. The *K-Punk* essays on Potter, of which there is no equivalent in the other anthologies, are the most important part of the section on television and film for understanding what it was about TV that mattered for Mark. Beginning with the two 1965 TV plays *Stand Up, Nigel Barton* and *Vote, Vote, Vote for Nigel Barton* – autobiographical works about an aspiring, Oxford-educated Labour politician from a mining family – Potter developed a fusion of Brechtian alienation effects, musicals, psychoanalysis, Christianity and an often bitter class politics, culminating in the kaleidoscopic *Singing Detective* in 1986. There are wonderful essays on both Nigel Barton plays, and on Potter's astonishing depiction of suburban fascism, *Brimstone and Treacle* – a step too far for the BBC, which banned it on the eve of its first screening in 1976. Mark, with his intense and dogmatic sense of ethics, his class background, his love of 'cheap music' and his openness to high-modernist experiment, understood Potter's work better than the critics who had written during Potter's lifetime; one of the many books I wish he'd written is a monograph on Potter. In the Nigel Barton post, Mark quotes Potter on why he used TV, rather than theatre or film or the novel, to convey his ideas.

> I knew that in small family groupings – that is, at their most vulnerable – both coalminers and Oxford dons would probably see the play. This could add enormously to the potency of a story which attempted to use the specially English embarrassment about class in a deliberately embarrassing series of confrontations ... there is no other medium which could virtually guarantee an audience of millions with a full quota of manual workers and stockbrokers for a 'serious' play about class.

Precisely. And that comes from the very limited nature of terrestrial TV, which, when Nigel Barton was shown, consisted of only three channels – up to four, when *The Singing Detective* was shown twenty years later (by comparison, the standard British digital TV package today has 105 channels, of which few develop original programming, and fewer still produce work of the slightest significance). That meant two state-funded BBC channels, with BBC2 having a remit to be relatively experimental; ITV, private and commercial but regionally dispersed, with northern and London-based production companies all developing distinct work; and from the early eighties, the private but regulated Channel 4, which would at first develop as a New Left–influenced 'alternative'. This ecology, which guaranteed that if something interesting was shown on one of these, you would probably see it and discuss it at work or at school the next day – an ecology also crucial in music, through the show *Top of the Pops* – was specific and unrepeatable. Mark would later become the TV critic for *New Humanist*, and wrote insightfully about the recent wave of 'literary' American serials: here, *Westworld*, *Breaking Bad* and specially *The Americans*, which was extremely K-Punk in its focus on sympathetic Soviet spies completely unaware of the imminent collapse of their 'future'. But he knew and we knew that this sort of niche marketing would never have the same cultural impact. Mark's stranger televisual fixations – a seemingly hate-fuelled addiction to news, sport and especially reality TV and talent shows, which feature often even in *Capitalist Realism* – were explicable by the fact that these things still happened in *real time*, with that same momentum of things that are *happening now*.

It's no accident that two of the essays in *K-Punk*'s 'Politics' section are about TV election coverage. One of the saddest things about the timing of Mark's death was an awareness of how *ecstatic* he would have been at the shock result of the June 2017 election, when a left-wing Labour party took the Conservative majority – seeing the utter amazement and horror of the Oxbridge-educated news anchors and Tory politicians could have worked better than a lifetime's SSRIs. The best of the *New Humanist* TV columns was on British satire, a smug and toothless creature largely responsible for the career of Boris Johnson, here considered via the stunning pointlessness of satirical news shows such as *This Week*: 'the programme was aimed at literally no-one: if you are staying up late to watch a programme devoted to politics, then presumably you are pretty serious about politics. Who wants this unfunny froth?' Nobody, it turns out, and dissatisfaction with the mainstream media has become endemic in Britain.

There is a socialist and democratic impulse in these writings on television, but they are not 'populist', and they are not 'levelling': Harold Bloom is a figure cited with approval. In a blog essay on actor-writer Patrick McGoohan's 1967 TV series *The Prisoner* – wherein a spy is captured, renamed Number Six and taken to a soft-totalitarian 'Village', set in the architect Clough Williams-Ellis's North Wales utopian neoclassical ideal town, Portmeirion – he places this ITV serial on the same level as Kafka's *The Castle*. The argument is that Patrick McGoohan was creating something *as good as* Kafka, not that Kafka was no better than ITV. We'll come back to this point later, on music, as it's key to understanding what Mark was up to. So too was his peculiar use of Nietzsche – a figure who might seem a strange reference point for a self-described communist and pop-culture enthusiast. But for Mark, Nietzsche's importance was as an 'aristocrat': he uses Nietzschean ideas to imagine a sort of proletarian aristocracy, while the 'herd' is recast as the Oxbridge-educated political and media class. So, in a post on the reality TV show *Big Brother*, then in its early stages, Mark takes righteous issue with the former *NME* journalist Julie Burchill – who was, like Mark, from a working-class background, but unlike him had been assimilated into the London media world when still a teenager (Mark was perhaps lucky to have been formed as a human being by years of unemployment and teaching, only being noticed as a writer in his late thirties). Burchill's 'endlessly reiterated polemic in favour of *Big Brother* – that it allows working-class people opportunities to break into a media dominated by the privileged' – is seen for what it is: patronising bullshit. 'The real beneficiaries' of the show are not the instant and instantly forgotten celebrities made out of its brief inmates, but the 'smug bureaucrats', its producers, Endemol; and the caricatures the inmates willingly make of themselves present a 'reductive' and crass version of what it is to be working class; but most importantly of all, the rise of reality TV – and the talent shows that would follow – have 'meant a defeat for that over-reaching proletarian desire to *be more*, a drive which negated Social Facts by inventing Sonic Fictions, which despised "ordinariness" in the name of the strange and the alien.'

This is explained further in a post about the notoriously oblique 1981 BBC science fiction play *Artemis 81*, which is used as a pretext to explore why the BBC would never conceive of funding or broadcasting something so ambitious, strange and modernist in the twenty-first century – largely because it's not 'what people want', unlike clip shows, nostalgia and reality and talent shows. This relates to an opposition Mark sees as central to actually existing capitalist culture.

The opposition that sets elitism against populism is one that neoliberalism has put in place, which is why it's a mistake to fall either side of it. The neoliberal attack on *cultural* elites has gone alongside the consolidation and extension of the power of an *economic* elite. But there's nothing 'elitist' about assuming intelligence on the part of an audience (just as there is nothing admirable about 'giving people what they want', as if that desire were a natural given rather than something that is mediated on multiple levels).

These writings on television are far too easily written off as nostalgia. Instead, they're about exploring something incredibly important: the formation of a generation of proletarian intellectuals, who would simply never have encountered these ideas otherwise.

The work on film is never quite as satisfying as the brilliant, hugely original essays on television. It bears the heavy influence of Slavoj Žižek (I remember Mark always in the front row of a series of 'masterclasses' led by the Slovenian philosopher at Birkbeck College in 2008, always the first to ask a – usually difficult – question) and his particular conception of 'ideology critique'. I'll admit that some of my lack of interest here is tied to specific figures in Mark's filmic canon, specially his baffling overrating of the ponderous and moronic Christopher Nolan. The best thing in these is a back-and-forth with Tim Fisken (Voyou), who gently scolds Mark's unusually facile account of the politics in Nolan's *Batman* films:

> ideology is not something foreign, something in a film with a strange power to impose itself on our minds; ideology is what we and the film share, what allows for the transfer of specific meanings between film and audience (a transfer which is not one way).

Much more interesting is a blog post on Chris Marker's epic film of 1968, *A Grin without a Cat*, and its aftermaths. Mark writes well on the film itself, but what is more important is the opportunity the account of campus radicalism gives him to talk about education – he was still an FE teacher at this point – and how the neoliberal reforms it has been subjected to have made institutions more, rather than less bureaucratic.

> It's hard to believe that public services are not more clogged with bureaucracy than they were pre-Thatcher. Certainly, education is choked with the stuff ... targets, action plans, log books, all of them required conditions for funding by the Learning and Skills Council, and assessed by Ofsted ... [surveillance] is introjected into the institution itself, through the permanent panoptic vigilance of a bloated managerial strata determined to over-compensate in order to fully ensure it is meeting central government's demands. This is the reality of 'market Stalinism' in education.

Watching a 1970s French avant-garde film was the ideal means by which to reflect on what it was like to teach working-class teenagers in 2006.

The section on music is named after 'Choose Your Weapons', an attack on what he called 'Popism', more of which later. For Mark, even more than television, music – pop music, dance music, occasionally rock music and more seldom jazz and modern composition – is what everything else revolves around. Early K-Punk pieces were efforts in furious canon-forming: some of the best of these, on Joy Division, on Japan, Tricky and Goldie, and on Burial, were included in *Ghosts of My Life* – a masterpiece of an essay on the Fall, worthy of Fredric Jameson at his best, was inexplicably heavily truncated in *The Weird and the Eerie*, and is happily included in full in *K-Punk*. But as with the Ballard essays in the 'Literature' section, what dominates here is glam Mark, which he had left out from his own published version of himself.

Chronological as it is, one of the first essays/posts here is a thing called 'K-Punk, or the Glampunk Art Pop Discontinuum'.

At the time this was published I was absolutely knocked down by this piece of writing, awed by its scope, its sweep, its rhetorical exuberance and violence. Looking at it now I'm less convinced, although I am now the age – thirty-seven – that Mark was when he wrote it. It sets up a series of linkages – mod (more the clothes than the music), glam (Roxy Music, much more than Bowie), post-punk (especially Siouxsie Sioux), and New Romanticism (especially Visage) – as examples of the 'proletarian aristocracy' Mark had developed out of his reading of Nietzsche. Mods started it off, because they 'embraced the hyper-artificial'; black American music, like drugs, was 'an accelerator, an intensifier, an artificial source of ecstasy', but it was not read by them as *soul*, as 'a timeless expression of pride and dignity'. Who did see it as such? *Hippies*. 'When hippies rose from their supine hedeno-haze to assume power (a very short step) they brought their contempt for sensuality with them.' Hippies get bashed in almost every K-Punk post written between 2003 and 2008. Fun as that is, as with the Meisel and *Crash* posts, there is some quite uncomfortable stuff here. A lot of this evident manifesto is made up of praise – and rightly so! – of Grace Jones, of the aesthetic she developed with Jean-Paul Goude at the start of the 1980s, and the magnificent series of records that came out of it, *Warm Leatherette*, *Nightclubbing* and *Living My Life*. But the rhetoric, in that *NME* version of William Burroughs and Deleuze and Guattari, is a little creepy.

> Jones is the sublime object before which (Bryan) Ferry
>   prostrated himself – and who talked back.
> Through vagina-dentatal teeth.
> Be careful of the womanimal machine. It bites

In this sublime and ridiculous prose poem to the 'neurobiotic femachine', you have to remind yourself this is a teacher in his late thirties writing. I also wonder what he made of Jones's own account, in her Paul Morley–ghosted autobiography, of just how exploitative her relationship with Jean-Paul Goude actually was – and whether this sexualised appearance of total control may be just another male fantasy. This writing – thrilling as it can be – represents Mark's last attempts to continue as his older incarnation, as one of the hardline theory soldiers of the Cybernetic Culture Research Unit. After that, Mark was preoccupied with trying to understand what had enabled his 'Kontinuum' to happen – and why it had ceased to happen.

Mark explained this partly by a shift from modernism to realism – not just in terms of representational and conservative art forms, but in terms of a 'realistic' idea of what is possible in culture and in politics. This meant downplaying just how strange, advanced and extreme pop culture could be.

> A certain notion of realism began not only to prescribe what could happen, but to airbrush out what had actually happened. The idea that pop could be more than a pleasant *divertissement* in the form of an easily consumable commodity, the idea that popular culture could play host to concepts that were difficult and demanding: it wasn't sufficient to disavow those possibilities, they had also to be *denied*.

In an era when these things were being denied, solace could be found in some strange places – namely, *goth*. In some ways, this is a measure of just how grim the pop cultural landscape was, but typically, the decision that goth was, as he writes in a post included here, both 'the last remnants of glam in popular culture' and also 'the last surviving post-punk cult' meant that some actual real-life experimentation in goth had to take place.

Another memory. Mark noticed my blog in spring 2005, linking to a hugely derivative post I had written (cut and pasted from an MA coursework essay) comparing Grace Jones's look to the constructivist clothes developed by Aleksandra Ekster and Varvara Stepanova. He had headed the post 'SOVIET GOTH'. As the goth post included in this anthology explains, Mark and 'I.T', i.e. Nina Power, had decided to go to goth clubs, specifically a night called 'Slimelight', a three-floor extravaganza in north London, which included three rooms of different kinds of goth – which also meant different outfits from the regulars: 'classic' Sisters of Mercy–style goth rock on the ground floor; electronic 'Euro-goth' on the second; and on the third, a punishing, instrumental 'noise goth', which was probably least bad, although all the music was terrible. Mark and Nina would do their hair and make-up (at this point, Mark had bright-red dyed hair, making him look a little Lydonesque) and put on their uniforms. I mean this not as a metaphor: they had decided, in their planned migration from normal London music festivals (one is described in *K-Punk*, a grim affair for which seeing Moloko, and particularly singer Róisín Murphy's outfits, was the only consolation) to seedy goth clubs, to invest in some Soviet army uniforms to wear. They gave me one to wear out too, as I had apparently been the inspiration for 'SOVIET GOTH'. The effect of these uniforms

Photograph of Author and K-Punk, Wearing a K-Punk T-Shirt, in 2005. Photograph by Ed Maw.

was to cause arguments in the club about 'communism', and when this happened I realised it was what Mark had really wanted, as we sat in the corners of the club and he explained to various puzzled but not unsympathetic goths why he was a communist. It might all sound a little silly, and that's because it was; but it was silly-serious, a way of working out an idea in reality, and doing so through dressing up and dancing to (in this case, dreadful) music.

This taking seriously of 'trash' was aimed at other ways of taking seriously 'trash', in terms which are remarkably similar to those Mark used to discuss TV. 'Choose Your Weapons', one of the pivotal K-Punk rants, is aimed at the critic Frank Kogan and, by implication, a network that partially intersected with the one around Mark, centred on the group blog Freaky Trigger and its forum, I Love Music. These had developed what they called 'poptimism', a celebration of the mainstream pop of the day: Girls Aloud, Rachel Stevens, Kylie, etc. On the face of it, this shouldn't have angered Mark, as he loved this music too. But he found the way it was often talked about, juxtaposing it with a contempt for 'rockist' values of seriousness and significance, infuriating – here, it grows out of Kogan's juxtaposition of the Backstreet Boys and Nirvana.

> The once-challenging claim that for certain listeners, the (likes of) the Backstreet Boys could have been as potent as (the likes of) Nirvana has been passive-nihilistically reversed – now, the message disseminated by the wider culture – if not necessarily by the popists themselves – is that nothing was ever better than the Backstreet Boys. The old high culture disdain for pop cultural objects is retained; what is destroyed is the notion that there is anything *more valuable* than those objects. If pop is no more than a question of hedonic stim, then so are Shakespeare and Dostoevsky.

His version of this dialectic (a word he was too much the Deleuzian to ever countenance using) was arrived at via the 'self-taught working-class intellectuals' Ian Penman and Paul Morley at the early eighties *NME*, and their creation and promotion of a 'New Pop' around ex-post-punk figures such as ABC and Scritti Politti, who shifted into creating their own versions of disco and pop.

The death of Michael Jackson led to Mark assembling these veteran writers, along with others on the blog, for an anthology called *The Resistible Demise of Michael Jackson*, for Zero; the continuity between these generations was obvious, both in the sometimes formidably dense use of theory to explain Jackson's music and life, and in the evident love for his music held by all of the contributors. The obverse, meanwhile, of a music paper aimed at teenagers and twentysomethings like the *NME* discussing Michael Jackson via Roland Barthes was *The Times* insisting that high politics and high art be treated with the same careless vacuity with which it treated pop music and fashion. In the midst of the essay, Mark detours into talking about an experience with 'Very Old Media (VOM)' requiring a piece of writing they had commissioned from him – he was starting to get noticed – be 'upbeat, witty and irreverent'. He doesn't mention that this was for *The Times* (which it was) or that it was a direct quote from the commission that led to his article being spiked.

Morley and Penman's claim, as Mark ventriloquises it, 'was that as much sophistication, intelligence and affect could be found in the pop song as anywhere else'. This is, I think, completely right; it's also strikingly at variance with how the division between high culture and pop culture is usually understood. Grace Jones is *as important* as the constructivists, Bryan Ferry every bit as much a pop artist as his teacher Richard Hamilton, and the Fall at their early 1980s peak were as weird, disjointed and experimental as one of Mark E. Smith's favourite authors, Wyndham Lewis. This is crucial to understanding why Mark's work is so original, because it theorises and explains something about pop music which many people know intuitively, but seldom spell out. The sheer *modernism* of, say, post-punk, glam, jungle turns upside-down the analysis of modernism that is popular in literature departments and, tellingly, in the media, where formal experimentation is a way of trying to stop the working classes from understanding what the writer is up to, a deliberate elitist strategy of obfuscation – an argument made at greatest length and influence in John Carey's book *The Intellectuals and the Masses*. This assumes that a working-class person – such as Mark E. Smith, or Ian Curtis, or Bryan Ferry, or Tricky, or, obviously, Mark Fisher – could not enjoy modernist culture, because it was specifically designed to exclude them. And yet, not only did they enjoy it, they also would then make their own modernist art, transforming the mass-market genre music invented on Tin Pan Alley into a modernist form all of its own, making their own shifts into obliqueness, fragmentation and dissonance (a similar story could be told about modern jazz in the US – but it has little to do with 'rock' or the question of whether the lyrics of Bob Dylan are or are not 'as good as' Keats). And whereas this 'anti-elitist' argument, as made by John Carey, comes from the political right, fairly similar versions of the thesis have come from the political left, from figures such as Jacques Rancière and Pierre Bourdieu, with their focus on education as a ruling-class tool, in the former case, and high art as a badge of bourgeois distinction in the latter. Mark would have none of this. If a Salford shipyard clerk like Mark E. Smith can make something as bizarre and endlessly complex a work of modernist art as *Hex Enduction Hour*, then the entire debate is meaningless.

For an example that connects these ideas with politics – not always obvious – we could turn to a somewhat later essay, on the industrial group Test Dept, where Mark's writing had become less vindictive, but had changed little in ethos. Test Dept produced a typical, if slightly late post-punk fusion of Soviet constructivist imagery, workerist rhetoric and metal-bashing rhythms borrowed from German groups such as Einstürzende Neubauten, which they tried to put in the direct service of socialist politics. The essay centres on their work during the miners' strike of 1984–85, when they recorded an album with the South Wales Miners Choir, *Shoulder to Shoulder*. The memory of the strike is explained more calmly than in the post on *GB84*, but is no less devastating for that.

> For any British, left-wing person, remembering the mid-1980s is liable to provoke a sadness that is visceral, choking, wrenching. I still can't recall without weeping the day when the miners returned to work in 1985 after a year on strike. What I have called capitalist realism – the deeply embedded belief that there is no alternative to capitalism – was definitively established in the UK during that period.

But *Shoulder to Shoulder* also offers the potential – to use a Deleuzism – of a 'line of flight', by which the miners' struggle could be seen not merely as a reactive attempt to preserve a nineteenth-century proletarian way of life, but as something which could go beyond it, forming solidarities with feminist and New Left currents, LGBT activists and pop culture, against both Thatcherism and the cowardice of the official labour movement (a similar line was carved out at the time by the Lesbians and Gays Support the Miners movement, organised by a gay Communist Party activist – this recently became the subject of a popular film, *Pride*, which would have been hard to imagine a decade ago).

My focus here on the music and culture and political struggles of the 1980s skews this portrait a little, suggesting that Mark had little interest in anything that came after. This isn't true, insofar as he maintained an interest in dance music – R&B, techno and especially the 'hardcore continuum' in Britain that ran from rave, through jungle, to UK garage and grime, although with a few exceptions he disdained hip hop for its machismo. A lot of his ideas around this date from the

CCRU days – the interview he carried out with Kodwo Eshun in the 1998 book *More Brilliant than the Sun* conveys Mark's ideas on the music of the 1990s, of the massive significance of the cybernetic 'rhythmic psychedelia' of jungle, better than anything here. But *K-Punk* includes an interesting dialogue with Simon Reynolds on these matters: Reynolds makes an empirical statement and then Mark moves to theorise and extrapolate from it – the anthology's best attempt at giving a sense of the fast-paced dialogues of the blogs.

But it's the disdain for so much of the music of the 2000s that marks a lot of what comes later. The slowdown of the pop-cultural machine of innovation was clearly a very important part of what drove Mark to the political left. The anarcho-capitalist infrastructure behind rave, jungle and UK garage – dubplates, pirate radio, warehouses – was not corporate, but it was hardly socialist either; it was undoubtedly modernist, in its sense of relentless forward motion (he points to all those jungle tracks that would literally declare, in their vocal refrains, 'I bring you the future') and its constant churn of experiment. When that slowed down, what was there to root for in contemporary culture? Of course, there were individual things, and there are decent essays here on those he did find sympathetic (Drake, Sleaford Mods) but the piece that I remember being impressed by at the time – in a 'he's still got it!' sense – was an utter evisceration of David Bowie's preposterously overrated 2013 comeback *The Next Day*, the fawning reception of which he puts down to a 'willingness to hallucinate' that the man who 'stands for all the lost possibilities going by the idea of art pop – which is to say, not only pop plus art, or pop as art, but a circuit where fashion, visual art and experimental culture connected up and renewed each other in unpredictable ways' could come back and save us. I don't know what he made of its vastly superior successor, *Blackstar*, but it could almost have been made as a response to the criticism, in its strikingly contemporary dialogue between

Kendrick Lamar, free jazz and the terminally ill Bowie's terror at his imminent death. In any case, the same criticism could have been levelled at Mark: his cultural ideas had by 2007 settled into a fairly comfortable refrain – lamenting the demise of his 'Glampunk Artpop Discontinuum' and the 'slow cancellation of the future' – and judging by *The Weird and the Eerie*, hadn't really developed over the succeeding ten years.

That's what I thought, at any rate. I was wrong: one thing this anthology reveals is a set of ideas he was developing in 2015 and 2016 with the soft-left philosopher Jeremy Gilbert, that were intended to be the basis of the real follow-up to *Capitalist Realism*. This comes out first in an essay-post on Gwen Guthrie's 1985 electro song 'Ain't Nothing Going On but the Rent', titled 'No Romance without Finance'. The song's narrator is a woman asserting that no man who doesn't have gainful employment is going to have sex with her – on the face of it, a cynical song, like TLC's 'No Scrubs', which is also discussed here. But that's not where Mark takes it at all: what is happening is instead a grim attempt at self-preservation and security when it has been taken away by mass unemployment and casualisation – and the immediate consequences for how people are forced to live their private lives. It is 'a song about security in conditions of radical uncertainty'. Similarly, 'the formula "no romance without finance" need not only be construed as merely some reactionary concession to capitalist realism. Rather, it can be heard as a rejection of the ideological sentimentality that separates out social reproduction from paid work.' He compares this to the feminist notion of 'consciousness-raising', popular in the 1970s, where autonomous groups of women would relate their experiences to the larger structures of patriarchy. For someone who in 2004 complained of 'feminazis' and celebrated a ruthless yet inhuman 'womanimal femachine', this is quite some shift – one which he may have arrived at through his enthusiasm for the communist-futurist xenofeminism popularised by the philosopher Helen Hester. 'The spreading of therapeutic narratives' in the consciousness-raising groups, he argues,

> was one way in which neoliberalism contained and privatised the molecular revolution that consciousness-raising was bringing about. Where consciousness-raising pointed to impersonal and collective structures – structures that capitalism and patriarchal ideology obscures – neoliberalism sees only individual choices and personal responsibility. Yet consciousness-raising practices weren't only at odds with capitalist ideology; they also marked a decisive break with Marxism-Leninism. Gone was the revolutionary eschatology and the militaristic machismo which made revolution the preserve of an avant-garde. Instead, consciousness-raising made revolutionary activity potentially available to everyone. As soon as two or more people gather together, they can start to collectivise the stress that capitalism ordinarily privatises. Personal shame becomes dissolved as its structural causes are collectively identified.

This is an astonishing leap from a disco track about feckless men, and one which I am completely surprised by: after years wondering what exactly it was Mark was doing, and why he was letting his ideas become flabby and familiar, it's a direction I hadn't expected, yet one which clearly connects with his earlier ideas in terms of the pivotal question of how to respond to the crisis of 'Fordism' and social democracy – long for the old days, or create anew?

By now, you'll have come to expect the sequence that emerges again in the book's 'Politics' section: early vehemence, bolstered and yet toned down around the time of *Capitalist Realism*, and then, a certain drift – the exceptions are two sharp, sudden moments when Mark imagines everything might be about to change, fast. So we begin as he watches the 2005 election coverage, when, with a record low turnout, Tony Blair and the fully neoliberal and increasingly nationalistic New Labour sailed past a hard-right Conservative Party.

Disgusted, he argues that 'New Labour is the worst of all worlds. Thatcherist managerialism without the Thatcherite attack on vested interests. In the pre-Thatcher 1970s, it took six carworkers to do the job of one; in the post-Thatcher Noughties, it takes six consultants to do the job of none.' That's the CCRU anarcho-capitalist disdain for 'sclerotic' social democracy coming out there, but it's something else, too – his experience of the massive bureaucracies created by the British version of neoliberalism, in which 'competition' is created by constant testing, auditing and metrics, and how that goes alongside employment insecurity, with the abolition of the 'job for life' and the demise of guaranteed pensions and sick pay. In 'October 6, 1979', a K-Punk post on the birth of neoliberalism, he explains this in terms indebted to the 1970s Italian far-left movement Autonomia Operaia. 'The horrors of these new working patterns are clear, but it is imperative that the left renounces one of its most dangerous addictions, its nostalgia for Fordism', given that 'the disintegration of stable working patterns was in part driven by the desires of workers – it was they who, quite rightly, did not want to work in the same factory for forty years.'

Five years later, Gordon Brown leads Labour to defeat in the 2010 election – and Mark writes another blog post (one of the few K-Punk posts that I was surprised is not included in the book is a brilliant portrait of Brown, a brooding, gothic and ethically compromised figure whom Mark clearly found fascinating; along with football, a hysterical essay on the film *Basic Instinct 2* and a post on Fleetwood Mac, it's one of the rare absences of which I thought, 'and where is *that*?'). In the post, the blanket denunciation has changed into the recognition of an opportunity. 'The fact that the post-Blair and Brown Labour Party is a hollowed-out shell means that it is a space, which it is at least plausible that could be filled with new ideas and strategies.' This would not happen for a few years, but it happened.

Mark's political writing gains enormously from his experience in the wave of student protests in late 2010 and early 2011, in response to the new coalition government of Conservatives and Liberal Democrats trebling tuition fees and abolishing the Education Maintenance Allowance, a grant for working-class sixteen-to-eighteen-year-olds to stay in further education – exactly the people Mark had been teaching in Orpington. His excitement crackles off the page.

> The only thing I can compare the current situation with is emerging from a deep depression. There's the rush that you get simply from not being depressed anymore – the occasional lurching anxieties, a sense of how precarious it all seems (don't drag me back into nothing) – and yet not only is it maintaining itself, it's proliferating, intensifying, feeding on itself – it's impossible, but it's happening.

This kind of rhetoric happened on K-Punk occasionally, and sometimes, it was just about seeing Moloko at a music festival. What makes this different is that he was absolutely right – something was changing here, and the number of people closely involved in the student protests who are now advisers or outliers to Jeremy Corbyn is an obvious indication of this.

Mark spotted the crucial importance early on of certain things that might, at the time, have seemed to be minor phenomena, and which were very seldom noticed by cultural critics. One is the way unemployment benefits and the remnants of the welfare state had become punitive and labyrinthine, a deterrent and a disciplinary measure – much of this discourse was a dialogue with one of the best Zero Books, Ivor Southwood's *Non-Stop Inertia*, an account of casual employment and the benefits system. The decisive event that would hand the Labour Party to its far left was its leadership voting for benefit cuts implemented by the Conservative government in 2015. Mark described this in terms of his own experience of tax credits. These had been brought in under New Labour to 'reward' people in poorly paid work, with the state stepping in to keep them from penury. These benefits were sharply reduced in 2015; Mark confesses via this anecdote he was wrong in claiming that New Labour was worse than Thatcherism, a rare moment acknowledging the development of his own ideas. But he continues to find the timidity of the very mildly further-left post–New Labour leadership under Ed Miliband (comically named 'Red Ed' by the tabloid press) deeply frustrating; even so, he joined the Labour Party after the student protests, largely, it seems, because it had something that the 'Neo-Anarchists' did not – 'institutional memory'.

The petty cruelties of the benefit system, it's now clear, had caused an undercurrent of rage which had been entirely missed in the mainstream media, with the exception of the young journalist Owen Jones, for whom Mark cheerleads in several of the later posts. His sympathy for Jones can't have had much to do with culture – by his own admission, Jones is a meat-and-potatoes, Oasis-listening chap – but was about his insistence on the salience of class, and his determination to be in the Labour Party and in the mainstream media, both of which made him unpopular in the online 'Left Twitter' circles that increasingly superseded the blogs, to Mark's great frustration. The media and the Labour Party, Mark argued, are 'mutable terrains to be struggled over'. The 'Neo-Anarchists', meanwhile, 'want to occupy everything except parliament and the mainstream media'. In 2018, reading these arguments from around 2012–14, it is interesting that he was right about the Labour Party, which really was transformed for a time into an organisation advocating a decisive break with neoliberalism – but wrong about the mainstream media, which, aside from admitting Jones and two photogenic former student protesters now running their own media organisation (Aaron Bastani and Ash Sarkar of Novara Media), has been extraordinarily closed, with both the BBC and Channel 4 (and, of course, the newspapers) adamantly refusing to tack even slightly to the left.

As with the unexpected ideas in the essay on Gwen Guthrie, you can see what Mark was planning to do next in some scattered posts and essays linked to a consciousness-raising group of which he was a participant, Plan C (you can guess what the C stands for). The idea that 'consciousness raising' could be a way of building anti-capitalist 'hegemony' is unusual; it shows a certain interest in *strategy*, and an increasing intellectual and political openness. He first mentions the idea in relation to people meeting in small groups to discuss economics, which appeals to him given his self-confessed illiteracy on that subject. In another election post – 'Abandon Hope (Summer is Coming)', on a briefly rejuvenated K-Punk, written after the Conservative victory in the 2015 election – he imagines small collectives working together to 'codify practices of collective re-habituation', which he lists as follows: 'talking to fellow workers about how we feel'; 'talk to opponents'; 'create knowledge exchange labs'; 'create social spaces'; 'use social media pro-actively, not reactively'; 'generate new figures of loathing in our propaganda'; 'engage in forms of activism aimed at logistical disruption'; 'develop hub struggles'. He had come a long way from 2005, and of these probably only 'logistical disruption' has not been done in some manner by Momentum, The World Transformed and other Corbynite networks. 'If they think Ed was Red, wait until they see the coming Red Swarm,' he concludes.

But the latest piece here, a never-uploaded K-Punk post on the election of Donald Trump, has none of this energy. Left unfinished and unpublished, it's obviously little more than a sketch, though it is interesting for relating the baleful effect of the distinction between 'economic' and 'cultural' elites that he'd previously outlined as part of the neutralisation of pop culture; and it has, at least, the following line. 'After Brexit and Trump, we can say with certainty: boring dystopia is over. We're in a whole other kind of dystopia now.'

Leaving aside a superfluous section of interviews – Mark was lucid enough in print and on the screen, so these conversations add little either of explanation or insight, particularly since he often *spoke exactly as he wrote* – the last and most questionable part of the collection is a set of 'Reflections', titled 'We Are Not Here To Entertain You'. This is a strange selection, and it reads as a way of contextualising what became, somewhat frustratingly, Mark's best-known piece of work after *Capitalist Realism*: the 2013 outburst 'Exiting the Vampire Castle', published on the small left-wing site the North Star and endlessly discussed since. The piece has been alternately praised for a 'class-first' attack on 'identity politics', and excoriated as crypto-racist or nationalist for the same reason. It's much more sophisticated than either of these factions give it credit for, but it was also in many ways a shift back to the 'you're either with us or against us' harshness of early K-Punk. So in order to make a case for the essay – I know people who were close to Mark and wanted it left out – Ambrose places it alongside a series of K-Punk posts from late 2004 and early 2005. I'm doubtful of the wisdom of this, but it appears to be a way of arguing that the deployment of deliberately cruel and divisive rhetoric was *always* part of what he did. There is some truth to this. But these explosions weren't just textual or theoretical – in my experience they always coincided with Mark suffering a manic episode of some kind. You knew they were happening when the gleeful, excited glint in his eye had hardened into a Lydonesque, slightly messianic stare. I hated these moments, because they were a reminder that he was ill. I can't read anything in this section without remembering that.

The posts are rants and denunciations aimed at various K-Punk interlocutors, and they were specifically directed – though Ambrose doesn't mention this – at two of his regular sparring partners: one of his CCRU colleagues and Luke Davis, an experimental poet whose evocations of East London peri-urban spaces on his blog Heronbone were once a huge influence on Mark, especially on his radio collage *London under London*. This was real, it wasn't just an online performance – the friendship with the old Warwick colleague recovered, the one with Davis did not. 'Feminazis, cult studs guilt mongers, passive consumer-"whingers", "friends" who occupy the moral high ground, misanthropes, gliberals, stoner pacifists, therapy-pushers' are firmly told they are unwelcome. We are also told that 'the purpose of the site is to build the Kollektive' – Ambrose doesn't footnote this, but it refers to a brief few months when Mark decided to throw open K-Punk to posts by his closest allies – at that point Nina Power and Siobhan McKeown. This was obviously not going to last, given how distinctive Mark's voice was, and so the idea was quietly and quickly abandoned. In the post 'How to Keep Oedipus Alive in Cyberspace', we are told to beware those who might 'contaminate k-space with the monkey superstition that there as such things as "persons"'.

This stuff mostly didn't continue, mainly because Mark grew up, but some of it returns in 2009, in the essay 'Break Through in Grey Lair'. This emerged from his dialogues with the philosopher Graham Harman, whose taxonomy of the human beings he didn't like as a bestiary of 'grey vampires' and 'trolls' Mark hailed as a useful way of understanding the reasons why the internet can be a horrible place to talk to people, as opposed to what it surely was – a way of making it even worse. Prepared for it by this scene-setting, I approached the 'Vampires Castle' with some trepidation, as I hadn't read it since 2013, and interpreted it then solely – and I know Mark would have hated me for this – as a symptom of a manic 'up', one which would soon enough be followed by a crash. In short, I thought he wasn't thinking straight. Actually, the essay is a lot sharper and more coherent than I remember, and five more years of Twitter, Facebook, Fake News, hashtag feuds and Guardian Comments idiots have made it very prescient.

It centres on Twitter, which Mark found hugely stressful and anxiety-inducing, and one of the regular 'pile-ons' to leftish figures, sometimes justified, always depressing, that are such a part of that site. He describes how he guiltily sat them out. What the subjects of the denunciations

> had said was sometimes objectionable; but nevertheless, the way in which they had been personally vilified and hounded left a horrible residue: the stench of bad conscience and witch-hunting moralism. The reason I didn't speak out on any of these incidents, I'm ashamed to say, was fear. The bulliest were in another part of the playground. I didn't want to attract their attention to me.

It's surely deluded not to recognise the accuracy of this description now. Where it gets difficult is the way that, influenced by Harman, he personifies the Twitter User That Piles-On as a 'Grey Vampire'. He tells us various things about the vampires, and their castle: they are anarchists, they are all middle class, they are obsessed with guilt, they want to reify identities in order to keep oppressed groups in their place while claiming to be their allies; like the Terminator – always a K-Punk favourite – they *can't be reasoned or bargained with*. That this is combined with a call for more reasoned and comradely debate is only half the problem.

I know he was talking about specific people, and some of those specific people enjoyed pointing out ways in which they did and didn't fit the grey vampire description. At one point, Mark tells us 'I definitely do not mean' those anarchists involved in the workplace and housing activism group Solidarity Federation – but in reality, as they gleefully pointed out, most of the 'Castle' were members of that very organisation. I think some of this came from Mark's lack of knowledge of how left-wing sects work, because of the fact he'd hitherto avoided them: the solidarity created by small groups struggling together can easily become paranoia and exclusion. The line between 'consciousness-raising' and 'Grey Vampirism' can be porous, to put it mildly.

However, some of the attacks on the essay were senseless and knee-jerk. Rather than being a 'class first' Old Labour worker-ist, Mark was a profoundly – in the old sense – *queer* thinker, and had never had the slightest allegiance until around 2011 to any kind of social-democratic reformism. He was pushed towards that in frustration with the tactics-free, emotive, spec-tacular and ineffectual actions embarked on by the sort of people who, as he put it, found it easier to imagine the end of capitalism than a left-wing Labour Party (the fact that this now exists has made these groups especially marginal since). So he is at pains in 'Exiting the Vampire Castle' to make clear that this *isn't* what he's doing:

> the danger in attacking the Vampires' Castle is that it can look as if – and it will do everything it can to reinforce this thought – that one is also attacking the struggles against racism, sexism, heterosexism. But far from being the only legitimate expression of such struggles, the Vampires' Castle is best understood as a bourgeois–liberal perversion and appropriation of the energy of these movements ... In all of the absurd and traumatic twit-terstorms about privilege earlier this year, it was noticeable that the discussion of *class* privilege was entirely absent. The task, as ever, remains the articulation of class, gender and race – but the founding move of the Vampires' Castle is the *dis*-articulation of class from other categories.

This, to me, sounds – if we ignore for a moment the personifica-tion of the pile-on as vampires – a highly accurate description of how 'call-out culture' works, and what it excludes. In a decade on Twitter, I've seldom seen a pile-on that has centred on the abuse of class privilege, and when figures are attacked for it, it is never an intra-left matter, as are other pile-ons, but rather the ire tends to be directed at conservative figures. But isn't this a good thing – would we want class to be used as a badge of identity? Isn't that what the likes of Julie Burchill, celebrating the moronism of *Big Brother*, are doing? It helps to explain why some Twitter moralists get upset when class is mentioned, but doesn't go far beyond that.

In any case, what everyone forgets about 'Exiting the Vampire Castle' is that around half of it was devoted to defending the comedian Russell Brand, whose brief intervention into politics in 2013, involving a widely shared, confrontational interview with the obnoxiously patrician news presenter Jeremy Paxman, hugely excited Mark; he believed Brand's appearance heralded a genuinely imminent revolution, a seismic cultural shift on the level of punk. The moment is now largely forgotten – including by advocates of the 'Vampire Castle' essay – for the reason that this never happened. What did happen was the rallying of forces radicalised after the financial crisis, Occupy and the student movement behind ageing, scruffy, slightly beatnik, even – horrors – slightly *hippy* New Left figures such as Bernie Sanders and Jeremy Corbyn, rather than strutting rock-star comedians. Being one of those whom Mark scorned at that point for not watching TV, only DVDs and box sets, I saw the interview with Paxman for the first time when writing this article. Some of it is silly and flirty, and Brand's insistence on not voting hasn't dated well; but sometimes, especially at the end of the interview, when Brand shifts from verbose preening and attempts to charm Paxman to savaging his complacency, quietly and eloquently, you can just about see what Mark saw in him.

> Defiantly pro-immigrant, pro-communist, anti-homophobic, saturated with working-class intelligence and not afraid to show it, and queer in the way that popular culture used to be (i.e., nothing to do with the sour-faced identitarian piety foisted upon us by moralists on the post-structuralist 'left') ... I couldn't remember the last time a person from a working-class background had been given the space to so consummately destroy a class 'superior' using intelligence and reason.

That's a measure of the moribundity around Brand, not of his own talents.

The fact remains, people who were in every other respect Mark's enemies – such as the drunken, vulgar, sentimental pro-war *Observer* journalist Nick Cohen, who is blasted several times *inter alia* in *K-Punk* – have found the 'Vampire Castle' essay useful. Cohen, for instance, has cited it as an explanation of how and why the 'online left' is terrible. There are reasons for this. One is that the creation of monsters is always appealing to newspapermen, as is bashing cultish lefties obsessed with such minor infractions as sexism and racism. Aside from this, Mark's enthusiasm for Brand not only antagonised the vampires – #vampbloc, as they smugly began to refer to themselves – but also damaged Mark's credibility as someone who cared about misogyny. Mark conceded here that Brand may have 'said' some things that could be 'construed' as sexist, but that it wasn't him talking about 'birds' or calling women 'darling' that people were upset by; it was his grossness and bullying behaviour, as for example when Brand, on a notorious radio show with presenter Jonathan Ross, telephoned the actor Andrew Sachs to inform him that Brand had 'fucked his granddaughter' – that and the occasional chirpy joke about rape and sexual assault. I don't think Brand should have been 'excluded' from the left for this, or subjected to one of Twitter's tedious grievance committees, but many really didn't want him as their figurehead for a new left, and I'm not sure that made them vampires. In fact, it transpired that they, and many others, preferred a morally spotless ageing hippy from the rural west country to represent them, and who can blame them? After this, and before he went back to being a celebrity comedian, Brand had a YouTube show called *The Trews*, where he interpreted news and current events from a broadly socialist perspective. It was written and produced by Johann Hari, a journalist sacked from his job at the *Independent* for a plagiarised interview with the autonomist Antonio Negri; Hari was someone whom Mark despised, and he's jabbed at several times in *K-Punk*.

That was the up; I don't know when the down first came for Mark, or if it had anything to do with the 'Castle' essay or his leaving Twitter. Given that he struggled with depression for his entire adult life, I very much doubt it. The suggestion made by some people that the fallout from this essay was linked to his suicide is offensive nonsense. In a subtly pointed editorial choice, Ambrose follows it here with 'Good for Nothing', a short account of depression that Mark published, again on a small left-wing site, the Occupied Times, in 2014. I thought we were meant to be occupying the mass media? No doubt I saw the piece at the time and didn't read it. Hadn't he said all this before? So I read it for the first time in the days after he died, and broke down reading the first paragraph. It is a beautiful, horribly moving essay, and I haven't reread it.

What is most heartbreaking is that the thirty or so pages of 'Acid Communism' – written in 2015, and with which the book ends – are the most serious and insightful he'd written since the publication of *Capitalist Realism*. When I got the book I read these first, and was shocked to realise that he clearly knew that his ideas had become repetitive, knew that in lesser hands they'd become alibis for nostalgia. He had planned a way out of it – a strange and compelling route. It begins with his familiar argument that neoliberalism was not merely about destroying social democracy or state socialism, but about destroying the possibility of thinking beyond them – hence, the first neoliberal experiment taking place in Chile after the violent crushing of Salvador Allende's attempt at introducing socialism through a democratic and constitutional government. 'Neoliberalism is best understood as a project aimed at destroying – to the point of making them unthinkable – the experiments in democratic socialism and libertarian communism that were efflorescing at the end of the sixties and the beginning of the seventies.'

Rather than seeing the culture of the 1960s and 1970s as being aimed against 'socialism' or 'communism', he sees it as providing glimpses of 'the possibility of a world beyond toil', a prospect that was 'raised most potently in culture – even, or perhaps especially, in culture which didn't necessarily think of itself as politically orientated'. He insists that 'to recall these multiple forms of collectivity is less an act of remembering than of *unforgetting*, a counter-exorcism of the spectre of a world that could be free'.

The reference points are mostly new. Bryan Ferry and J. G. Ballard are conspicuously absent, replaced with the American feminist critic Ellen Willis, Motown producer Norman Whitfield, Sly Stone, Herbert Marcuse and a gorgeous anecdote from the radio and TV presenter and former *NME* writer Danny Baker that recalls sailing through the mid-1960s on a boat called *The Constellation* – an image echoed, I think, in *K-Punk*'s cover art, with Mark's visage outlined in stars. He hated pictures of himself, but then he hadn't ever seen himself rendered as a constellation. 'The concept of Acid Communism', he asserts, explaining the book's bizarre name, 'is a provocation and a promise. It is a joke of sorts, but one with very serious purpose' – that is, to explain how there could be a convergence of 'class consciousness, socialist-feminist consciousness-raising and psychedelic consciousness, the fusion of new social movements with a communist project, an unprecedented aestheticisation of everyday life'. It's about both 'actual historical developments' and an imaginary 'virtual confluence that has not yet come together in actuality'. Could he really have done this, and made it stick, made it coherent? On the basis of these pages, yes. He explains what acid communism is via a 'Psychedelic Shack', borrowed from a Temptations song, written and produced in heady, panoramic form by Norman Whitfield. Here, the psychedelic experience is a *place*, not merely an individual experience (its bleak flipside is the drug-assisted solipsism of the same group's 'Cloud

Nine'), a communal thing, kaleidoscopic, head-spinning and compulsive, but also rhythmic, filled with onward momentum. Part of what makes acid communism 'communist' is that this experimentation with psychedelics had no 'shamans and sorcerers'; its 'experiments with consciousness were in principle open to anyone'. By this point, I'm assuming the Russian reader will want to know why he opted to call this *communism*. Of course, part of it comes from his proletarian distrust of the middle class – he doesn't want to compromise with it, he wants it abolished, and the proletariat with it. Part of it is his dislike of the fusty term 'socialism', which he would associate with unsexy, un-K-Punk tweedy figures of righteous dissent such as Tony Benn or Michael Foot or, surely, Jeremy Corbyn. But it's also because of what he glimpses in the psychedelic shack, where all those intense, head-spinning three-minute moments become a lifetime of intensities, experienced by everyone at once, in the present.

In that, it's a late attempt to argue for the significance of pop culture full stop, something which is, to a large degree, retrospective (this is not, as he always made clear, to say that there aren't still great pop-cultural pleasures – records, TV appearances, videos, albums, micro-genres – but that their seismic wider cultural effect is a thing of the past). In a hilarious attack on the Live 8 pop charity events, in a blog post of over a decade ago included in *K-Punk*, he quotes, to his own surprise, the exceptionally capitalist-realist ex-*NME* journalist and hack romantic novelist 'Tony Parsons, of all people'. This is because he 'made the very good point in the *Mirror* today that the generation of the Thirties and the Forties did not expect Crosby and Sinatra to change the world – but, he says, many of them had either risked or given up their lives to change things.' I don't know if he really thought this through. Similarly, the generation that created the welfare state neither had nor needed a Dennis Potter or a Mark E. Smith, let alone a Bryan Ferry – neither do the millennials of the UK, who are frequently politically committed, and just as frequently culturally indifferent.

And yet, Mark Fisher is a hero among them. After his death, his students at Goldsmiths created a mural in his name, and his books have been circulated and cited among the young new left in Britain and America perhaps more than any other recent writer. I think this is in part because they feel the *absence* of a counterculture, and the huge charge it would give to the left if it could be created. That's partly because they know that culture is an aid to understanding and interpreting. In a late essay included here on 'Anti-Therapy', Mark recapitulates, in the clearest terms, one of the arguments for modernism – that you cannot understand contemporary capitalism, and even less, the malevolence of the ruling class, as expressed in the Jimmy Savile or Hillsborough scandals, in a realist way.

> The representational frameworks which have served British capitalism so well since the 1980s clearly cannot accommodate the trauma of the establishment paedophilia scandals, any more than they can accommodate popular mobilisations against neoliberalism. You would indeed need the formal inventiveness of a David Lynch or a David Peace to do justice to the extremity of what the English ruling class has got up to.

That's one explanation. The other is provided in that glimpse of 'Acid Communism'. So much of this book is about the memory of having your own world transformed, your world in Loughborough in the 1970s, completely transformed and turned upside-down by a record, a children's programme, a TV play, which has beamed in from another dimension and taken you elsewhere, and offered you one of Herbert Marcuse's moments of prefigurative utopia. Expanded out of his own head, out of his own time, Mark demands that everyone have access to this experience, and not as individuals struggling with their own ill-adapted mind and body – but as a collective, as a social body, as communism.

Winter 2018

Acknowledgements

All photographs are my own except for the one in the last essay, and most of those in 'Arab Villages' – these are taken from public domain sources, indicated in the names of the captions. This is an anthology, so I should thank those who commissioned or published these essays and articles in their original form. So gratitude is due to: Lisa Blanning at *Electronic Beats*; Paul Myerscough, Daniel Soar and Thomas Jones at the *London Review of Books*; Amanda Baillieu and Ellis Woodman at *Building Design*; Ian Irvine at *Prospect*; Jonathan Charley, who published the original version of 'False Landscape Syndrome'; Amy Frearson at *Dezeen*; John Jourden at *Archinect*; Nancy Levinson at *Places Journal*; Chris Foges at *Architecture Today*; Josephine Berry Slater at *Mute*; Dan Fox at *Frieze*; Mark Krotov at *n+1*; and to Kirill Kobrin and Anna Aslanyan at *NZ*.

Thanks to Leo Hollis at Verso and my agent Nicola Barr for their efforts in making this into a book rather than a scrapbook, to Mark Martin and the production and proofing team at Verso for helping to even out a rather chaotic collection of texts, and special thanks to Lynsey Hanley, Juliet Jacques and Carla Whalen for their strong yet tactful advice on the various drafts of its introduction, which was by far the most difficult part to write; and with love to Carla for everything else.

These pieces were originally published in the following places – though in most cases I have used my original drafts rather than the published versions.

'Want to Buy Some Illusions?', originally published on *The Measures Taken*, October 2005

'Hurrah for the Black Box Recorder', originally published on *Sit Down Man, You're a Bloody Tragedy*, November 2007

'From Revolution to Revelation: The Politics of the Pet Shop Boys', originally published in *Electronic Beats*, July 2013

'Dancing to Numbers', originally published on the *London Review of Books* blog, May 2020

'The New and Closed Libraries of Britain', originally published in *Building Design*, June 2013

'Edinburgh's Golden Turds', first published in *Prospect*, March 2017

'False Landscape Syndrome: The Poetry and Propaganda of Andrew Jordan', originally published in *The Routledge Companion to Architecture, Literature and the City*, edited by Jonathan Charley, 2018

'The Shop Signs of Walthamstow High Street', originally published in *Dezeen*, November 2017

'Arab Villages: Architecture and War in Israel–Palestine, Sixty Years On', originally published in *Archinect*, May 2008

'Socialism and Nationalism on the Danube: Architecture and Politics in Budapest and Vienna', originally published in *Places Journal*, May 2017

'Fragments of German Expressionism', unpublished, October 2019

ACKNOWLEDGEMENTS

'My Kind of Town: Warszawa', published in *Architecture Today*, September 2012

'A High-Performance Contemporary Life Process: Zaha Hadid Architects and the Neoliberal Avant-Garde', originally published in *Mute*, October 2010

'Strange, Angry Objects: The Brutalist Decades', published by the *London Review of Books*, November 2016

'Jane Jacobs Says No', originally published in the *London Review of Books*, July 2017

'The Socialist Lavatory League', originally published in the *London Review of Books*, May 2019

'Decadent Action: Věra Chytilová's *Daisies*', originally published on *The Measures Taken*, January 2006

'The Petroleum Sublime', originally published in *Frieze*, January 2011

'And Then the Strangest Thing Happened …', originally published by *n+1*, March 2017

'From Boring Dystopia to Acid Communism', originally published in Russian translation in *Neprikosnovenniy Zapas (Emergency Rations)*, winter 2018